HUMAN RIGHTS AND STATE SOVEREIGNTY

Written under the auspices of the Center of International Studies, Princeton University. A list of other books written under Center auspices appears at the back of this book.

HUMAN RIGHTS and STATE SOVEREIGNTY

RICHARD FALK

HOLMES & MEIER PUBLISHERS, INC.
NEW YORK • LONDON

First published in the United States of America 1981 by
Holmes & Meier Publishers, Inc.
30 Irving Place
New York, N.Y. 10003

Great Britain:
Holmes & Meier Publishers, Ltd.
131 Trafalgar Road
Greenwich, London SE10 9TX

Library of Congress Cataloging in Publication Data

Falk, Richard A
  Human rights and state sovereignty.

  Includes index.
  1. Civil rights.   2. Comparative government.
I. Title.
JC571.F24   1980   323.4   80-22620

ISBN 0-8419-0619-X
ISBN 0-8419-0620-3 (pbk.)

Manufactured in the United States of America

For

Kim Chi Ha
Kim Dae Jung

beacons of bravery
and hope
in the stern and ceaseless
struggle for human rights
and humane governance
that goes on in Korea
and in many other countries,
including especially here,
in our own country

Contents

Prefatory Note

Writing on the eve of the Reagan presidency hardly seems like an auspicious moment to champion human rights. And yet, the ebb and flow of official support for human rights is itself an enduring feature of the subject, an aspect of what is to be expected. In any event, the main inquiry of this volume is into structural issues—how the promotion of human rights works in a world order system dominated, but not nearly yet monopolized, by the realities of state sovereignty. Such an inquiry takes a longer view of human rights than that associated with the vagaries of national foreign policies, and hopefully, examines aspects of the subject that are of more persisting interest.

My understanding of human rights has been shaped by friends and colleagues, especially those whose background and experience has brought them into contact with peoples struggling against various contemporary forms of repression. I would mention, in particular, Georges Abi-Saab, Eqbal Ahmad, Fouad Ajami, Walden Bello, Joel Carlson, Burgess Carr, Noam Chomsky, Abdelhai Chouikha, John Dugard, Daniel Ellsberg, Mansour Farhang, Herbert Feith, Farideh Gueramy, Rajni Kothari, Don Luce, Ali Mazrui, Russell Means, Edward Said, Stuart Schaar, Ralph Schoenman, Nathan Shamuyarira, and George Wald. I could easily have lengthened this list. Each of those mentioned here has, in some definite sense, shaped my vision of what the pursuit of human rights means in the concrete encounter with state power. Of course, I do not mean to suggest that any member of this diverse group necessarily shares the outlook or interpretations found here.

The other special influence I would acknowledge is that of the late Lelio Basso. His extraordinary insistence on creating a permanent mechanism to examine and censure crimes of state has begun to take shape in the early operations in Europe of the Permanent Peoples Tribunal during 1980. I have been privileged to work closely on this project since its inception in the mid-1970s, and believe deeply in the legitimacy of such an initiative on behalf of human rights in a world order system in which every prominent government turns its deaf ear to its own earlier promises to protect the peoples of the world from the kind of criminality that was defined and punished at the Nuremberg and Tokyo trials of defeated war leaders held shortly after the end of World War II. Lelio Basso remains one of the yet insufficiently sung heroes of the struggle to create a human rights process entirely worthy of world order values, rather than one reflective of what is currently acceptable to governments and official leaderships.

I also have learned more than my fair share about human rights from some recent Princeton students, and I would mention Jo Backer, Robin Broad, John Cavanagh, and Andrew Reding as prominent instances. This book has benefited as well, in countless ways from the talents and dedication of my research assistants in recent years: Janet Lowenthal, Charlotte Ebel, and Jack Sanderson, who prepared the index to this book. Finally, my secretary, June Garson, has far exceeded the call of duty in all respects, with a rare blend of joyfulness and efficiency, as has her principal colleague in the Center of International Studies, Gladys Starkey, who cheerfully and skillfully helped all along lighten the heavy typing burdens. As has been the case for many years, my work has been supported by and has benefited from the Center's congenial atmosphere, established especially by the efforts of its gifted director, Cyril E. Black, and its spirited logistical leader, Jean McDowall.

I also wish to acknowledge the prior publication of material used here, although in each instance revisions have been made: Chapter 2—published by permission of Transaction, Inc. from *The Dynamics of Human Rights in United States Foreign Policy* edited by Natalie Kaufman Hevener, copyright © 1980 by Transaction, Inc; Chapter 3—reprinted from *The Politics of Human Rights* edited by Paula R. Newberg, copyright © UNA-USA 1980, published by New York University Press; Chapter 4—"A World Order Perspective on Authoritarianism," *Alternatives* V, No. 2 (August 1979): 127–194; Chapter 5—"Comparative Protection of Human Rights in Capitalist and Socialist Third World Countries," *Universal Human Rights* 1, No. 2 (April/June 1979): 3–29; Chapter 6—From *Enhancing Global Human Rights* by Dominguez et al., copyright © 1979 by the Council on Foreign Relations, Inc., used with permission of McGraw-Hill Book Company; Chapter 7—"The Algiers Declaration of the Rights of Peoples and the Struggle for Human Rights" from *UN Law/Fundamental Rights,* edited by Antonio Cassese (published by Sijthoff and Noordhoff, 1979), pp. 225–235; Chapter 8—"Keeping Nuremberg Alive" in Giuliano Amato and others, eds., *Homage to Lelio Basso* (published by Franco Angeli Editore, 1979), pp. 811–820; Chapter 9—"Geopolitics and Law: A Brief for New Rules," from *Christianity and Crisis* 40, No. 3 (March 3, 1980): 44–48; "Human Rights in a Rivalry Situation: Preliminary Observations on the Iranian Case," *Bulletin of Peace Proposals,* X, No. 2 (1979): 179–184 (also published in *Islamic Review,* 10–15); "The Iran Hostage Crisis: Easy Answers and Hard Questions," *American Journal of International Law, 1980.* I also want to thank the American Map Company for their permission to use adaptations of several of their maps in Chapter 4.

RICHARD FALK
Princeton, New Jersey

I

Introduction

Human rights as a focus of concern have come alive politically and intellectually, especially in the United States, but also worldwide, in the last few years. Certainly President Jimmy Carter's human rights diplomacy has played a part in this process. Other developments have also helped: the award of a Nobel Peace Prize to Amnesty International, the inclusion of a human rights section in the Helsinki Final Act, the general acceptance of basic economic needs as an element of human rights, as well as the humanitarian rhetoric habitually used by such symbolic global figures as the secretary general of the United Nations and the Pope.

It is, as yet, too soon to appraise this new prominence. Is it one more fad in world affairs that will pass from the scene shortly, perhaps even before the disappearance of Jimmy Carter from the White House? Recall how quickly after the ending of the Vietnam War the ecology movement was put back "on the shelf." And yet, something nonfaddish has persisted in the shape of an abiding environmental constituency long since the faddists dropped out. I suspect it will be the same with human rights. The prominence won't last, but neither will the obscurity return. Some fundamental things have happened in relation to concern about human rights nationally and globally that will not be easily reversed.

There has always existed the danger that human rights would become the preserve of sentimental legalists and dogged propagandists, that is, of those who thought the world automatically became a better place every time platitudes were inscribed in a legal form and of Cold Warriors who used some of these platitudes to increase international tensions and military spending through their strident denunciations of "the enemy" state and its ideology.[1] There is emerging now, I think, a more sophisticated appreciation of human rights among mainstream students of international relations, although this deepening appreciation should not be confused with a new consensus. Indeed, there is more disagreement than ever in foreign policy circles about whether and to what extent it is a good idea to take human rights seriously as an instrument for the pursuit of national interests.

At principal issue is the basic understanding of international society as a political system. The main contours of debate can be suggested. On one side is the belief, perhaps best represented in the writings of Hedley Bull and R. J. Vincent, that the promotion of human rights is at odds with the proper functioning of the states system.[2] Their outlook, put simply, rests on the conviction that any serious implementation of human rights is necessarily interventionary, and interventionary in a particularly dubious way—strong states with imperial interests and expansionist tendencies acting against weak states situated in "alien" cultural and ideological regions of the world. The historical record of so-called humanitarian intervention bears out their skeptical response to those governments who currently proclaim themselves the global guardians of human rights.

This skeptical view also stresses the diversity of conceptions about the real content of human rights that exists today despite the quasi-universal adherence of governments to a common normative language such as is embedded in the Universal Declaration of Human Rights and other widely endorsed legal instruments. This diversity is a natural expression of the conflict between individualist and collectivist images of societal fulfillment, evident in the clash between socialist and capitalist forms of organization, as well as in certain antagonisms between Western and non-Western cultural traditions. In any event, the reality of these diversities is used by Bull and Vincent to reinforce their claims on behalf of an international morality of nonintervention. To such skeptics, human rights activism leads to warfare by way of imperialism. If benevolent spirits want to help the world, then they should cease and desist from these misguided efforts to induce governments to promote human rights as a matter of foreign policy. The best that can be done in this kind of world system is to reinforce the autonomy of all sovereign states. Global reform that rests on the opposite conviction, that the world can be made a better place by the application of higher standards to every state, is either irrelevant or has an effect that is the opposite of its lofty goals. I identify this kind of position as that of "liberal statism."

It contrasts with the outlook of the "liberal internationalists," which includes the Carter Administration and such institutions as Freedom House, as well as a variety of academic champions of human rights in foreign policy including Tom Farer, Louis Henkin, Richard Lillich, John Norton Moore, and Michael Reisman.[3] In their view, the world is an imperfect place where many terrible abuses of state power occur. For this reason, carefully confined interventionary missions can be beneficially undertaken even by strong states to alleviate some of the suffering. As a Freedom House document puts it, "We believe that democratic states must be concerned with the internal affairs of other states. Intervention is not always wrong. . . ."[4] Do we have to sit by while tyrants commit genocide? Since the United Nations can't or won't act to overcome some of these extreme cases, isn't it desirable to encourage interventionary pressures, even including an occasional recourse to military action if necessary and possible, to rescue a foreign population or some tormented section of it?

This positive view of human rights tends to be associated with a belief in moderate degrees of global reform beyond the confines of statism. We are not stuck with the state system in its pure form as the best of possible worlds. We can modify it through enlightened behavior. Part of that enlightening process consists of the near universal acceptance of a growing list of human rights standards. This public acknowledgment, no matter by whom or for what motive, builds expectations and moves in the direction of a more peaceful and just world. Liberal internationalists are aware that some repressive governments endorse human rights treaties because they regard them as "soft law," with no enforcement prospects. They believe, however, that cumulative effects arise from human rights concerns in various policy-making arenas, and that while there are many abuses of human rights that cannot be corrected, there are many others that can, and that it is worth the effort. And especially, when a powerful government commits itself to the promotion of human rights, even acknowledging an element of selectivity arising from security considerations, the world generally becomes a more decent place.

I suspect that it is no accident that liberal statism has been most sensitively formulated by two gifted specialists in international relations living in England. In their lifetime, they have witnessed the baton of humanitarian imperialism pass across the Atlantic from London to Washington. Similarly, the upsurge of liberal internationalism in the United States during this century is surely associated with tensions between the global role and the moral heritage of the United States, and represents an inevitable, and even laudable, attempt to bridge that gap through positive action.

My own approach to human rights starts off with an appreciation and criticism of both these attitudes toward the place of human rights in foreign policy generally, and in the foreign policy of the United States specifically. I believe the Bull/Vincent approach overdoes statism both descriptively and prescriptively. As a consequence, their preoccupation with intervention is misleading. Their focus of concern assumes that the value of human rights depends almost exclusively on impartial enforcement, and since this statist outlook finds no prospect of this other than by Great Power intervention, it seeks to discredit altogether the international protection of human rights. But there are other actors than governments and other instruments than intervention by which governments (or parts of governments) can promote human rights.[5] To advocate human rights is to inform people about their violation, to fortify the morale of certain resistance efforts, to create "space" for human rights concerns within and without the governmental apparatus, and to set in motion a positive transnational momentum on behalf of peace and justice in the world.[6] As such, the advocacy of human rights provides some foundation for hope and progress, and generally strengthens the more reformist elements in national bureaucracies. At the same time, the Bull/Vincent contention that human rights can easily serve as a cover for humanitarian imperialism is well-taken, especially if advanced as a critique of the pretensions of United States foreign policy since World War II.

In contrast to the liberal statists, the Freedom House approach is unduly innocent about the imperial tendencies of big, dominant states, whatever their rhetoric and their domestic record of observance. Part of this innocence is expressed by the implicit assumption that humanitarian intervention is something that only happens to "others." The targets are always *foreign* societies. No consideration is given to whether other governments might have the right to intervene or exert pressure here on behalf of perceived victims of abuse—say, the American Indians or other minorities. Therefore, an artificial quality arises when the only operational policy question is deciding how far the United States should go in helping out victims of human rights abuses *abroad*.

Similarly, there is insufficient attention given by liberal internationalists to the influence and sorting of mixed motives in interventionary settings. International experience, including United States diplomatic history, suggests that altruistic concerns play a very subsidiary role in the execution of foreign policy, especially where military force is contemplated or important economic interests are at stake. For this reason, it seems prudent to encourage a noninterventionist foreign policy (when it comes to unilateral use of military power) in *all* its aspects, especially on the part of a country with as widespread material and ideological interests as the United States, and where the confusion between moral purpose and selfish interest seems so pervasive.[7]

Getting at the actual role of human rights requires more attention to the nongovernmental dimension of international life than either liberal statists or liberal internationalists are willing to accord. Both outlooks share an overriding concern about government policy, the former seeking to inhibit activism while the latter seeks to stimulate it within guidelines. Neither outlook is much interested in the role of transnational actors, the stimulation and support of resistance efforts within countries, the extension of human rights criteria to the domestic political arena, and the strengthening of the United Nations role vis-à-vis severe human rights abuses. It is here, in the interstices of statism, that the greatest promise for human rights lies.

To begin with, it is important to inquire into the manipulation of the human rights agenda by various elites with vested interests of one kind or another. There are two sides of this issue—what I would call the "politics of invisibility" and the "politics of supervisibility"—that reveal much about how the human rights agenda is orchestrated by a tacit relationship between the state and mainstream media, even in a country such as the United States, which enjoys all of the formal endowments of democracy.[8] Of the politics of invisibility there are many examples, but among the most poignant is the virtual media blackout, despite abundant documentation, on news about the tragic decimation of the Timorese people as a consequence of the Indonesian conquest and pacification of East Timor, an operation filled with barbarities and taking several hundred thousand lives. Another "invisible" context relates to the plight of the hundred million or so "untouchables" in India, who suffer a daily existence, by and large, that is quite as humiliating as that endured by black South Africans. Or, turning to the politics of supervisibility, one notes the relish with which postrevolutionary abuses of human rights have been reported in Iran and Vietnam. And, of course, there is a self-fulfilling feature here. A new revolutionary leadership, sensitive about its image, is likely to retaliate against hostile and often exaggerated representations of its policies by initiating press censorship. The poles of invisibility and supervisibility correlate closely with the American foreign policy imperatives of supporting certain repressive regimes and discouraging recourse to revolutionary politics. Human rights violations—keeping them hidden or magnifying their occurrence—become, then, part of the battle for the hearts and minds of Americans (and others).

Or, on another front, there is the question of asylum and extradition for deposed tyrants. At what point, if any, is it an abuse of sovereignty to shield an individual wanted for state crime in his native country? Is it an exercise or abuse of human rights to grant asylum to such deposed tyrants as the Shah of Iran or Anastasio Somoza Debayle? The idea of individual responsibility initiated so impressively, if imperfectly, at Nuremberg, needs to be extended to perpetrators of "crimes against humanity" even when the abuses are not associated in any way with a foreign war.[9]

There are also issues about alleged "new frontiers" for human rights. Increasingly, there are claims that subjecting individual workers to health hazards without adequately informing them is a violation of their human rights. This issue has been raised in more general terms by the dangers attributed to low-level radiation emitted by nuclear reactors. And it is possible that "ecological intervention" will become a ground for infringing on the sovereignty of foreign societies. The extension of human rights to new battlefields enlists new constituencies, but it also attenuates the clarity of the more traditional focus and by so doing confirms skeptical perceptions of human rights concerns as just words.

The question of the ways and means to promote human rights at home and abroad is a matter of policy, whether the arena is governmental or nongovernmental, whether the instruments available are potent or feeble. Devising policy is, however, constrained by structure, as already illustrated by the controversy over whether, on balance, it is beneficial to encourage under certain conditions intervention on behalf of human rights. The structure of the state system is hierarchical; that is, only a few powerful states are in a position to use their economic, cultural, and military power on behalf of human rights. And yet a norm of the system is the protection of the autonomy of each sovereign state, and self-determination is widely regarded as a critical human right, perhaps even overriding the protection of individual rights.

It is here that a world order perspective enters. Human rights that can be promoted by regional and global institutions on the one side (central normative guidance) and by citizen movements on the other (global populism) represent the two main structural challenges to the primacy of the state in world affairs. These challenges to statism, variously estimated, suggest the relevance of levels of analysis above and below the level of the state, as well as a call for a more complicated image of "actor" with respect to human rights.

There are contradictory trends present. The state mechanism is getting stronger almost everywhere, more "modernized" in all regions of the world; this strengthening has meant also, in most cases, more militarized. Greater attention is given to "control" of the people, especially as pressures of population growth and poverty mount and tax the capacities of governments. Governments are augmenting their capacity to repress, while they move also to insulate their society against various forms of penetration from without. Authoritarian tendencies are intensifying, especially in the Third World, although the picture is not entirely bleak. The "efficiency" and "invulnerability" of authoritarian systems have been refuted by a series of developments late in the 1970s in such key countries as India, Iran, and Brazil. It is far from clear how the net effects of these authoritarian rhythms will work out in the 1980s.

Underlying these various tendencies is the question of structural transformation. Is the state system compatible with the substantial realization of human rights? If not, can we envisage a preferable system emerging within the next several decades? If so, can positive steps relative to human rights be taken in the interim? The essays that follow proceed from an affirmative, if guarded, answer to each of these three questions: structural transformation is needed to realize human rights on a global scale, it will not come soon, and its coming can be hastened and the transitional experience enhanced by sensitive support for human rights.

Human rights are not, in the main, legal or moral abstractions. They are embedded in historical process. More concretely, this process at this time is closely intertwined with the ongoing anti-imperial struggle against political, economic, and cultural structures of international domination. This struggle can be conceived of as the quest for self-determination by population groups at the scale of the state. Deferred, by and large, is the related struggle for internal self-determination at the level of the nation, tribe, sect, or ethnic/religious minority. Deferred, also, as a matter of *international* priority is the fundamental quest by women to unravel the oppressive features of patriarchal political life that exists everywhere, although in various intensities and forms.

Hence, there may appear to be a certain selectivity, or even bias, in my treatment of human rights. I believe that the flow of history and of international morality sanctions the antiimperial struggle, and that this struggle is the principal arena for realizing (or thwarting) human rights in the years ahead. Such an assertion is made despite the evidence that some postcolonial states have been the scene of far worse betrayals of human rights than anything that occurred in the colonial period. In effect, I maintain that the antiimperial struggle must be waged to completion so as to set the stage for the subsequent realization of human rights *within* the state, however traumatic these traumas may turn out to be. Naturally, especially in light of the bloody record of abuse in many postcolonial societies, a more sensitive stress on other dimensions of human rights during decolonialization and thereafter assumes an especial urgency.

This urgency exists for both Marxist and capitalist polities. Here again in a world of mass poverty and rising resource costs, it seems preferable, by and large, to move in a socialist direction to satisfy those human rights concerned with the basic needs of people. This preference persists in my view despite the disappointing record of socialist states with respect to safeguarding the political, civil, and cultural rights of their citizens. For ecological reasons, as much as for political relationships, a humanistic socialism seems to be the best hope for the future for the overwhelming majority of societies in the world.

The promotion of human rights is certainly not a panacea, nor is it a substitute for a wider program of global reform. At the same time, taking human rights seriously is one dimension of that wider shift in consciousness entailing the gradual displacement of statist modes of political organization and their replacement by a new repertoire of local and global orientations.[10]

The chapters in this volume explore these themes. Chapter II initiates the inquiry by considering the rhythm of United States support for international human rights, as well as the realistic limits on this support given domestic configurations of political power. In Chapter III the thorny question of the theoretical basis of human rights in a world of sovereign states is addressed, especially to clarify the main lines of reconciliation between international claim and internal prerogative that have developed over the years.

Chapter IV surveys the varieties of authoritarianism in the contemporary world, thereby showing the extent of domestic resistance to the implementation of human rights that it is reasonable to expect in various parts of the world. This chapter also raises the question as to whether the generality of governing processes failing to observe human rights is not a reflection of the character of world order, as well as a matter of specific types of domestic order. This line of inquiry is extended in Chapter V to explore the human rights records of capitalist and socialist countries, especially in the Third World. And Chapter VI looks at the promotion of human rights from an international point of view, asking the basic question as to what is possible, even for extreme instances of persisting violation, given the structure and operation of the state system.

In Chapters VII and VIII unconventional topics are explored. Chapter VII considers the content and character of a specific effort by a group of individuals from various countries to generate standards of human rights that will be binding on governments despite their lack of participation or consent. In effect, the possibility of populist forms of law creation in the human rights area is taken seriously. Chapter VIII also rests on the same possibility, although in relation to the concrete instance of extending the populist role to the application of law in the context of holding governmental leaders accountable for gross violation of human rights. In effect, Chapter VIII argues that ordinary citizens have the right to act if governments fail to carry out the promise made after World War II at Nuremberg that henceforth *all* leaders would be individually accountable for crimes against humanity.

The final essay, Chapter IX, discusses various human rights issues raised in Iran during the first month after the fall of the Shah in early 1979. Its tone is conjectural and exploratory. The reason for including this chapter is to confront an issue that tends to be neglected—namely, what is it appropriate to expect by way of human rights in the aftermath of a successful revolution? On the one side, the idealistic claims of the revolutionaries raise expectations. On the other, the reality of recreating institutions and procedures of state authority in a setting of turmoil tends to produce arbitrary and even repressive forms of governance.

We cannot expect rapid success or even steady progress. The struggle for human rights is bound to ebb and flow, and yet in an era of increasing global awareness, this is a time for perseverance. In the end, I feel about human rights the way Vincent van Gogh felt about painting: ". . . be sure of this: when a thing turns out wrong, that's no reason for me to admit that I ought not to have begun it; on the contrary, if it fails many a time it is a reason for me to try again; even if the same thing is not possible, I can always try again in the same direction, as my views are well-considered and calculated, and have their *raison d'être*."[11] With human rights, as with painting well, we enter a realm of moral necessity, where the quest is itself an aspect of our dignity as individuals, as collective entities, and even as a species. The disappointing record of observance and implementation may suggest the need to reconsider our means, but it should not, for that reason alone, draw our ends into question.

The Evolution of American Foreign Policy on Human Rights: 1945–1978

Issues of Perspective

Assessing the American record on human rights during the period since World War II is problematic on several counts. For one thing, there is no agreement on what is the proper scope of inquiry for such an assessment. Does one consider the broad geopolitical sweep of American foreign policy that includes lending support to a wide variety of repressive governments provided only that they are anticommunist? Does one include the goals and effects of covert operations by the CIA? Or, in contrast, does one take account of the linkages that some claim make the cause of world peace depend on not pressing the Soviet Union or its close allies too hard on human rights? Also, to what extent do we base our assessment on the human rights situation in the United States? And if we do base them on the United States, then do we make our judgments rest upon a comparison between American society and foreign societies at similar levels of economic achievement or by reference to the standards and norms embodied in international law? And, finally, do we conceive of the relevant portion of international law to consist only of validly ratified treaties or do we include authoritative declaratory documents (especially the Universal Declaration of Human Rights) and widely endorsed treaties (e.g., Genocide Convention) as embodying an international consensus that qualifies either as customary international law or as an instance of *jus cogens?*

Second, literature and statecraft on human rights seemed dominated in the United States by pieties and formalism. For various reasons, until very recently and with notable exceptions, many of those attracted to human rights as a subject of academic concern were bewitched by words and international legal standards. Hence, the American record often seemed to be assessed primarily by how many human rights treaties were supported and ratified at a given time. This sort of formalism rests upon the twin pillars of legalism and moralism, postures that make the pursuit of human rights in the world seem apolitical, involving neither costs nor effects. Such an approach also presupposes that issues of human rights were exclusively concerned with what happens in foreign societies, and not at all directed at correcting abuses in America itself.

Third, the promotion of human rights has often served as a propaganda vehicle for a particular foreign policy. The political right has favored emphasis on repression in communist countries as a way of stirring trouble in those societies and reinforcing a hard-line approach to Soviet-American relations; this emphasis tends to be complemented by a refusal to be troubled by even the most severe violations in anticommunist countries. On the left the reverse pattern is evident. The emphasis is placed on human rights violations in the capitalist countries (or in America itself), where American responsibility (and leverage) is greatest. By now, most of the left is also disturbed by repression in communist countries, but is either reluctant to enter terrain dominated by militant reactionaries or believes that it is both futile and dangerous to press the Soviet Union too hard on human rights.

Fourth, there often appears to be a very opportunistic quality about human rights diplomacy. In the most recent period, it seems obvious that President Jimmy Carter stumbled across the human rights theme on his way to the White House. Once used, it seemed to fit with his temperament, as well as fill an important need to engender domestic support for an activist foreign policy in a period of wide popular depression among the American citizenry after Vietnam and Watergate. Human rights built up some moral enthusiasm for United States world leadership without necessarily reviving the tensions of the Cold War. In such an analysis, human rights are taken seriously as a concern because of their value in domestic politics, and the international effects of the campaign are incidental, and in certain instances may even be unwanted. In fact, pressing hard on human rights will cause antagonisms abroad with both friends and rivals and may complicate prospects for economic cooperation, arms control agreements, and alliance relations. Such a realization has evidently led President Carter to adopt a more "realistic" and low-profile approach in reaction to the negative after-effects of his ebullient advocacy of human rights in the first months of his presidency.

Underneath these various factors is the elusiveness of policy in international relations. The reality of the state system, the diversity of social, economic, and political life on a national level, and the importance of fostering international cooperation make it difficult to assess the proper place for human rights in the foreign policy of a state, especially in the foreign policy of a superpower such as the United States. We do not even know with certainty what actions are effective, so we cannot have confidence that a given strategy will promote a desired result. Some argue that support for Soviet dissenters induces a decrease in repression; others feel it results in increased repression; others, a tightening; each view seems persuasive at different times.

However, despite all these difficulties, many people feel that indifference to the abuse of rights elsewhere is not the answer, that it would only reinforce the most power-oriented conception of international relations. Besides, even a highly selective pattern of help may still bring relief to a specific group or individual caught in a particular situation. Also, there may be unintended beneficial secondary effects arising from an activist human rights policy, such as stimulating opposition movements in repressive societies, giving dedicated civil servants within the American bureaucracy a mandate to pursue more enlightened policies, encouraging public support for nongovernmental activities in the human rights field, and exposing the gap between the moralistic creed of human rights and the imperialistic logic of geopolitics. Finally, dealing with the dangers and contradictions of the state system ultimately involves moving toward some kind of more integrated form of world order that would presuppose a sense of global community. The most critical foundation for such an evolution is the growth of sentiments and attitudes of human solidarity, which in turn rests upon a concern for the well-being of people as people, regardless of their geographical location or their ethnic, linguistic, religious, cultural, or ideological identity. Such a prospect seems intimately connected with deepening the sensitivity of peoples everywhere to human rights issues.

A Moderate Human Rights Cycle

If a conventional perception of human rights, as expressed in formal acts (treaty-making, United States voting) and official discourse (emphasis in statements by leaders), is accepted, we notice a rather clear pattern of fluctuation in American behavior. The pattern takes the form of a cycle that seems constrained within certain definite boundaries established by mainstream American political attitudes.

Figure 2-1 portrays the United States record in a crude and schematic form. The vertical axis suggests the level of support for human rights. The trend line from 1940 to 1978 fluctuates between the political center and the right, whereas line B suggests the boundary between the center and the right. The space between A and B represents the political center in which both national parties operate, with the Republican Party more consistently in the space between A and C, and the Democratic Party hovering more consistently around C, or even occasionally straying across the C boundary into the CB space.

The main trend line takes note of four turning points that mark shifts in the phases of the cycle. From 1940 to 1948 was a waxing phase associated with the presidency of Franklin Roosevelt. This period is identified with the proclamation of the Four Freedoms in 1941. This idealistic mood persisted, in a diminished form, for several years after Roosevelt's death in 1944. X_1 is located at 1948, when the postwar emphasis on human rights

FIGURE 2-1
U.S. Record on Human Rights

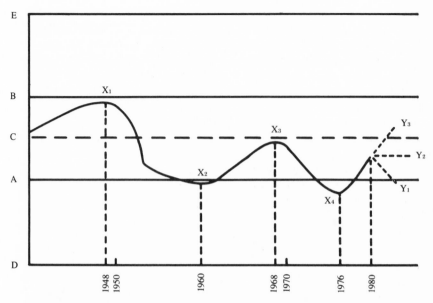

X_1 = 1948 = Universal Declaration of Human Rights
X_2 = 1960 = Truman Doctrine
X_3 = 1968 = Nixon presidency begins
X_4 = 1976 = Carter presidency begins

reached its culmination under U.S. leadership in the drafting and en-dorsement of the Universal Declaration of Human Rights. Nineteen forty-eight also initiated a waning phase in the human rights cycle as it is the year that most conveniently marks the real beginning of the Cold War, epitomized by the proclamation of the Truman Doctrine, which offered economic and military aid to the Greek and Turkish governments to support their struggles against Communist encroachment.

The period from 1948 to 1960, consisting of four Truman years and eight Eisenhower years, was dominated by Cold War stridency. An important domestic backlash to the liberal internationalist outlook of the New Deal occurred in the late 1940s and 1950s. One aspect of this backlash was its attack on any abridgments of American sovereignty. Human rights obli-gations were seen as encroaching upon the United States Constitution and upon the residual sovereignty of the (then) forty-eight states. Senator John Bricker, a conservative Republican from Ohio, working in conjunc-tion with various pressure groups, led a fight to prevent the ratification of human rights treaties, including the Genocide Convention. The Bricker efforts were so successful that by 1953, the Eisenhower Administration, through its secretary of state, John Foster Dulles, abandoned any effort to increase the promotion of human rights by the United States, and indeed, until 1960 no further efforts to strengthen international human rights by way of treaty obligation were made by either the president or Congress. Dulles was the most characteristic figure of the period, devoting his energies to building a global network of anticommunist treaty arrangements and abandoning any serious effort to promote human rights except in the ideological sense of claiming that the anticommunist group of states constituted the "free world" in distinction to the totalitarian realm constituted by the Soviet bloc, which was assumed in that period to be a monolithic system completely subject to the will of the Kremlin. In such an adversary climate, the stress on geopolitics and military approaches to security dominated the foreign policy process.

A second turning point, X_2 (1960), marks the beginning of the Kennedy presidency, a period of expansive international liberalism typified by the Peace Corps, the Alliance for Progress, and global involvement in the internal affairs of foreign societies. The United States under Kennedy was perceived as an idealistic force in international society, despite such contradictory features as anti-Castro interventionary tactics and the escalating involvement in the Vietnam War. After Kennedy's assassination, Lyndon Johnson pressed forward on civil rights for blacks, although such developments as the Dominican intervention of 1965 and government moves to intimidate domestic antiwar activists tarnished the Johnson image. Nevertheless, the Kennedy-Johnson period, 1960 to 1968, can be viewed as a positive period in terms of support for human rights.

The inauguration of Richard Nixon as president in 1968 brought a reversal of mood in American foreign policy that was also expressed as a downward turning point, X_3, in human rights. The Nixon years were premised on intergovernmental relations that generally accepted the legitimacy of territorial sovereignty and exhibited a notable insensitivity to the rights of citizens, whether at home or abroad. The pursuit of human rights, even in the communist countries, was largely ignored in this period, which is exemplified by Nixon's China initiative and his coordinated effort to achieve détente in relations with the Soviet Union. Kissinger, the dominant presence in American foreign policy during the Nixon–Ford years, was openly scornful of introducing human rights concerns into serious diplomacy, treating such concerns as moralistic encumbrances upon the serious business of negotiating stable arrangements of state power. This was evident in the United Nations, where the United States, during Moynihan's tenure, stridently used human rights as an ideological tool against the Third World in an effort to dilute the antiapartheid campaign. Of course, some minor countercurrents were evident even during this time, such as Nixon's support, although quite bland, for the ratification of the Genocide Convention, as well as moves to protect individuals and societies from unofficial international terrorism.

Despite this adverse trend at the presidential level, an important countertrend took hold in Congress during the 1970s. As of 1973, under the spirited leadership of Congressman Donald Fraser, a series of hearings on human rights issues were held virtually every year. These hearings substantiated the contention that the United States, as a matter of often covertly implemented official policy, had abetted violations of human rights. The congressional mood also reflected the conviction arising in response to the Vietnam experience that it was not sensible foreign policy to support foreign governments just because they were anticommunist, and, further, that in an era of détente, it was again possible to insist upon some moral content in American foreign policy. Such an insistence was in part an aspect of congressional assertiveness in the foreign policy domain after a decade of relative passivity in deference to the prerogatives of the imperial presidency during the Vietnam War.

Tangible evidence of congressional concern about United States support for foreign governments that engaged in violations of human rights was introduced in a variety of respects into foreign assistance legislation.[1] The basic legislative tactic was embodied in section 502B of the Foreign Assistance Act, which called upon the president to reduce substantially or terminate "security assistance to any country which engages in a consistent pattern of gross violations of internationally recognized human rights." There was an unspecified "exceptional circumstances" provision that enabled a president to overlook human rights abuses if so inclined by other considerations. These initial congressional efforts were substantially thwarted by the Kissinger-Ford dislike of any effort to bring human rights factors to bear on the foreign policy process.

Congress, however, gradually became more vigilant, and in 1975 enacted a revised section 116 to the International Development and Food Assistance Act that extended the approach of section 502B to the area of economic assistance. According to section 116, economic assistance could not be provided by the United States unless it "will directly benefit the needy people in such country." Here again, in effect the responsible part of the governmental bureaucracy—in this case the Agency for International Development—has great discretion to determine whether recommended assistance is for the benefit of "needy people."

It remains difficult to assess how much this congressional human rights pressure meant prior to the Carter Administration. President Ford refused to cut aid to such human rights violators as Argentina, Haiti, Indonesia, Iran, Peru, and the Philippines. Some impact probably resulted from the reporting requirements of the legislation, which imposed an obligation on the State Department to submit annual reports on the human rights records of all aid-receiving countries. Also of some durable consequence was the creation of a distinct human rights identity within the State Department bureaucracy. Such initiatives took on much greater significance when, in the early Carter years, the executive branch was given a bright green light on human rights; but even earlier, Congress had created certain expectations and conditions that moved the subject matter of human rights ever so slightly closer to the policy-forming process. As the 1980s commence in a spirit of a renewed preoccupation with the Soviet menace, it is to be expected that congressional support for human rights initiatives will ebb even more than they have at the presidential level. In fact, it would be possible to depict the ebb and flow of congressional attitudes toward human rights in a figure that parallels the pattern of national policy depicted in figure 2-1, but whose gyrations are more drastic.

At the beginning of the Carter presidency, X_4, a new surge of positive emphasis on human rights commenced. Indeed, the focus on human rights was given unprecedented attention as a dimension of foreign policy during Carter's first year in office. An explicit claim was made that relations with both allies and adversaries would be shaped by human rights considerations. Whether this human rights emphasis has been consequential and will be sustainable is a matter of conjecture. From the outset the tension between human rights aspirations and geopolitical goals was evident, with the latter normally given priority. Administration leaders acknowledged that human rights concerns, however serious, should not be allowed to impair the quality of United States relations with strategic countries such as Iran, South Korea, and the Philippines. Similarly, although Soviet dissenters were given some early aid and comfort, later stages in the Carter Administration suggest that arms control and trade relations are more significant features of the American relationship with the Soviet Union and cannot be successfully pursued if the stress on human rights is too strong. In effect, Soviet countermoves involve linking human rights attacks on their society with their denial of other forms of cooperation important to American leaders and make it clear that the American hope of separating various aspects of Soviet-American relations is unacceptable to the Soviet Union. Such an interaction has forced American leaders to concede, at least tacitly, the reality of linkage, and then to rank order their various objectives. In such an ordering, economic cooperation and arms control definitely outrank human rights.

As of mid-1980 the record of the Carter Administration, at least in its first term, seems reasonably clear on the human rights front. Throughout the Carter period a general concern with human rights was sustained and support lent to mild institutional initiatives at the United Nations. Few serious pressures on behalf of human rights have been mounted since mid-1978. Hence whether the years ahead will be properly interpreted as Y_1, Y_2, or Y_3 is uncertain (see figure 2-1). Y_2 seems the most probable future course at this time, reflecting the downward pressure exerted by geopolitical developments in a period of economic anxiety and related concern about energy prices and availability. This pressure, however, is likely to be almost neutralized by the bureaucratic momentum created by the endorsement of human rights as the anchor in American foreign policy, giving bureaucrats and officials more of a mandate than at any time except in the Roosevelt years to treat human rights concerns in a serious, positive way. This prospect was diminished somewhat by Andrew Young's resignation as chief United States representative in the United Nations. It will be undoubtedly diminished still further given Ronald Reagan's victory in the 1980 elections.

The political assessment offered here suggests that the status of human rights issues is resolved within the American political center, and is most characteristically located below midpoint on line C. Nevertheless, from a conservative perspective—that is, below line A—the profession of human rights concern is perceived and attacked as if it were an aspect of left politics, an instance of "creeping socialism" that erodes American sovereign rights and interferes with the pursuit of national interests. In contrast, those who can be associated with the political left—that is, above line B—perceive the progression of human rights as a deliberate mystification, by those in or close to power, disguising an imperialistic foreign policy with liberal rhetoric. Figure 2-2 represents, in crude terms, these diverse perceptions of the political identity of the human rights agenda.

The mainstream perceptions of human rights is indicated by trend-line I, the rightist* perception by II, the leftist perception by III. Figure 2-2 is

FIGURE 2-2
U.S. Record on Human Rights as Perceived

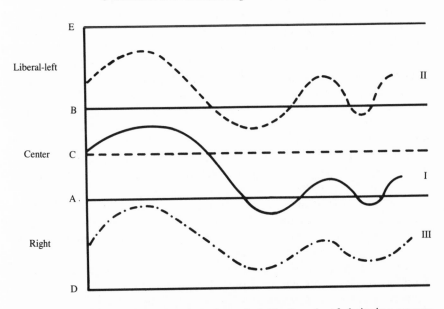

*"Rightist" and "leftist" are used here denotatively for the sake of clarity in a manner that corresponds with conventional perceptions of political orientation.

intended only to suggest the range of ideological debate pertaining to human rights issues. It makes no claim to assess the accuracy of these perceptions in relation to the *actual* course of human rights developments.

There are several observations that can be made about this attempt to graph the United States record on human rights:

- It is based on a subjective appreciation of the degree of human rights emphasis generally perceived to exist at a given time; others could challenge the depiction of the trend by projecting a divergent subjective trend or by relying upon some indicators that might objectify the trend-line in relation to one or more variables.

- The United States record as projected indicates the degree to which human rights policies are rooted in the overall setting of centrist politics and indeed are mainly a feature of right-leaning centrism, as expressed by the A–C space on the graph. In fact, as portrayed, the waning periods have dipped below line A, indicating a rightist approach, while never penetrating line B, beyond which a leftist approach would be indicated.

- The trend-line suggests a cyclical pattern that is generally correlated with presidential and party politics; turning points, except in the case of X_1, associated with the serious initiation of the Cold War, coincide with changes in the person and party affiliation of the president. The more waxing phases have been periods when a Democrat was in the White House, and the waning phases those when the president was a Republican. The cycle is self-generating, the idealistic phases inducing a concern with a foreign policy based on real interests, whereas the realist phases induce an idealistic impulse to vindicate the use of power with an active sense of moral purpose. This alternation in emphasis corresponds to deeply held attitudes embodied in American political culture and diplomatic history. The duration of these phases reflects, in part, the period of time which it normally takes for disillusionment to shift the political mood. If the economic or security situation worsens, the idealistic strand will probably be eliminated, whereas if it improves it will be strengthened.

- The perceived reality reflects political orientation; those in the mainstream of American politics would regard the trend-line as generally reasonable. Those to the left would shift the line lower, while those to the right would shift it higher.

- The purpose of this mode of presentation is to offer in concise form an overall image and impression of the United States record on human rights; it attempts to depict general relationships and to regard the controversy about the proper place of human rights in American foreign policy as an intramural concern of centrist politics.

Human Rights in the Domestic Political Arena

Part of the argument of the previous section was that support for human rights oscillates within a relatively narrow ideological range. In this section, the implications of these constraints for policy will be explored somewhat further. It is hardly necessary to add qualifiers, especially to underscore the limited utility of such rough and subjective political designations as "left," "right," and "center." The justification for this type of analysis is that it reinvests the subject of human rights with political content, thereby challenging lawyers and moralists, as well as cynics, to offer a richer, more relevant type of analysis of the politics of human rights.

FIGURE 2-3
U.S. Political Spectrum

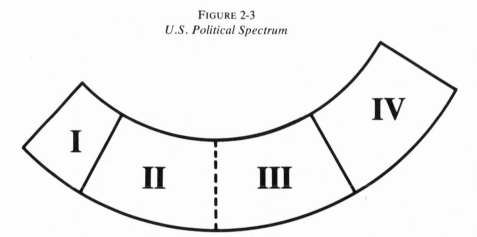

In figure 2-3, Roman numeral I represents the left, II represents the more liberal position of the center, III represents the more conservative portion of the center, and IV represents the right. Sections II, III, and IV are represented as occupying equivalent political space and as being each twice the size of I. Of course, this representation is crude and static. The relative strengths of these various positions are more elusive and vary from issue to issue and over time. The purpose here is to encourage a way of thinking that is generally in touch with the concrete situation. In a variety of respects, I is far weaker than IV, although IV, while influential, has also been excluded from a commanding position in relation to United States policy-making since World War II. The political direction of the United States has been generally positioned in III, the conservative-center space, with periodic enlargements of ideological orientation to embrace the more moderate fringe of II or the more moderate fringe of IV. The coalition-building space in American politics, then, can be extended from mid-II to mid-IV.

For a foreign policy position's visability to be assured it must have a secure identity within II, and for it to be genuinely sustainable, it must also have some appeal to the moderate fringe of IV. In crude terms, a supportive coalition needs to be able to command two thirds of the relevant space, a degree of support that happens to coincide with the constitutional requirements for treaty ratification by the United States Senate. The search for a left-leaning coalition based on support from II–III can rarely command a sufficient majority to achieve a two-thirds consensus, whereas a right-leaning can produce effective results. The strength of IV rests on its influence in Congress, in the Republican Party, in business, in military and media circles, in corresponding sectors of the bureaucracy, in grassroots support in the South and West, and in influential national professional and voluntary organizations. In contrast, I has virtually no "presence" in any of these domains, and II has only a shaky, marginal episodic presence, except in some important segments of the media. Political figures such as Robert Taft, Barry Goldwater, and Ronald Reagan are associated with IV, whereas George McGovern, Eugene McCarthy, and Ramsey Clark can be associated with II. Both Goldwater and McGovern won presidential nominations and were decisively defeated at the polls, reinforcing the political dominance in this period of the political center, and II has been only very episodically relevant, and really only influential during the short period in the later 1960s and early 1970s when anti-Vietnam sentiments crested.

In 1978, the debate over the Panama Canal Treaties illustrated in a vivid form the veto power of the American moderate right in the context of coalition-building for foreign policy purposes. Of course, the nostalgic significance of the Panama Canal, its national security role, and Ronald Reagan's emphatic and continuing opposition to the treaties all accentuated the normal circumstances. What is evident, however, is the need of the centrist Carter leadership to move right so as to diminish popular opposition and build sufficient support for the treaties. The support of conservative senators, of the Joint Chiefs of Staff, and of Henry Kissinger, Gerald Ford, and William F. Buckley, rather than that of prominent liberals, is what the Carter Administration relied upon in its struggle to build a ratifying coalition. Such a reliance meant making the treaties more attractive to conservatives, and this was done by acquiescing in a series of amendments and reservations. In actuality, the colonial features of the treaties, as well as their ambiguity about the occasion of United States intervention, makes them substantively, if not politically, vulnerable to rejection from the left.[2]

The relevance to human rights issues is apparent. No firm national commitments pertaining to human rights can be undertaken if viewed as objectionable by the more conservative fringe of III or the more moderate fringe of IV. For this reason, it is not surprising that the American record on ratification of international human rights instruments lags so far behind the actual standards of domestic observance in the United States. Presidential discretion is not so constrained, especially at the symbolic level. To make presidential initiatives into a durable line of policy, however, eventually requires a normal supportive coalition.

The ideological constraints on human rights derive from several general concerns held by adherents of conservative III, moderate IV outlooks. Broad perceptions of human nature and international relations play some role. These outlooks tend to take a skeptical, Hobbesian view of human nature and regard the world as an anarchic arena of conflict. Such views lead to a stress upon the supposed realities of power, as well as to the conviction that "peace" is promoted by "balance," "stability," and "control," rather than by the promotion of decency within and harmony among states. In this regard, the advocacy of human rights, except as an instrument for exposing the moral vulnerability of ideological and geopolitical adversaries, is dismissed as wooly-headed, pie-in-the-sky moralism associated with the left-liberals who inhabit space II.

The strength of this (III–IV) critique of human rights induces compromises with centrist political leaders. For instance, centrist policymakers couple universal rhetoric with highly selective application of human rights concerns so that the realist world view generally prevails, although somewhat disguised by the assertion of humanistic pretensions. In turn, left-liberals in II seek to be taken seriously by claiming that their more sweeping endorsement of human rights is not only righteous, but efficacious in conventional national-interest terms; that is, the right-leaning coalition requirements skew the whole debate on human rights policy in a pragmatic direction, thereby eroding idealistic claims of principled behavior, as well as constraining the policy potential of a human rights emphasis.

The schematic division of approaches can be illustrated by representative voices. On the left, a moderate version of I is the kind of position set forth by Noam Chomsky and Edward Herman:

> Human rights have tended to stand in the way of the satisfactory pursuit of U.S. economic interests, and they have, accordingly, been brushed aside, systematically. U.S. economic interests in the Third World have dictated a policy of containing revolution, preserving an open door for U.S. investment, and assuring favorable conditions of investment. Reformist efforts to improve the lot of the poor and oppressed including the encouragement of independent trade unions, are not conducive to a favorable climate of investment. . . . For most of the sample countries U.S.-controlled aid has been positively related to investment climate and inversely realted to the maintenance of a democratic order and human rights.[3]

Characteristic features of position I are illustrated in this Chomsky-Herman passage: a stress on economic rather than ideological or geopolitical motivation, no attention at all to formalistic criteria of support for human rights, and a guiding conception of human rights based on humanistic values. This left outlook is anti-imperialist and refuses to qualify its endorsement of human rights at all by reference to overriding geopolitical considerations. Indeed, a distinguishing feature of I is to repudiate altogether geopolitical calculations in evaluating the moral content of foreign policy. The position is also critical of Soviet behavior, and more generally, of statism, except in the context of Third World struggles to establish their independent states so as to be free from outside control. The spokespeople for I rarely gain access to mainstream forums and tend to be read mainly by others who share their general orientation.

Position II, the more liberal sector of the political center, is intensely concerned with promoting symbolic, small-scale, gradual gains. Congressman Donald Fraser, who energetically works to expose human rights abuses and seeks to incorporate into United States foreign policy a genuine concern about human rights, is an excellent example of this outlook. In support of the early emphasis by the Carter Administration Fraser writes, "I believe that Carter can not only make good in his commitment, but that American interests will be advanced by doing so."[4] Fraser's conviction rests on the view that "societies cannot long be governed peacefully in the absence of mutual respect among citizens and between their citizens and their government."[5] In effect, protection of human rights is a precondition for political stability and a convenient belief for an advocate of human rights to hold, but a difficult argument to sustain with evidence. The empirical record is too mixed; many highly repressive societies seem ultrastable. And, in a broader setting of time and space, Fraser associates American national interests with the "gradual evolution toward a peaceful international system" which he believes requires "the protection of human rights as a foundation for such a system."[6]

To demonstrate that he is not alienated from the political mainstream, Fraser analyzes the policy option for the United States in the context of South Korea and the Philippines, two states with whom the United States has a significant security interest. In both instances, Fraser questions the objective character of this interest and suggests instead that if the observance of human rights standards does not improve, the United States should modify these relationships. In the Korean context, Fraser argues that the "United States must be prepared to disengage from South Korea carefully and in full consultation with Japan on a step-by-step basis," while Fraser hazards the view on the American military bases in the Philippines that "the need for these bases . . . should be studied, because a reasoned argument can be made that they are not important to U.S. security."[7] Note that Fraser's tone is tentative, there is no stress on the economic underpinnings of geopolitics, and the argument is formulated without questioning the security assumptions or framework of the mainstream. Position II does have a minority presence in all significant

arenas (government, media, public opinion), but its specific policy recommendations rarely prevail. The tone of position II may exert a genuine
influence in periods of Democratic Party occupation of the White House,
and the concerns of its adherents are useful at all times in exposing the
realities of human rights abuse. It is important to emphasize the absence
of communication between adherents of positions I and II, and the mutual
exclusiveness of their respective views of the world. In this regard, II is
much closer to III than to I; also IV is much closer to III than I is to II. II
tends to be more optimistic about the potential for human nature and
global community within the existing world order system than I, III, or
IV, although I is more receptive to revolutionary and utopian possibilities.

Position III, the mainstream right-leaning coalition, emphasizes the
primacy of geopolitics, although in periods of liberal Democratic presidencies, it seeks to couple this orientation with a moral posture, including
the appointment of representative figures associated with II to positions of
symbolic leadership. The Carter Administration, more than any other, has
sought to make the promotion of human rights the moral centerpiece of its
foreign policy, which in other respects maintains the priorities and assumptions associated with III. In his first major address on foreign policy
in May of 1977 at Notre Dame, President Carter said, "We have
reaffirmed America's commitment to human rights as a fundamental tenet
of our foreign policy."[8]

Carter was careful to emphasize the limited significance of the posture:

> We want the world to know that our nation stands for more than financial
> prosperity. This does not mean we can conduct our foreign policy by rigid
> moral maxims. We live in a world that is imperfect, and which will always
> be imperfect. . . . I understand fully the limits of moral suasion. We have no
> illusion that changes will come easily or soon. But I believe that it is a
> mistake to undervalue the power of words and the ideas that words
> embody.[9]

In effect, Carter associates human rights with a posture of moral concern,
rather than with the sort of policy and behavioral shifts that are stressed
by adherents of position I. And unlike II, Carter's stress on the "imper-
fection" of the world signals a recognition that conventional American
interests will not be jeopardized by the new emphasis on human rights.
Geopolitics will continue to be given priority and policy will not be
re-examined or reformulated in light of human rights ideals (i.e., the value
of military bases in the Philippines or the commitment to uphold, by force
if necessary, the status quo in Korea will not be questioned).

Such selective concern for human rights becomes more apparent in the
statement of secondary officials responsible for shaping actual policy.
When asked about selectivity, Zbigniew Brzezinski responded:

> I'm sure you must have confronted this same issue in different walks of life.
> . . . If you cannot punish all the criminals, is it fair to punish the one that

you can punish? The same thing applies to the international community. If, in fact, you are in a position, without damaging your other relationships, to make progress in the case of country A but not progress in the case of country B, should you therefore abstain from making progress in country A? I would say no.[10]

Selectivity is defended here in general terms of capability, although it is clear from the context that Brzezinski intends that human rights must be subordinated to geopolitics, and that this meaning should be read into the phrase "without damaging your other relationships." The United States' relationship with the Shah of Iran during the early Carter period was, perhaps, the most dramatic instance of this selectivity. Iran under the Shah was a country with one of the worst records in human rights, and yet its leader was welcomed at the White House as "strong, stable, and progressive"; it was supplied with the most modern weaponry in great quantities, and an individual, William Sullivan, whose career featured counterinsurgency operations more than diplomacy was appointed by Jimmy Carter as American ambassador.

Since III is the prevailing policy it is important to ask whether gains have been recorded. Of course, the basic claim is, in the words of Cyrus Vance, that "We are embarked on a long journey," and hence that "We can nourish no illusions that a call to the banner of human rights will bring sudden transformations in authoritarian societies."[11] On occasion, more tangible short-term gains are claimed. For instance, Brzezinski, reacting to the charge that we can do virtually nothing about human rights because almost every important country has something we want or need, replied with the boast: "Is it really unimportant that we can get 10,000 political prisoners released in Indonesia? Is it really unimportant that, in the case of East European or Latin American countries, with some caution and without fanfare, things may have improved because of our concerns?"[12] Of course, the causal connections are elusive since a target government will never acknowledge that it is acting under pressure. Certainly the Indonesian government will never acknowledge that their prisoner releases were stimulated by pressure from the Carter Administration. Both II and III share the view that idealism and realism must and can be reconciled, although the emphasis is somewhat different because II tends to reformulate realism in longer-term horizons and, therefore, raises questions about whether the presumed security preoccupations of inherited policy are really warranted.

Of course, the specific content of III shifts through time, partly in response to the growth of external pressures. For instance, minimum human rights credibility in global arenas in the late 1970s requires a much higher level of support for the anti-apartheid campaign than was expected a decade earlier. The international consensus on this human rights issue has hardened, and its proponents have escalated their demands in reaction to the frustration of their inability to achieve their goals.

Similarly, there has been a rise in the global acceptance of expectations that the satisfaction of basic human needs is necessary to any general conception of human rights. Earlier, in the formulation of the Four Freedoms and the Universal Declaration, such economic concerns were acknowledged, but only minimally. The Carter Administration has consistently defined human rights as including three main clusters of concerns: rights of the person to be free from government abuse; "right to the fulfillment of such vital needs as food, shelter, health care and education"; and the right to enjoy civil and political liberties.[13]

Carter went further in accenting this imperative: "More than 100 years ago Abraham Lincoln said that our nation could not exist half slave and half free. We know a peaceful world cannot long exist one-third rich and two-thirds poor.[14] At the same time, the human rights initiatives and claims directed at concrete circumstances of foreign societies have all concerned noneconomic violations of human rights, especially abuses of the person. The Carter Administration has not been forthcoming with actual plans to restructure the international economy so as to give poor countries a favorable prospect for solving problems of domestic poverty. Thus, the expansion of the conception of human rights to include economic rights has been mostly verbal up to this point and hardly evident in policy settings.

Position IV is rather diverse in composition. Its adherents are not isolated from the mainstream political process as are adherents of I, and its more moderate representatives participate actively in the coalition-forming process. Indeed, even the more extreme adherents of IV, through commanding positions in politics, media, the military, or business, exert considerable influence, and in this sense the outlook associated with IV exceeds II in its impact on the right-leaning coalition process located mainly in the political space of III. The concerns of IV need to be consistently taken into some account at the level of political action, as the adherents of IV possess an effective veto power over political initiatives proposed by American leaders. As a consequence, for value-sensitive subject matter such as human rights, the capability of III to sustain its policy depends eventually on attracting sufficient support, or at least avoiding active opposition, from IV

The essential goal of IV during this period is to invest foreign policy with a heavily ideological character, stressing the fundamental conflict with the Soviet Union and Communism, and emphasizing the moral superiority of the United States and Western allies in that struggle. Furthermore, that struggle takes precedence over other concerns, and waging it successfully should override by a wide margin all other goals of foreign policy. The more moderate adherents of IV have an affinity with the more conservative adherents of III in their insistence that human rights should be construed in political terms, should emphasize the concrete failings of communist societies, and should give aid and comfort to opponents of state policy within those societies. The more militant adherents of IV would take any steps in their effort to transform communist societies, risking even war to do so. In this regard adherents of III tend to be much more cautious in practice, even though they share many of IV's views on what is desirable. Adherents of IV also tend to regard human rights as mainly, if not exclusively, devoted to the failings and struggles associated with communist societies; with other states they either consider human rights violations subordinate or neglect them altogether. Concerns with communist societies exhaust the legitimate agenda on human rights, and adverse pressure should not be placed on governments that are our geopolitical allies.

Daniel Patrick Moynihan is a clear example of a political personality who is in the border region of III–IV. He argues:

> . . . the Soviets are necessarily singled out by any serious human rights offensive . . . they are the most powerful opponents of liberty on earth today . . . their ideology . . . since the passing of Nazism and the eclipse of fascism as a school of thought . . . remains the only major political doctrine that challenges human rights *in principle*.[15]

Hence to promote human rights necessarily implies mounting an anticommunist ideological attack, with all that this portends for deteriorating Soviet-American relations.

It also means repudiating sharply the effort of the General Assembly of the United Nations, acknowledged as valid in the Carter diplomacy, to shift the emphasis of human rights from the defense of liberty to the pursuit of equality. Moynihan explicitly attacks Carter on these grounds and is particularly scornful of the view that on North-South issues the United States and USSR might cooperate to mitigate the burdens of poverty. Moynihan believes that Carter's conceptual approach to human rights is objectionable to the extent that it diverts "our attention from the central political struggle of our time—that between liberal democracy and totalitarian Communism—and focuses instead on something else, namely, the concerns and quests of Third World peoples.[16] Even more pointedly, Moynihan rehabilitates the justification for Vietnam, acknowledging only that "the enterprise was doomed, because it was misconceived and mismanaged," not because it is "wrong or immoral to resist the advance of totalitarian Communism."[17] Indeed, he argues that the failure of Vietnam, if anything, has "added enormously to the importance of ideological resistance, and this precisely is the role of 'Human Rights in Foreign Policy.'"[18]

Moynihan's outlook differs revealingly from that of Fraser. For Fraser the human rights stress should be mainly associated with the international relationship in which American responsibility exists. While he is quite prepared to condemn communist abuses of human rights, his main concern is with encouraging liberal democratic values in noncommunist societies, partly on the basis of values, partly as a practical step to assure societal stability. From this perspective, the proper role of human rights is to shape policy that will reduce suffering and produce a more humane world; such a policy objective is not effectively advanced by exposing Soviet failures, about which the United States can do little, and may even be counterproductive by creating more tension and less cooperation.

Hardcore adherents of position IV, especially in the 1950s, tended to view the espousal of human rights in general terms as the province of ultraliberals associated with position II. The earlier battleground involved sovereign rights and their alleged compromise by the submission of national behavior to international standards, procedures, and scrutiny. These concerns crystallized in a domestic political struggle relating to treaty-making, climaxed by the narrow defeat of the Bricker Amendment, which was designed to confine the president's authority to bind the country and to confine treaties within constitutional limits. Even though this initiative associated with position IV was defeated, the closeness and intensity of the struggle has inhibited III and reinforced the perception of IV as a potent blocking force in the human rights area. The poor ratification record of the United States in relation to major human rights instruments has reflected this domestic political situation.

More recently, these hardcore adherents of IV dissent from the Moynihan view that the universal character of human rights standards is an appropriate basis of foreign policy, provided the focus of emphasis is placed on the main danger posed by left-authoritarianism associated with the Soviet Union. Their emphasis is upon disentangling geopolitical priorities from liberal moralizing. Such views surface especially in relation to criticism of United States policy toward South Africa. On the right there is strong resistance to the antiapartheid campaign, to the attitude that was epitomized for a time by Andrew Young's outspoken attacks on racism, to the whole insistence that race is an international issue. In essence, the right regards American hostility to an economically, strategically, and ideologically useful ally in Pretoria as a self-negating and stupid policy. Underneath this criticism is more general opposition by hardcore IV to taking American foreign policy initiatives in close association with the United Nations. This opposition arises from bedrock nationalism, which is threatened by any claims advanced on behalf of humanity or the global community. These anti-United Nations views held by IV are confirmed and inflamed by the tendency in recent years for the main political organs of the United Nations, especially the General Assembly, to take positions opposed by the United States and to be the scene of a rising tide of anti-American rhetoric.

We can draw several conclusions from this analysis of principal political positions in the American policy. First, human rights policy, to be a sustainable aspect of American foreign policy, must be supported by a right-leaning centrist coalition associated with space III; for formal initiatives such as treaties or legislative actions, this coalition must normally extend across the boundary of III into space IV; for policy-making purposes space I is irrelevant and virtually "invisible"; that is, its adherents lack "weight" except in some limited intellectual circles. Space II provides the inspirational leadership for human rights activities, as prod in times of liberal ascendency, and as goad in times of conservative ascendency; the influence of space II is to provide data, ideas, rhetoric, and leadership personnel, but its positions are perceived as generally "unrealistic," and receive only diluted endorsement by the actual leadership of the country.

Second, the character of mainstream political coalitions means that leaders must reconcile human rights initiatives with significant short- and long-term geopolitical interests of the United States, including especially its role as leader of a global anticommunist network of alliances; such a requirement also means that the promotion of human rights must not be achieved at the cost of any significant domestic economic interests; these requirements severely constrain policy-makers' freedom of action in the human rights field.

Third, the United States is one of the few countries in the world in which the left, space I, is neither active nor repressed. As a result, the perception of "balance" in the American system is different from what it is elsewhere, even among the Trilateral (or Organization for Economic Cooperation and Development) group of countries. For this reason, the attitudes of the General Assembly are discounted in the United States as "radical" and "extreme" rather than being received as "mainstream" expressions of international public opinion. Furthermore, American debate on human rights is rarely informed by or sensitive to more radical analyses of international developments; consequently there is serious distortion of political discourse in this country and a genuine difficulty in communicating official American policy abroad. Such difficulty is somewhat offset by the relatively high standards of human rights within the United States and by the degree to which idealistic American presidents are taken at their word, rather than their deeds, in many other parts of the world.

A Conjecture on Results

What can we expect to happen over various periods of time in relation to a variety of proposed human rights initiatives? What steps would be necessary to attain particular human rights goals? These are enormously complex questions. Policymaking that bears on human rights occurs in a wide variety of arenas. Also, human rights realities can be deeply influenced by a variety of policies that are undertaken for geopolitical reasons, ranging from covert operations in foreign societies to international trade and monetary moves. As a consequence, there is a tendency to fall back on traditional criteria of human rights progress: How many treaties are proposed, signed, ratified? Has the number of political prisoners changed? Has the incidence of torture been reduced? Obviously, there is no objection to the consideration of such developments, only to their being used as a sufficient indication of progress.

It seems helpful to adopt a politically more sophisticated framework of assessment. This means, above all else, that the behavioral patterns of United States policy will be weighted more heavily than the rhetorical patterns. Hence, if United States leadership in public arenas advocates support for needs-oriented development in Third World countries, but uses the CIA to destabilize or overthrow governments so oriented, then that apparent incoherence should be exposed.

Also, if a forward rhetorical stand on human rights by the United States government encourages Americans and others to increase their financial support for human rights organizations and thereby gives these organizations a greater opportunity to exert influence, this result should be noticed and appreciated. In effect, we need to be sensitive to the secondary and tertiary, possibly unintended, effects of a particular human rights policy. A systematic attempt to do this is beyond the scope of this chapter, but a schematic outline of what is contemplated is suggested in the following list.

Checklist for Assessing Human Rights Policy

  I. Diplomatic Settings
      1. Persuasive diplomacy
         a. Raising awareness
         b. Symbolic actions and omissions (*e.g.,* honoring dissenters, avoiding ports of call, ambassadorial and other appointments)
         c. Private communications (*e.g.,* ambassadorial representations to foreign governments)
      2. Coercive diplomacy
         a. Criticism and censure
         b. Military and economic aid tied to human rights
         c. Boycotts
         d. Sanctions
            i. psychological (*e.g.,* preventing athletic contact), economic, public and private, diplomatic (*e.g.,* breaking relations), and military
           ii. formal, informal
          iii. unilateral, collective
 II. Governmental Settings
      1. Executive branch
         a. Upgrading human rights concern via budgetary allocations, machinery, and appointments
         b. Cooperation with other branches of government, with international institutions, with nongovernmental organizations (NGOs)

      c. Operational support by leadership of active concern by diplomats, bureaucrats

      d. Subordinating government programs, including CIA activities, to human rights objectives

      e. Discretionary leadership with respect to refugees, asylum, immigration policy

      f. Information and educational activities associated with United States Information Agency, Voice of America, and so forth

  2. Legislative branch

      a. Insistence on compliance with legislative initiatives bearing on human rights

      b. Critical scrutiny of executive branch country reports on human rights situations

      c. Ratification of basic international human rights instruments, such as the Convention on the Crime of Genocide, International Covenant on Economic, Social, and Cultural Rights; International Covenant on Civil and Political Rights; International Convention on the Elimination of all forms of Racial Discrimination

      d. Hearings and reports on serious human rights situations identified by the United Nations and respected nongovernmental organizations

      e. Support for presidential initiatives

      f. Initiatives in response to severe deprivations (*e.g.,* boycotts on critical imports and exports from worst violators)

      g. Review of human rights impact of United States foreign investment

III. Policy Domains

  1. Rights of the person

  2. Economic rights and duties

      a. Support for new international economic order

      b. Priorities in aid and loans

      c. Trade liberalization for poor countries

      d. Democratization of international economic institutions

  3. Civil and political rights

  4. Reduction of arms sales and defense budget

IV. Domestic Implementation in United States

  1. National self-determination for Indian peoples

  2. Satisfaction of basic needs for the poor

  3. Rights of minority peoples

  4. Rights of extreme opponents of government

  5. Control of infringement of rights by official agencies (*e.g.,* FBI, CIA, etc.)

This tentative checklist is designed only to encourage politically more sensitive styles of assessment of human rights activity than have been generally undertaken in the past. Obviously, the checklist can and should be refined continually through time.

A Note on the Carter Approach

Although we have emphasized the Carter approach to human rights as a typical waxing phase of a cyclical pattern, it also has a certain distinctiveness that should be noticed. Unlike earlier moralistic periods in American foreign policy that tended to be oriented around creating conditions for world peace (Wilson, Roosevelt, Kennedy), the Carter initiative is centered on human rights as an end in itself. Never before has concern for the way governments treat their populations been given so much importance in the formulation of foreign policy, a presidential initiative that originally, also, was reinforced by strong congressional support.

As we have suggested, this embrace of human rights diplomacy by President Carter has weakened considerably since its earliest period, especially in controversial contexts of specific country policies. Nevertheless, in the first retrospective glance at the Carter presidency, its emphasis on human rights is its hallmark, aside from its revival of the Cold War at the beginning of 1980. Until the hostage crisis in Iran and the Soviet invasion of Afghanistan, critics or supporters of the Carter foreign policy often concentrated on human rights. Even a geopolitical hardliner, such as Brzezinski, has rested his defense of Carter's foreign policy, of which he is, of course, principal acrobat (architect), on claims of success in infusing "American foreign policy again with a certain moral content. The human rights issue is very pertinent here."[19] Even with the tendency of 1979–1980 geopolitical developments to supercede other aspects of foreign policy, no other American presidency ever rested so much of its credibility on its performance in the human rights sphere of policy.

In this respect, the stakes are raised. If the Carter emphasis is abandoned or leads to his electoral repudiation, the status and cause of human rights is likely to be set back seriously. If it succeeds, even in part, the whole cycle of waning and waxing may be shifted slightly to the left, making space II rather than IV the main focus for coalition-building activities. Such an outcome at this writing seems unlikely because of the wider rightward drift of American politics that is likely to erode Carter's broad emphasis on human rights and, more generally, stifle further whatever liberalizing tendencies still remaining active in the American political mainstream.

In conclusion, the Carter experiment on human rights diplomacy has revealed the basic dynamic of the American political scene and will not persist, much less prevail, because of the character of this dynamic. At the same time, the global setting of American policy has its own dynamic, which is resulting in more external pressure for human rights implementation and internal pressure to commit violations since governments are relying on increasingly coercive approaches to contain their own populations. For a variety of reasons beyond the scope of this chapter, moderate politics is in decline throughout the globe.[20] The human rights policy likely to emerge from the limited contemporary United States political spectrum may make a positive contribution to the emerging global consensus on human rights but will, at best, have a modest impact on the domestic affairs of regimes that fail to meet this international standard of human rights.

III

Theoretical Foundations of Human Rights

In most respects national sovereignty at the state level is stronger than ever. Such a political reality restricts the potential scope for applying rules of international law to those subject matters where governments give their consent to be bound and are prepared to implement their consent with a high degree of compliance. The protection of human rights is in a very special category. For various reasons associated with public opinion and pride, governments are quite ready to endorse (even formally) standards of human rights despite their unwillingness to uphold these standards in practice. Occasionally, for internal political reasons, the reverse situation pertains, such that a government is unwilling to endorse in a formal manner standards of human rights that are characteristically upheld; the United States, of course, is the prime instance of this latter observation, beset by social forces with political leverage that are reluctant to validate any external claims on the shape and substance of the internal governing process.

At the heart of the matter is the peculiar status of enforcement in international society. Given the absence of community enforcement capabilities, the system depends on voluntary patterns of compliance, the effectiveness of which depends, in turn, on perceived self-interest. Normally, governments don't agree to norms unless, at least at the moment of their creation, compliance seems consistent with the national interest. But human rights are different, at least for many governments. In this instance, some governments have an interest in subscribing to the norms even when there is absent any serious intention to comply, and vice versa: some have an interest in avoiding subscribing even when their intention to comply is evident. In the former case, the absence of any *real* enforcement prospect makes it feasible to give lip service to human rights, while in the latter case the *theoretical* possibility of enforcement inhibits certain governments from regarding human rights as binding rules of international law.

Such a situation creates the temptation to adopt a cynical view of efforts to protect human rights, a view to some qualified extent justified by patterns of state practice. However, a more subtle appreciation of the relationship between norms of law and the behavior of states in international society suggests that the protection of human rights through their formulation as norms may achieve certain limited results. The tension between normative aspiration and political constraint in relation to the protection of human rights needs to be better understood.

To depict this tension requires an image of the overall system of world order, defined here as the main patterns and principles by which sovereign states and other actors interact with one another. One dimension of world order consists of a series of competing normative logics, each of which purports to provide an independent basis for structuring behavior in prescribed directions. A normative logic refers to a set of propositions about what ought to happen with respect to the exercise of authority in the world political system.* In a sense, each normative logic can be thought of as an independent line of ethical or legal argument about how to relate values or societal goals to behavior, given the reality of sovereign states.

These several complementary ordering logics are of greatly unequal political weight. Each logic generates a distinctive normative approach. The assessment of these distinct logics determines the relationship of human rights to the world legal order at a given period in international history. To think of human rights in the world as a whole, as distinct from some particular transgression (treatment of Indians, slavery, genocide), is a recent phenomenon and, to date, partly an American preoccupation and partly a consequence of the greater prominence achieved by human rights organizations that consider the world as a whole their proper domain of concern. Such a global focus is itself a reflection of the emergence, however weakly, of a planetary perspective based on the notion that persons, not just juristic entities like states, warrant our normative attention.

First, we will describe these ordering logics highlighting their distinctive relevance to human rights concerns. In a subsequent section their relative weight will be considered, as well as the "ordering mix" pertinent for human rights. It should be emphasized that the protection of human rights is dependent on the interplay of normative standards and social forces committed to their implementation. Pressure to violate human rights also reflects social forces, especially as these take shape within governmental bureaucracies at the state level. In essence, then, the protection of human rights is an outcome of struggle between opposed social forces and cannot be understood primarily as an exercise in law-creation or rational persuasion. Similarly, the ordering logics specified below are arenas of struggle, as well as foundations of authority.

---

*Perhaps the word *logic* conveys an overly rigorous image of the relationship between premises and application. It seems preferable, however, to *approach* or *perspective*, as the main intention is to suggest that a line of analysis *follows from* (in a logical sense) the adoption of an initial premise about the foundation of political authority in the world system.

Statist Logic

The predominant ordering logic since the Peace of Westphalia has been associated with the "will" of the territorial sovereign state. The government of a state has been its exclusive agent with respect to formulating its will in external relations. The juridical framework of relations worked out in the West has been gradually generalized to apply throughout the globe. The mainstream of international law has evolved out of the predominance of the state and of the states system. Notions of rights evolved within the context of domestic political struggles. However, from Greek, Stoic, and Christian roots came ideas of humane governance associated with relations between rulers and ruled anywhere. While medieval ideas of Christian unity and natural law were influential, theorists of the emergent states system were ambivalent about such critical issues as rights of resistance, tyrannicide, and humanitarian intervention. That is, the prerogatives of the state were balanced against notions of "higher law."

Jean Bodin, writing in the sixteenth century, set forth the decisive argument in favor of centralized secular authority, prefiguring the actual emergence of strong governments enjoying the realities of sovereign control over domestic society. The Swiss eighteenth-century jurist Vattel extended Bodin's views of sovereignty to the external relations of states, providing an application of statist logic to the conduct of interstate or international relations accepted as authoritative virtually until the present time. He separated natural law from positive law, placing emphasis on the requirement of governmental consent as critical to the formulation of international law obligations. Also, Vattel underscored the importance of accepting a government's own interpretation of its obligations, especially in relation to its own citizenry, or those present within its territory. External actors had no standing to complain in the absence of very specific agreements affording protection to aliens.

That is, human rights were not a fit subject for global concern unless a particular government so agreed. The positivist idea of sovereignty shielded abuses of rights committed within state territory. Some tension arose from the status of aliens abused by the territorial government, especially when the abuse was committed outside the European center of the world political system. Thus, "capitulary regimes" and doctrines on "the diplomatic protection of aliens abroad" complemented notions of nonintervention in the colonial period. With the collapse of colonial legitimacy, ideas of granting special status to privileged aliens and the more general approach of diplomatic protection lost their influence. Powerful governments continue to maintain a residual claim to intervene to protect their nations in a situation of jeopardy, but the claim is controversial and regarded by the Third World as colonialist behavior. The Stanleyville Operation of 1964, in which Belgian and French paratroopers with the benefit of United States logistical support rescued a thousand or so white hostages caught up in the swirls of civil war in the Congo (later renamed Zaire), illustrates the pattern of claim and response. Third World attitudes were sharply conveyed in the subsequent Security Council debate, much to the dismay of Western diplomats, who insisted on the "humanitarian" character of the mission.[1]

The pure morality of the states system is, in its essence, both antiinterventionary and antiimperial. The main contention, which continues to attract modern champions, is that only imperial actors have, in general, the will and capabilities to do anything significant about abuses of human rights, and yet it is precisely these actors that are least trustworthy because of their own wider, selfish interests.[2] John Vincent upholds the morality of nonintervention even "in the face of outrageous conduct within the state" (as in relation to Nazi persecution of Jews or mistreatment of blacks as a result of apartheid). Vincent argues that there are, on balance, insufficient grounds for trust in the impartiality of the intervenor and that there are reasons to suppose that the consequences of intervention will extend beyond the correction of the perceived evil.[3] In effect, an absolute doctrine of nonintervention (at least by forcible means) is an ordering choice that acknowledges that some particular instances might justify intervention, but not sufficiently to create a precedent that other potential intervenors could invoke.

This view of world legal order rests heavily on the juridical ideas of equality of states and sanctity of treaties and on the geopolitical ideology of a pure states system. It presupposes the absence of imperial actors serving as global enforcers, or, put differently, of strong states assuming the role of assuring compliance by weak states. This model of juridical and political equality, of a world of states mutually respectful of each other's sovereign prerogatives, necessarily precludes any missionary claim to intervene for humanitarian purposes. The highest goal in such a system is the autonomy of state actors protected through maximum adherence to the norm of nonintervention.

The statist matrix of political life also means that the most substantial contributions to the realization of human rights arise from the internal dynamics of domestic politics. Far more significant than imposing human rights policies from outside is an effective commitment to their protection arising from within the body politic. Political theorists as different as Kant and Lenin have argued that the realization of human rights is an automatic consequence of adopting the proper form of domestic government; in Kant's case, a liberal republic, and in Lenin's a radical socialist state established after an armed struggle that overcame the old order. That is, the achievement of human rights is a matter primarily for domestic reform; global concern is neither necessary nor effective.

Of course, there are connections between domestic political changes and external stimuli. The point, however, is that a repressive structure of governance cannot be transformed by marginal, voluntary remedial steps taken under pressure from without of the sort associated with human rights initiatives. The maximum impact of human rights pressures, absent enforcement mechanisms is to isolate a target government, perhaps denying it some of the benefits of trade and aid. There are no positive examples where such pressure has led to abandonment of the pattern of violation or to a collapse of the governing process responsible for such abuses of human rights.

However, a domestic challenge, if it succeeds, may indeed lead to a new political arrangment untainted by human rights abridgments. For instance, the Indian electoral repudiation of Mrs. Gandhi's "emergency" in 1977 was an enormous if perhaps temporary, victory for the cause of civil and political liberties in a polity containing almost one fifth of the world's population. The Iranian Revolution of 1978–1979 represented an extraordinary unarmed popular uprising against an extreme form of tyranny. These evolutions in national circumstances were largely achieved through the domestic play of forces, although the challenge and outcome may have been influenced to some small extent by the international endorsement of human rights. In addition, the failure in the Iranian case of pro-Shah forces to intervene assured the primacy of domestic factors.

The critical political arena for human rights, then, is most often internal to sovereign states. To the extent that repressive regimes are sustained by outside support via arms and capital, however, policies of governments and international financial institutions have some relationship to ongoing struggles between those who seek to promote human rights and those opposing them. An important implication of this way of thinking is that noninterference with the dynamics of self-determination is the most solid external contribution foreign governments can make to the promotion of human rights. Noninterference includes, of course, refraining from covert operations intended to alter the domestic play of forces.

But what of antirepressive interference? Here, I think, the reality of hegemonial and transnational patterns of self-interest are such that likely intervenors are predisposed in favor of the status quo or of some new configuration of control manipulated from outside. States are by and large oriented around selfish ends of power, wealth, and prestige; they are not reliably enough committed to human rights to be endowed with interventionary discretion, at least in the absence of a global community mandate that would shift the ordering logic to that of supranationalist logic (see below).

And what of counterinterventionary moves designed to neutralize the intervention of others? The interdependence of international political life means that to stay out while others go in can amount to a form of intervention. The dictates of statist logic suggest that if one state intervenes in a given country, counterintervention of a proportional character may be appropriate. Of course, such relations are imprecise, and each side is interested in prevailing over rather than neutralizing its adversary. Nevertheless, these considerations inevitably enter into an assessment of what must be done to allow the domestic arena to operate as effectively as possible to uphold human rights in light of statist logic.

Hegemonial Logic

Juridical equality has been up against the geopolitical reality of gross inequality since the inception of the states system. As a consequence, some polities have been much more penetrated than others. The colonial system, assimilated into world legal order with different degrees of formality in the nineteenth century, upheld imperial patterns of control. These patterns were justified by the colonizers, as had been the conquest of the New World some centuries earlier, by humanitarian, civilizing claims, and were formalized in such legal doctrines as state responsibility, diplomatic protection, and extraterritoriality. These humanitarian rationalizations and their doctrinal embodiment have been totally discredited during the decolonizing period, losing by now their earlier status of legal and moral right. Both international law and morality rest to some extent on a consensus among actors; if that consensus is eroded or shattered, the norms it had earlier supported are weakened or destroyed. The hegemonial relationship persists in informal and covert patterns, although it is everywhere renounced as a valid ordering logic, except possibly in the form of support for humanitarian intervention undertaken by states.[4] Nevertheless, the United States proclamation of a human rights diplomacy to be implemented as an element of its foreign policy, entails a hegemonial attitude toward the internal affairs of some other foreign countries to the extent that the attitude has consequences, as through diplomatic pressure, withholding aid or credits, and giving aid and comfort to dissident elements. Of course, unintended consequences occur. The promotion of human rights by the Carter Administration was never intended to overlook strategic considerations by undermining or alienating governments friendly to the United States; in fact, however, the evidence suggests that opposition groups in such countries as Iran, South Korea, and Tunisia were emboldened by Carter's encouragement of human rights in foreign societies. Indeed, Mehdi Bazargan has confirmed, unwittingly, Henry Kissinger's attack on Carter's human rights diplomacy as a factor in the collapse of the Shah's regime in Iran early in 1979. If such a result had been anticipated, it seems assured that the Carter Administration would have refrained from its posture of human rights support. Nevertheless, such interactions with internal struggles do not contradict earlier assertions that the destiny of human rights is overwhelmingly shaped by domestic factors.

The hegemonial outlook is not a reciprocal tolerance of the sort appropriate to contractual relations among equals in the statist framework. On occasion, it may involve some efforts to bargain concessions in human rights for economic assets with foreign states (such as the Soviet Union) of equivalent power; the effectiveness and side-benefits (and costs) of "linkage" geopolitics are controversial and should be considered a special instance of statist behavior rather than an exercise in hegemony. Hegemonial logic is an acknowledgment of the structuring role of power in a political system lacking an established governing process. In this regard, it is international relations as explained by Thomas Hobbes. In essence, there is no such thing as equality in international life on the level of states, no matter how much equality is achieved on the level of persons.

Hegemonial claims may be promoted by regional or even subregional actors, possessing relatively greater power within their relative domain and possibly motivated, in part at least, by human rights concerns. It seems evident, for instance, that both the Vietnamese-backed invasion of Cambodia and the Tanzanian-backed invasion of Uganda in 1979 were motivated (and tolerated, if not endorsed) but *not* legitimated as such because the target regimes were guilty of such flagrant, extreme abuses of elemental human rights. In effect, there is an ordering logic relevant to human rights that is associated with the capacity and will of governments or groups of governments to intervene in foreign societies to insist on political adjustments of a fairly fundamental character. The principal locus of this hegemonial capacity and disposition is in the leading global states, which take a definite interest in events in all regions of the world, but exceptional circumstances of abuse and relative capability to act, as we suggest above, may create a much more geographically limited conception of hegemonial role in certain settings, as between neighboring small countries.

The normative underpinning for the hegemonial logic is connected with "leadership": the supposition that there is some implicit correlation between power and virtue giving powerful states a mandate to impose their will on weaker states and that, on balance, this works out positively. Such a hegemonial process may obtain the acquiescence, tacit approval, and/or cooperation of other like-minded states. This kind of support, even if limited to the absence of censure for violating nonintervention norms, operates to confer a weak form of legitimation on *certain* hegemonial claims based on human rights abuses. Usually the hegemonial features are omitted from any argument in justification. The claim is projected as a matter of acting to overcome societal evil elsewhere, as the adoption of a policy by a given government to promote the well-being of others. India made such a claim to justify intervening to promote the secession of Bangladesh from Pakistan in 1971. Here, the element of geopolitical ambition—splitting asunder Pakistan, a traditional enemy— coincided with liberating the people of East Pakistan from abuses of their human rights that reached genocidal proportions. The United States, given its political traditions, is peculiarly prone to suppose that its exertions of influence on other societies are selfless undertakings for the benefit of foreign peoples. Throughout the Cold War, interventionary diplomacy in all forms was justified in large part by United States policymakers as a commitment to "freedom" (by which was meant, as it became increasingly clear in the Vietnam era, merely that the regime was noncommunist or non-Marxist, no matter how repressive of elemental human rights it might be otherwise). Thus, a human rights rationale was used as one rallying cry to engender support for waging a geopolitical struggle, the goals of which were quite unrelated to human rights.

On the other side of the struggle, the Soviet pattern of response amounted to an ideological mirror image of the Western crusade. The Soviet conception of freedom has been associated with nothing more substantive than the pro-Soviet orientation of a foreign government. Taking a more extreme approach, the Chinese People's Republic has deliberately subordinated political virtue to geopolitical preoccupation by its tendency to give moral endorsements to virtually *any* regime that adopts an anti-Soviet stand, even if it is also extremely anticommunist (e.g., Chinese positive response to Pinochet's accession to power in Chile or its positive association with the Shah's rule in Iran).

It is one thing to believe that the spread of a certain ideological orientation toward governance has human rights benefits. It is plausible for Democrats (or Republicans) to believe that liberty for the citizenry and checks on governmental power will produce a polity respectful of human rights. It is also plausible for socialists to believe that a polity governed by the working classes will produce a polity respectful of human rights. In both empirical instances, such beliefs have proven naive given repressive tendencies operative *within* each ideological frame. It is complex and controversial whether the repressive features of communist or capitalist societies inheres in the orientation toward governance. It would seem evident that the protection of basic human rights for most sectors of the population has been achieved in some advanced industrial countries with noncommunist governments in the North (that is, among the OECD membership). Very few states in the South have been able to realize political and civil rights, although it has been argued by Jorge Dominguez that Third World capitalist countries have a generally better record when it comes to political and social rights, whereas socialist countries do better with respect to economic rights.[5]

The more elusive case for hegemonial claims arises in relation to building up a defense against international aggression. Here the argument is that the overriding normative issue is maintaining a context for national self-determination in the face of a serious threat posed by an expanding imperial actor. As such, weaker countries are faced with an either/or prospect and would serve the cause of domestic political virtue by accepting a subordinate relationship to the more benign of the rival imperial actors. Such was the diplomatic posture of the United States in the first phases of the Cold War, dramatized by John Foster Dulles's contentions that nonalignment by Third World governments was "immoral." Such a hegemonial logic vindicates for *its* constituency the overthrow of Dubček in Czechoslovakia, Allende in Chile, or Mossedegh in Iran, as well as support for their far more repressive successor regimes. Of course, the more severe repression that arises after the hegemonial intervention is never acknowledged by the intervening government(s). Hence the contradiction between the liberating claim and the oppressive reality is never confronted. It is inevitable that the intertwining of hegemonial logic and statist behavior would produce these patterns of behavior. In one central respect, "hegemonial logic" is nothing more than an exemption for the strong from the constraints of "statist logic." Its "justifications," based on benevolent motivation, have not been validated by patterns of great power practice through history and seem flawed by the difficulty of separating the pursuit of interests at the expense of a weaker foreign society from the promotion of its well-being. In this regard a case could be made for stripping away the normative pretensions that cover the exercise of power in international relations with fig-leaf claims of moral and legal purpose.

The Third World stress from the outset has been on the primacy of nonintervention as a stance, at least with respect to "legitimate" regimes (*i.e.*, noncolonial, nonracist). The disintegration of colonialism together with the postindependence interventions of the superpowers in Africa and Asia have strengthened, at least temporarily, the antihegemonial posture. Also, the greater political self-consciousness of the Third World on a world level since the early 1960s, both in its own arenas and in the United Nations, has deprived the United States of global support for hegemonial geopolitics.

In some Third World settings, a regime in power solicits hegemonial intervention to sustain control in the face of rising domestic opposition or declining governing capacity. Mobutu's regime in Zaire did this in 1978 by turning over the internal administration of economic policy to IMF guidelines and guidance, with the IMF serving as an instrument for the diplomacy of the noncommunist leading states in the North. The consequence is a penetration of sovereignty, the subordination of the dependent state to an extent comparable to what occurred during the colonial period. Of course, at times the only sovereign option is to alienate normal prerogatives so as to promote national goals. The idea of intervention by invitation is at one level self-contradictory. At another level it reflects the hierarchical structure of the world political economy, which coerces weaker states to compromise their independence so as to avoid internal dissolution.

At what point a regime loses "legitimacy" under statist logic by inviting intervention is partly a factual question (extent of prior intervention by others) and partly a theoretical question (extent of governmental authority to alienate sovereign right of self-determination). From an international law perspective, if a foreign power is engaged on one side of a self-determination struggle, this weakens, in general, the prohibition on intervention by others. In fact, since at least the time of John Stuart Mill, prior intervention has generated a case for counterintervention so as to restore the dynamic of self-determination. That is, to the extent that overlapping and antagonistic hegemonial claims exist and are tied to contradictory images of the political preconditions for human rights, hegemonial logic has the effect of escalating and internationalizing political struggles in the modern world, causing additional loss of life and devastation. The Indochina War illustrates this destructive pattern. In this light, the statist stress on nonintervention seems normatively more beneficial in most circumstances than the hegemonial stress on benevolent intervention. This priority is a historical judgment assessing the imperial motivations of leading governments, as well as the tendency for ideological adversity to incite competitive patterns of intervention carried out at the expense of weaker polities. It is relevant to note that most of the fighting and dying since World War II has been done along the Third World periphery of the world political system. That is, "peace" is preserved at the core, even among bitter antagonists, because war is too costly in such arenas when the stakes are so high, as they are in the nuclear age. The political space outside the core (in the North) is where contending power positions can be tested at "acceptable risk" to the hegemonial actors, even if "unacceptable costs" are imposed on weak states. Such considerations form part of a critique of the role of hegemonial logic under present international circumstances. In an altered global setting one can imagine a more positive view of hegemonial logic, especially if imperial goals were credibly renounced and a broad consensus on human rights justifications existed among the potential range of hegemonial actors.

Naturalist Logic

Far less consequential in its behavioral impact than either statist or hegemonial logic, is the naturalist notion that certain rights inhere in human nature and should be respected by all organized societies. Here, the basis of human rights is prior to politics; the absence of consent by a sovereign authority is not necessarily an excuse for nonobservance. To the extent that human rights rest on a moral imperative, their status is both prior to and independent of their formal acceptance by a government. If a legal imperative is asserted, most jurists require some form of acceptance of norms to occur, although the process can be an implied one, as through the formation of customary international law. In part, the naturalist case is an appeal to the conscience of the rulers, or, more broadly, to the conscience of every political actor in the world, including private citizens, and even more, a plea to all to become "political" in their actions as they regard rights. It is the essential ground for claiming that human rights are universally valid.

Whereas statist logic accords primacy to jurisdictional principles, naturalist logic accords primacy to normative standards. Ideally, the state machinery would use its power to act within the guidelines of natural rights. The main difficulty with naturalist logic relates to the vagueness of the norms and ambiguity of the mandate. Those with power lay down what often appear as self-serving interpretations of what natural law requires, usually on the basis of nonnaturalist goals that rest on statist or hegemonial analysis. In this regard, disembodied naturalism (that which is right) is disregarded by policymakers and leaders as sentimental and moralistic. At the other extreme, a naturalist justification for controversial behavior may provide a government with a normative rationalization for what appears from an impartial perspective to be an imperial adventure.

In recent years, claims to topple regimes in Uganda and Cambodia raised an extreme naturalist case for outsider intervention. In effect, the naturalist contention was that the regimes in place were so shockingly bad by objective moral standards that the only appropriate question for outsiders was whether in the specific circumstances it was possible to intervene effectively. Vietnam's role in "liberating" Cambodia was not phrased by its leaders in Hanoi in naturalist/humanitarian terms, but rather as a matter of statist prerogatives to uphold its own sovereign status. Tanzania's role in toppling Amin's regime was more directly justified along naturalist lines. It was only because Amin's barbaric practices caused such widespread outrage that Tanzania's violation of Uganda's sovereign rights was overlooked. In Third World settings, especially Africa, the noninterventionist features of statist logic are generally given precedence over naturalist claims because of the fear that such claims could generate warfare and new patterns of imperial abuse disguised by a regional variant of hegemonial logic.

Given this sensitivity about hegemonial behavior in the Third World, it is necessary to organize interventionary missions of this sort with wide community support if possible. The difficulty of doing this effectively even in extreme cases suggests the vitality of statist logic, or put differently, the political weakness of naturalist logic standing on its own. If a course of action dictated by naturalist logic also coincides with the perceived implications of other logics (especially, statist and hegemonial), an improved prospect for effective action exists. In such an instance, however, motives are clouded, and cynical observers (often accurately) attribute the real motive to the practical influences and dismiss the naturalist argument as window-dressing. This either/or style of analysis misses the instances where naturalist considerations exert some influence, but not necessarily *sufficient* or *decisive* influence that might have been sufficient on its own to explain an interventionary act.

Naturalist logic does have a bearing on public opinion, and may inhibit some repressive policies. It may provide the most effective case to build popular support for taking human rights seriously. In addition, the influence of naturalist logic may express itself in relation to the normal desire that most rulers and ruling groups have to be regarded with respect, if not esteem. With transnational groups active in publicizing gross violations of human rights, there seems to be some incentive to avoid censure even when no government or international institution is prepared to object strenuously to a pattern of violation in a particular foreign society.

A final aspect of naturalist logic is its attractive doctrine that all persons, not just citizens, should be protected against state abuse. As such, the particular politics associated with the serious promotion of human rights contributes to the formulation of a movement for global reform in which the central objective is the well-being of people rather than the sanctity of juristic persons called states.

Governing by naturalist logic is up against a variety of constraints, especially to the extent that the existing national systems of political order lose legitimacy in the eyes of the masses. Given the dynamics of power and economic scarcity, there is a persistent need to coerce and mystify to protect the rich and deter the poor. The bureaucratic character of the modern state also renders naturalist logic less relevant to the decisional process. Political leadership in large organizational settings tends to be dominated by a variety of competing pressure groups representing differing parts of the government. Under these conditions a government will more readily use the rhetoric of high ideals while ignoring them in practice. Public policy is set by reference to a pragmatic calculus, partly shaped by pressure, partly by perceptions of interest. The spirit of doing right by doing good cannot prevail in such an atmosphere. Yet there is a subsidiary trend, exemplified by the notion of war crimes as prosecuted at Nuremberg in 1945, that violations of minimum rights are criminal acts even if committed by the highest public officials acting in the course of their bureaucratic duty. Although the Nuremberg Judgment was set in a framework of positive law, its validity rested more on the public consensus that Nazi leaders had acted in defiance of naturalist logic.

Naturalist logic remains, however, the underpinning of human rights, validating in the most fundamental way certain minimum standards of behavior. Such validation is prior to and takes precedence over any agreement to uphold certain rights that may exist, even if it is binding by way of treaty commitment. There is in all societal spheres an active moral force that is sensitive to patterns of abuse deemed contrary to nature; such patterns are perceived as wrong, as justifying resistance, opposition, and even outside financial and military assistance. The various forms of support given by outsiders to those engaged in the struggle against apartheid in South Africa draws on this naturalist logic. There is a core sense of decency and fairness that gives human rights their motive power in the popular imagination despite an understanding that the influence of these norms on governmental policy often tends to be at most honorific, minimal. It is this potency attached to moral claims that produces various forms and enthusiasms for populism, including shouts of "power to the people," "take it to the people," and so forth.

Supranationalist Logic

Here, we move to a different kind of logic, based on the inability to deal with the questions of human rights by reference to the relations among and within sovereign states. The creation of a supranational logic as an act of will by national governments complements the traditional language of diplomacy by a metalanguage of supranationalism. Whereas the lines of argument arising from statist, hegemonial, and naturalist logic are based on the *horizontal* ordering of separate states, supranational logic aspires to vertical ordering from above.

A weak sense of supranational community is operative at both the regional and global level and has been given increasing institutional expression in recent decades. This sense is conventionally associated with expressions of collective action by governments representing states in permanent international organizations. The League of Nations and the United Nations are the most prominent examples of such organizations; their shortcomings rarely lead even their critics to propose a world without such a central global actor. Globalist logic also characterizes various groupings of governments sharing a common position (Third World, OECD) or goal (nuclear suppliers, OPEC). Also, regional logic is operative to a limited and uneven extent in different parts of the world, with an impressive record of achievement and growth in Western Europe.

The regional context is very uneven and complex. The European record since World War II stands out in the human rights framework. The European Convention on Human Rights and the European Court of Human Rights give human rights a solid institutional foundation; several of the participating governments have accepted compulsory jurisdiction of disputes, granting individuals an opportunity to submit human rights complaints about abuses by even their own governments. This innovation, by acknowledging that nationals as well as aliens are victimized by human rights abuse and giving all victims of abuse the procedural basis for securing relief, has practical and theoretical importance. Of course, the relatively secure protection of human rights by governments in the region makes this acceptance of supranationalist review less of a threat to statist logic than might be supposed. Nevertheless, it represents a breakthrough. Recent positive achievements by the Organization of American States include issuing reports on systematic patterns of human rights violations occurring within particular states in the Western hemisphere; especially useful have been reports on abuse in Chile since 1973.[6] Elsewhere regional developments have proceeded less far, although in Africa and in the Middle East organizational frameworks exist, and some attention has been given to organizing responses to violations of human rights, but on a selective basis, generally limited to regional outcasts not permitted to participate as normal regional members. Here, the distinction between regional aggression and enforcement may grow blurred. We need to have recourse to the criteria of naturalist logic to assess whether such regional interventionary diplomacy seems to possess an authentic justification in human rights. Even if such a justification exists, it remains necessary to question whether the encroachment of statist logic is a positive contribution to the overall quality of world order at the current stage of international relations. These questions can be considered concretely with respect to Cuba since Castro in relation to the OAS, Israel in relation to the Arab League, and Africa in relation to the OAU.

With respect to human rights, the main global arena of supranationalist logic is the General Assembly of the United Nations. In its initial decade, dominated by the United States, the General Assembly was principally a bearer of Western hegemonial logic. Since then, it has become increasingly a bearer of both statist and naturalist logic, being an arena dominated by governments concerned with the protection of state sovereignty and at the same time being a forum in which the principal normative concerns of world public opinion were given expression. As such, it transmits contradictory signals, exhibiting strong rhetoric, selective moral perception, and, finally, expressing a political will that is constrained by the overall calculus of statist and hegemonial interests. The escalating line of United Nations response on southern African issues is indicative of the furthest reach of its activist stance based on a virtually global consensus on the level of rhetoric. Such results are deceptive. With the exception of the sanctions experiment in response to the Unilateral Declaration of Independence by Rhodesia (1965–1979) and the Security Council initiatives prohibiting export of arms for South Africa and supporting the independence claims of Namibia, little action has been taken in the United Nations despite years of condemnation and the many calls directed at the South African government demanding the abandonment of apartheid. Some states, especially the United States and Great Britain, have strong economic and geopolitical interests in South African stability. These countries, together with others, are glad to condemn apartheid, even as they act behind the scenes in various ways to assure the stability of the government in Pretoria, which acts in defiance of the demands issuing out of the United Nations. Hegemonial divisions and statist anxieties stymied efforts to fashion a response in the United Nations to reported mass atrocities in Cambodia after 1975 and in Uganda during

Amin's rule. Such passivity in the United Nations, given the grave circumstances in these two countries, which are only two examples among many, discloses the inability to deal evenhandedly at the supranational level with the broad array of international human rights concerns.

An aspect of this limitation on supranationalist logic arises from the inability of the United Nations to escape from its womb of hegemonial and statist logic. The activities of the United Nations are deeply constrained by the *will* of hegemonial actors, especially the two superpowers, and by deference to a statist conception of the *structure* of world order. These constraints are manifest in the lack of financial independence or sanctioning authority and capabilities. The United Nations lacks financial independence or sanctioning capabilities. The structures of authority in the United States represent a compromise between statist and hegemonial logic. Superpower veto rights in the Security Council, together with the Charter pledge in article 2(7) to prohibit intervention in the domestic jurisdiction of member states, are expressive of the formal extent to which the United Nations is derivative from and dependent upon other, stronger ordering logics. Some activity by the General Assembly suggests the opposite potentiality, namely, the inability of formal constraints alone to prevent the United Nations from playing an active norm-related role where a consensus of governments exists (as was the case with respect to demands for a new international economic order). Whether perceived as the conscience of the world or as an unconstitutional encroachment on statist prerogatives, the reality of the General Assembly's role in certain human rights contexts is undeniable, principally because it establishes a climate of concern about particular patterns of abuse that encourages sanctions or even intervention.

In addition, the rhetoric of the secretariat of the United Nations creates a weak independent sense of global identity that arises from some identification with longer range planetary concerns. The secretary general, perhaps even more than the Pope, speaks as a voice of conscience oriented toward the morality of the whole human species, rather than on behalf of a particular segment. Although constrained by practical inhibitions, the secretary general is expected to be a voice of globalist logic, reinforced by the content of naturalist logic. By way of contrast, the Pope is expected to speak as an interpreter of naturalist logic whose voice is entitled to great respect by non-Catholics, especially when reinforced by supranational logic (that is, on issues of war and peace as opposed to distinctively Catholic positions as on birth control).

The secretary general does not now possess an important voice. It is not expected to challenge successfully the main policies of the superpowers, except in very marginal ways, and the effort to mount such challenges is more likely to weaken the United Nations than inhibit a hegemonial actor like the Soviet Union or the United States. Dag Hammarskjöld challenged Soviet policy as related to the Congo struggle in the early

1960s and was eventually rebuffed, while U Thant's criticism of American policy in Indochina caused a hostile reaction in Washington but no shift in policy.

More generally, the United Nations can, at best, provide a global frame for statist logic. Efforts to hold world conferences under United Nations auspices on such global issues as oceans, environment, population, food, human settlement, and disarmament have mainly served as vehicles for statist propaganda. Only governmental representatives participate in a formal way. With the exception of the law of the sea negotiations, where a serious if difficult bargaining process has been underway, the outcomes of such United Nations spectacles are rhetorical flashes in the pan. It is true that the technical and political preparations for such a conference are a learning experience for the delegations and their support groups, perhaps influencing national policy. For instance, there is no question that environmental protection by states throughout the world was encouraged by the United Nations Stockholm Conference on the Human Environment in 1972 even though its supranational initiatives of a normative and institutional character have been of only minor significance. Another virtue of global conferences of this sort is that they provide a dramatic context for nongovernmental, populist groups that would otherwise lack the resources to organize a global presence or gain access to the media.

Despite the spread of repressive tactics of governance, it is significant that the United Nations has never sponsored a global conference on human rights. Indeed, governmental pressure a few years ago led UNESCO to withdraw from Amnesty International even the right to use its facilities to discuss the worldwide practice of torture; in the main report to support the contention of widespread torture, evidence was presented that implicated more than sixty members of the United Nations. It is no wonder disaffiliation by the United Nations occurred; it is some wonder that some slight affiliation was contemplated.

What the United Nations does in the human rights area is to set standards and generate norms, as well as put pressure on a few politically isolated states whose abuses are serious (e.g., Chile, Israel) although by no means the worst, if severity of abuse were the principal criterion for agenda attention. In this regard, the United Nations role is restricted and arbitrary, and its impact quite limited even where its concern is great (e.g., southern Africa). This appraisal may underestimate the United Nations' contribution by way of formulating an authoritative framework for human rights in the form of a series of instruments, including the Universal Declaration of Human Rights (1948), the International Covenant on Economic, Social, and Cultural Rights (1966), and the International Covenant on the Elimination of All Forms of Racial Discrimination (1966); in addition, the International Labour Organisation has generated a series of conventions pertaining to work and workers' rights. The Commission on Human Rights attached to the United Nations Economic and

Social Council has been disappointingly constrained in its activities by the lowest common denominator of statism—that is, high levels of mutual forbearance with respect to human rights violations.

The Charter of the United Nations also sets forth a compromise between dominant logics, although it seems oriented toward a more globalist set of goals, especially war prevention. The Charter could support a political shift in the direction of a more cooperative, centrally guided world legal order, but as matters stand, the potentiality of the Charter is totally dependent for realization upon governments of sovereign states. As such, it is not realistic to expect an expanded role for supranationalist logic until there is a significant shift in outlook by several leading governmental participants as a result of domestic cultural revolution or international ecological or security trauma. Something has to shake down the power-oriented, territorially based morality of statist logic before a more autonomous type of globalist logic can gain influence. Unless and until this happens, the United Nations is present mainly as the chrysalis for a different set of world order solutions and as a supplemental instrument of convenience when normal statist modes break down or are stymied. Because its procedures can be manipulated by tides of opinion, outcomes in the United Nations may appear arbitrary, or even contrary to the dictates of naturalist logic. To the extent that this happens, it undermines the slight additional weight accorded to the supranational logic by virtue of its status as a metalogic. Indeed, such a deterioration in the perception of the United Nations leads to a reinforcement of statist logic, and for powerful states, to a strengthening of hegemonial logic.

Transnational Logic

A variety of ordering activities in world society occur across national boundaries, reflecting neither statist territoriality nor the universalist sweep of globalist logic. In essence, the distinctive transnational aspect is the initiation of a stimulus in one state so as to have an impact elsewhere. The growing significance of a transnational perspective reflects the increasing interdependence of international life combined with the persisting weakness of global institutions. The transnational focus is an ordering halfway house responding to global needs, yet accepting the territoriality of power and authority. Transnational order as a logic is intermediate between the horizontal language of statism and hegemony, and the vertical language of supranationalism. Although they often base their claims on an alleged universality of outlook detached from other ordering logics, transnational actors are situated within sovereign states and subject to their control, except to the extent that some transnational economic actors can overwhelm the statist capabilities of weak states either on their own or through the support of hegemonial actors.

The identity of transnational actors is formally nongovernmental, although in certain settings links with some governments exist. The multinational corporation, the modern successor to the royal chartering of trading companies, is the most formidable and salient instance of a transnational actor. There is a dazzling array of transnational actors in all those sectors of modern life where activity is of concern to more than one territorial polity and where the multistate concern cannot be effectively represented by the direct cooperation of governments.

The transnational context of human rights is obvious. Interventionary obstacles restrict what governments or intergovernmental institutions will do, while geopolitical considerations may insulate some polities from human rights criticism or make their leaders reject such criticism as politically motivated. Therefore, it is not surprising that nongovernmental organizations devoted to the promotion of human rights have emerged in recent years. Amnesty International, International League for Human Rights, and the International Commission of Jurists are among the most significant transnational actors whose special concern is the human rights field. By issuing reports, applying informal pressure on foreign officials, and keeping in touch with victims of human rights abuse, these organizations exert an important, if selective, influence. Of course, statism intrudes as a constraint. Access to facts can be seriously curtailed by governments eager to avoid adverse publicity. No enforcement or sanctioning processes are directly available, although the impartial disclosures by these transnational actors may create a climate in some countries that builds pressure for more coercive stands on human rights in official arenas. The various moves against racism in southern Africa reflect this interactive process.

Transnational actors in the human rights area are private associations that depend for their existence on voluntary contributions of money. Their stature is partly a reflection of the quality of their work, their freedom from partisan causes, and their commitment to widely shared values. Hence, their influence results from having an impact on public opinion in all relevant arenas.

These initiatives focus on civil and political rights that have been globally and nationally endorsed through their embodiment in the Universal Declaration, the main global and regional human rights covenants, as well as in national constitutions and statutes. As a consequence, even many repressive governments are technically committed to these norms, and may be marginally vulnerable to arguments from within or without that the call for human rights is nothing more than the call for domestic law enforcement.

Within the wider conception of human rights as extending to the right of every person to the basic necessities of life, especially those transnational groups associated with religious and educational organizations have been important. The World Council of Churches, the National Council of Churches, the Third World Forum, and the World Order Models Project are examples of transnational actors seeking to generate support for humane patterns of governance that center on the full realization of human rights. Some of these groups take an active stand that is political in character; for instance, church organizations that give funds to liberation groups engaged in armed struggle, especially those in southern Africa.

In terms of ordering logics, normative transnationality is fragile and vulnerable, depending for its very formal existence on statist indulgence and voluntary private financing. And yet, given the "space" available in democratic polities, these transnational initiatives are relatively well established, enjoying a large measure of autonomy, and able to maintain contact with oppositional groups in many repressive societies. Awarding Amnesty International the Nobel Peace Prize in 1972 confirmed, in one sense, the contribution and prominence of the transnational approach to the promotion of human rights.

Populist Logic

The weakest, potentially most subversive, of ordering logics is that of "the people," taken in Rousseau's sense of being the ultimate repository of sovereign rights. Governments, institutions of any character, are derivative, and corrupting to the extent that they substitute various particular interests for the promotion of general interests. All political institutions are imperfectly representative, whatever their claim. And yet governments, especially, have at their disposal overwhelming capabilities to resist all challenges except occasionally those that arise from revolutionary groups seeking themselves to take over control of state power.

At the margins of power are a growing number of individuals and loosely organized groups that distrust the capacity, *in general,* of any government to uphold basic human well-being, including individual and group rights. These individuals and groups deny governmental and intergovernmental claims to possess a monopoly of legitimated authority. Often in the context of human rights these groups react to the failure of governments to follow through on their own promises, such as those contained in the Nuremberg Principles or the Helsinki Accords. Positive populist initiatives include the Bertrand Russell War Crimes Tribunal (originally organized in response to the Vietnam War, more recently perpetuated as a commission of inquiry into the denial of human rights in Latin America and West Germany, and now carried forward in a proposed permanent form by the Lelio Basso Foundation), the proclamation at Algiers on July 4, 1976, of the Universal Declaration of the Rights of Peoples (which supplements conventional international law with a series of claims based on the inalienable rights of peoples), and aspects of the counterconferences at major United Nations conclaves on global policy issues. Various individuals and groups adopt a perspective of planetary citizens, especially in imperial actors who tolerate oppositional activity, to emphasize the degree to which supranationalist logic needs to be strengthened by agitational activity.

At this stage, populist initiatives are significant mainly as thorns in the side of certain state and imperial actors. In human rights contexts, this means mobilizing public awareness about certain categories of abuse. It is a moral logic based on declaring what is right, as such, drawing its inspiration from naturalist logic.

The populist approach is distinguished from the transnationalist approach by its rejection of statist legitimacy. Transnational actors tend to accept the legitimacy of the overall world order system, seeking to induce governments to do what they are obliged to do with respect to specific claims of right. Populist actors insist that statist prerogatives are derivative from popular sovereignty and fully accountable to it; their thrust is more radical, and often their attacks on abuses of human rights rest upon more fundamental indictments of repressive structures of governance (e.g., imperialism, fascism). Of course, the interaction of logics is evident here. Some transnational actors have arisen as a consequence of populist pressure and have adopted as their goal a populist program of action. Environment groups, especially those with an antinuclear focus, such as Friends of the Earth, are illustrative of this admixture of populism and transnationalism. Other forms of populism become co-opted by statist logic, operating virtually as an adjunct to governmental authority and accepting as a constraint the consent of the territorial sovereign; the International Red Cross, for instance, has assumed this basic character. Still other types of populism act essentially as pressure groups on behalf of supranationalist logic, as is the case with the United World Federalists, or, perhaps, the United Nations Association.

In effect, populism is a protean logic that can act either independently or to reinforce the thrust of any of the other logics in a wide variety of respects. It can also act to oppose other logics, as is the case of the interaction between revolutionary populism, with its antecedents in movements associated with philosophical anarchism, and statism.

Conceived of as a logic, then, populism, like supranationalism, is operative at a different level of social organization. If supranationalism provides a metalanguage or logic in relation to logics associated with statism, then populism provides a sublanguage, taking a stance that is "below" the state.

The present system of world order is evolving in ways significant for the protection of human rights. To grasp this process of evolution it is helpful to distinguish among the six principal ordering logics that together comprise what we mean by the present world order system. Figure 3-1 conveys an impressionistic sense of the changing relative importance of these ordering logics since World War II, projecting trends speculatively into the near future of 1985.

In the specific setting of human rights, the relative importance of these

FIGURE 3-1
Ordering Logics since World War II

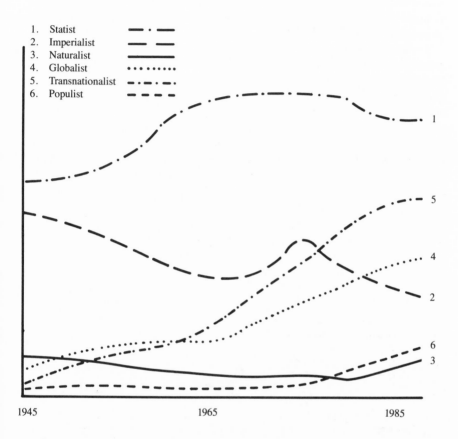

logics is somewhat different from its relation to the overall character of world order. For one thing, imperial geopolitics does not frequently promote human rights in dependent polities; its overriding quest for reliable control over foreign societies tends itself to involve serious deprivations of human rights. Even here no easy conclusions are possible. Uganda under British rule certainly achieved a better record of compliance with minimum standards of human rights than during the period of Idi Amin's reign, yet the sequel to Amin in Uganda seems more positive in human rights terms than colonial Uganda. In general, political independence for a national society is a necessary but not sufficent condition for the realization of human rights in the contemporary world. Why? it might be asked. Because explicit colonial rule runs so contrary to popular aspiration and to legitimate political arrangements (as defined by international consensus, manifest in General Assembly resolutions) that severe forms of repression are required to sustain stability. The colonial holdouts in southern Africa reinforce this line of reasoning.

Figure 3-2 tries in rough terms to suggest the relative significance of the six ordering logics for the protection of human rights. Note, especially, that this indication of relative importance should not be confused with degrees of effectiveness. That is, the world order system as a whole has a poor record with respect to the promotion of human rights. The basic mixture of statism and imperial geopolitics that dominates international politics is not conducive to the promotion of minimum human rights, especially given patterns of gross inequality, ethnic animosities, high population growth, and mass poverty that are characteristic for such a large part of the planet. In effect, state power is typically exercised on behalf of a privileged minority of the total society, while the majority population of most national societies endures misery of various types and is repressed to the extent that its representatives challenge as unacceptable the patterns of benefits and burdens prevailing in a particular polity.

FIGURE 3-2
*Ordering Logics since World War II Relative to
Human Rights*

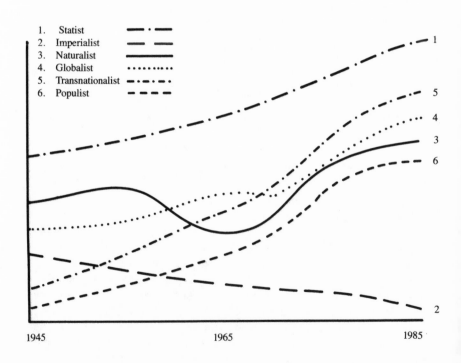

This primary domestic hierarchy is reinforced by imperial geopolitics, which create and shape relationships of mutual benefit between the hegemonial elites of dominant governments and their counterparts in dependent, weaker states. In effect, then, the basic structuring of power is statist-imperialist in a manner that entails only very modest opportunities for the international implementation of human rights.[7] Neither the incentives nor the capabilities for enforcement exist, given the present character of world order, except in aberrational circumstances where a target polity can be isolated from geopolitical support. Given this limited possibility, the instances of international enforcement may seem arbitrary in the sense that they do not present necessarily the most serious violations. At the same time, to date, the target polities are genuine and gross violators (e.g., Rhodesia, South Africa) of minimum standards of human rights.

This skeptical assessment of world order capacity can be expressed differently. A given system of political order can be evaluated with reference to its capacity to realize particular world order values. Again, such an evaluation is somewhat subjective, as we lack "hard," agreed indicators, as well as relevant, comprehensive, and reliable data. Nevertheless, the crude quality of a particular system of world order can be expressed by its relative value realization for a given array: peace, economic well-being, human rights, environmental quality, and humane governance viewed as a cumulative assessment of the other four value dimensions. The idea of appraisal is a matter of past record, present assessment, and future prospects. Figures 3-3, 3-4, and 3-5 offer a judgment about value attainment and expectations, based on a hypotheti-

FIGURE 3-3

Value Attainments in Present System of World Order

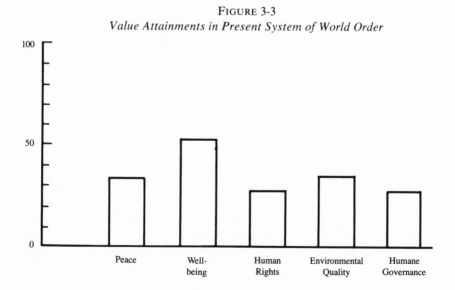

cal scale of 100 as an acceptable minimum. These are crude simplifica-
tions of reality designed only to be suggestive in relation to prior analysis
of ordering logics. To be more useful, the scaling of value attainments
would have to be justified by some objective method and the emphasis on
values correlated with each of the six ordering logics.

These figures summarize a developmental view of the world order
system, its deficiencies and its prospects.[8] Figure 3-5 selects one scenario
of the future, perhaps an optimistic one, that anticipates significant
progress with respect to satisfying the basic economic needs of people on
the planet, but accompanied by further deterioration along the other value

FIGURE 3-4

Value Attainments in World Order System 50–75 Years Ago

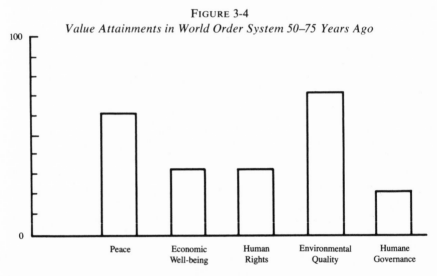

FIGURE 3-5

*Projected Value Expectations in World Order
System for Year 2010*

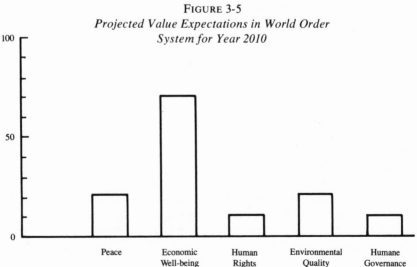

dimensions. The reasoning behind this view is based on the priority accorded to economic production and distribution, partly expressed by a continuing trend toward various forms of socialist organization at the state level and by a refusal in such circumstances to allow much space for dissent or competitive politics. The countries in the South will be faced by a fundamental challenge to expand production and employment to keep pace with a growing population and work force. The countries in the North will be confronted by increasingly costly trade-offs between health and affluence, as well as by a decline in relative economic power that may result in a falling standard of living on the average.

This view of the future is structural in the sense that it insists that little can be done to promote human rights given the geopolitical reality of the persisting dominance of the state and system, including patterns of imperial spheres of influence and, more recently, the emergence of a complex network of transnational social, economic, and cultural forces. The overall point is that the present world order system does not appear to have a very satisfactory value-realizing capacity. This deficiency is mainly a consequence of its organizational fragmentation in a setting of high-technology weaponry, rapid population growth, pervasive inequalities correlated with patterns of racial domination, and a governing process on the state level that is overwhelmingly dependent on coercion to secure the compliance with the imperatives of minimum order of distinct national populations. In such a political framework the promotion of human rights across boundaries is sporadic and arbitrary, depending, above all else, on the occasional convergence of geopolitical goals with the promotion of human rights.

For instance, the promotion of human rights by the United States in the early years of the Carter presidency reinforced the domestic process of moral recovery from Vietnam and Watergate and served to expose the relative deficiencies of Soviet society. By resetting the global moral agenda around rights, the Carter initiative also diverted attention from and eroded the morale of Third World advocacy of a new international economic order. Such a result was not, in all probability, a planned side-effect of the human rights diplomacy; however, since many of the flagrant abuses of human rights were in Third World countries, the effect of the focus was to deprive the Third World of much of its moral advantage vis-à-vis the world economic system. As such, United States human rights diplomacy initially served the practical ends of American foreign policy, although in a generally controversial and nonsustainable way. Positive relations with the Soviet Union seemed obstructed and worse by the linkage of superpower relations to human rights. Besides, it was questionable whether the rhetoric of concern about foreign abuses of human rights was being translated into improved patterns of observance. Causal calculations of impact are notoriously difficult to make, especially as official elites of target polities will never acknowledge the reforming influence of outside criticism on their patterns of governance. Thus, the increased rates of Jewish emigration and the release of prominent Soviet dissidents in April 1979 are being hailed as a belated tribute to the trade linkages of the Jackson-Vanik legislation and to Carter's human rights diplomacy. Other analysts with equivalent plausibility consider the apparent Soviet shift of policy to be part of an effort to establish a political climate in the United States that will enhance prospects for the ratification of the SALT II treaty. Such an illustration suggests the complexity present here. At issue is the effectiveness of a reward-incentive-punishment policy under a variety of conditions and with respect to diverse sets of actors.

Another kind of alleged impact of human rights diplomacy eroded the grip of repressive friendly governments on their populations, alienating present leaders and stimulating the opposition to act more boldly. We have here primarily an interaction between statist and populist logics as ordering processes. The assumption in the modern world is that there has been a decisive shift in the balance of forces within the state to the mechanisms of government. And yet popular movements from below are under certain circumstances capable of mobilizing sufficient support to overthrow even a brutal, ruthless tyranny. Part of the motivating energy in such a context is the conviction of the people and their leaders that they have been denied certain rights that are worth fighting, and even dying, to secure. In effect, populist logic is reinforced in a repressive national setting by naturalist logic. It may be further reinforced by transnational and supranational logics, as well, to the extent that such actors help identify and censure the pattern of human rights abuse. Even hegemonial support for human rights of the sort associated with President Carter's advocacy contributes, even if unintentionally, to the outcome of a struggle against repression in a foreign society.

The struggle between the Shah's government and the Khomeini movement is a spectacular instance of this dynamic. Leaders of the Iranian Revolution, as well as such critics of the human rights diplomacy as Henry Kissinger, share the judgment that the movement against the Shah was tangibly helped by Carter's general posture of support for human rights. Relevant here is not only the reality of the causal link, but the evident unwillingness of the Carter leadership to acknowledge that adverse political consequences in geopolitical terms might on occasion follow, or seem to some observers to follow, from a genuine commitment to human rights as an element of American foreign policy. The prevailing assumption, borne out by the virtual disappearance of human rights from the United States foreign policy agenda since the start of 1978,* is that

*The attention given Cuban refugees in early 1980 is not primarily a matter of human rights, but part of a continuing United States effort to discredit the Castro government. The official indifference for years to refugees from the same region, for instance from Haiti, suggests that United States receptivity to Cubans is, in large part, cynically motivated.

geopolitics takes clear priority over human rights and that, given the actualities of the world, reconciliation is not generally sustainable over time. In addition, adverse domestic consequences are perceived to follow for a politican who sacrifices tangible national interests for the sake of such intangible goals as the promotion of human rights. And indeed it may be that this domestic backlash operates as a more powerful inhibitor on the promotion of human rights by American political leaders than do the supposed adverse overseas consequences as measured by rising tensions or weakened alliances. Experience is so limited, however, that other factors should be considered: for instance, perhaps the perceived failure of Carter's human rights policy was a matter of insufficient persistence and patience, of an outmoded calculus of gains and losses in foreign policy, or of an inadequate campaign to build popular support.

On the record to date, even the verbal endorsement of human rights by the Carter Administration, with relatively little effort at follow-through, has proved nonsustainable, at least for now. In effect, unless human rights can be successfully combined with geopolitics, as it might be by concentrating on violations in the Soviet sphere during periods of East/West tension, it seems like an inappropriate emphasis in the current world order system. This is the point of Kissinger's critique. Foreign policy is concerned with the promotion of national interests, as related to the power, security, wealth, and prestige of a state. Human rights do not fit into such an outlook, except under special, limited, pragmatic circumstances. At most, however, this assessment suggests that statist and hegemonial logics seem organized around the pursuit of ends which rarely include a serious commitment of national resources to the promotion of human rights.

Given systematic reliance on repressive methods of rule by the great majority of states, any international body such as the United Nations, which depends on overwhelming levels of support to take any kind of action, is bound to have its role confined, at best, to "special cases." By a special case is meant one which seems to present a human rights issue with features restricting its applicability to the situation pertaining in one or two states. In contrast is an abuse such as torture, which is attributable to a large proportion of states, or terrorism, which enjoys tacit support under certain circumstances. General condemnation is possible, but in such a form as to assure no systematic consideration of the range of violations. If spectacular abuses of human rights occur that offend a major state, a vague rhetorical posture might be adopted by one or more of the political organs of the United Nations, but nothing more substantive is likely to be done.

In these respects, apartheid is the perfect special case, while torture is an apt illustration of a general systemic condition too sensitive to examine (except occasionally in a specific instance—for example, Chile—where its occurrence could be associated with the consequences of the CIA's intervention against Allende). In addition, the United Nations as a global arena is not accorded independent capabilities to alter behavior at the state level and rarely has such capabilities delegated to it. The United Nations is barred by the domestic jurisdiction provision in its own Charter from more than symbolic and verbal initiatives. Such initiatives can significantly shift the balance of legitimacy by, for instance, vindicating support for armed struggle against racism, but they can also engender frustration, expose weakness, and create a mood of futility by having repeated resolutions calling for change lead to no consequence more substantive than a subsequent resolution.

The main conclusion, at once obvious and fundamental, is that the cause of human rights in the present world system is overwhelmingly dependent on the normative orientation of the governing process at the state level. Some pressures can be brought on this process from outside, as by impartial transnational organizations whose motives are harder to discredit in certain situations, especially where the leadership in the target polity seeks to avoid having an international reputation as repressive and the abuse can be corrected without seeming to erode the quality of governmental control. Yet this pressure can only be marginal, perhaps leading to some cosmetic changes in judicial procedures, in improved conditions of confinement, or possibly even release for prominent prisoners of conscience. Nevertheless, the governing orientation of states is primarily shaped by internal factors, especially by attitudes of domestic leaders relating to the retention of power and maintenance of domestic order, what has been called "the rulers' imperative."

The world order limits on the promotion of human rights seem firm, at least in the short run of say five to ten years. A different perspective arises if one considers the present historical period to be one of transition to a new political frame of reference that involves some drastic changes in the state, regional, and supranational levels of organization. There is disagreement about the extent, pace, and even reality of transition. Some consider the "crisis of world order" to be one of simply adjusting to the passing of American primacy that helped organize international relations after World War II. Such adjustments, involving a more pluralistic, complex variant of world order, require neither structural change nor normative shifts in emphasis.

A second more fundamental view of transition suggests that the interdependent character of security, and of economic and ecological life requires greater capabilities for "management," perhaps even central guidance. Here, too, the functional shift toward central guidance does not imply any reduction in the internal political autonomy of state actors. Perhaps, over time, a more integrated world system would begin to translate awareness about abuses of human rights into a more formidable role for the supranational ordering logic at the expense of both statist and hegemonial logic. This move toward the "management of interdependence" is sometimes described as a "moderate" (as compared to the present and past) world order system in which cooperative aspects of relations between state actors are augmented while competitive aspects are diminished. It may be that the attainment of moderation would encourage gentler modes of governance, resting on more consent and less coercion. Such a development is feasible if the relationship between economic and demographic growth can be reconciled with improved life circumstances for most inhabitants of most polities in the world.

A third, even deeper, view of transition exists. Its time horizon is a matter of decades. It views the crisis of world order as involving the disintegration of the state system as it emerged from European regional politics in the middle of the seventeenth century, a development often conveniently associated with the Peace of Westphalia, concluded in 1648 at the end of the Thirty Years War. From this perspective a new world order system is emergent that will combine an organizational framework suitable for a planetary polity with appropriate new beliefs, values, and myths. The essence of such a system, if it is to achieve transition, is the attainment of stability on a planetary scale. This could take either of two principal forms. It could be a centralized tyranny that imposes its will on the various peoples of the world. It could also be a relatively decentralized form of central guidance (combining functional specialization with the deconcentration of power at the state level) premised on symbiotic link between leadership and consent, which manages to combine stability with equity as the essence of the new world order system. The idea of "equity" covers a range of substantive arrangements proceeding from a minimalist commitment to assure satisfaction of basic material needs as a matter of right for everyone to a maximalist commitment to a just polity that achieves substantial equality among its inhabitants, as well as equality among such collectivities as sovereign states. Nonutopian conceptions of equity could not do more than reach a compromise between a basic needs approach and the achievement of genuine equality.

In the negative variant of the poststatal system, human rights will be denied in more systematic and flagrant ways than is currently the case. In terms of ordering logics, the supranational logic (or conceivably the hegemonial logic via world conquest, condominium, or oligopoly) would be greatly expanded at the expense of both statist and populist logic, the latter being already trivial. Supranational logic would assume a hierarchical relationship of repressive superiority that would extend to the strict control of even regional and subregional expressions of supranational logic. In the positive variant, the essence of world order will be the progressive realization of human rights by means of a combined strengthening of populist and global logic, mainly at the expense of statist logic.

In this conjectural spirit it is worth noticing the following aspect. The protection of human rights in a given world order system is not rigidly the exclusive preserve of any one of the ordering logics. It all depends on the value base that animates a given political actor at any level of social organization. As racist and religious militants' movements have demonstrated, repressive intolerance can rise from below (via populist logic) as well as be imposed from above (via statist logic). Similarly, holders of effective power may, under certain circumstances, act to remove human rights abuses within their own policy (e.g., civil rights in the United States).

From a formal point of view, a balance among ordering logics is important as a check against tendencies to abuse authority. The present world order system, confronted by an insidious mixture of inequality, misery, and scarcity, is most profoundly obstructed by the imbalanced domination of ordering logic by the sovereign state. Yet supplanting the state by a centralizing mutation is unlikely to diminish its repressive features for very long. Besides, the state helps to neutralize certain adverse features of the hegemonial logic. Strengthening weak states and weakening strong states, seem like reasonable short-term approaches to the role of the state in the world system. It is for this reason that the positive direction of global reform at this historical stage seems to require a simultaneous strengthening of supranational (global and regional), naturalist, transnational, and populist logics at the expense of the statist and hegemonial logics.

In one respect, strengthening the naturalist logic may be the most important emphasis at this point in the transition process. It helps to orient other ordering logics around emergent values, building a normative foundation and social consensus that will help create the sort of community sentiments needed if a beneficial form of world order is to be brought into being some time early in the twenty-first century.

A World Order Perspective on Authoritarian Tendencies

Abuses of human rights on a systematic basis are almost always associated with certain repressive features of the governing process. In this respect, patterns of authoritarian rule, if widespread, limit greatly prospects for implementing human rights. In part, this limitation expresses the extent to which states are resistant to *external* normative pressures, and in part, it expresses the reluctance of repressive leaders to support international initiatives designed to withdraw legitimacy from or otherwise impair the sovereignty of human rights violators. Therefore, the drift toward authoritarian rule is not only itself a negative trend vis-à-vis human rights, but it conditions the international climate as well.

Approaches to world order that neglect the internal life of sovereign states tend to be sterile. The main social forces active in human affairs are concentrated within national boundaries, although these are increasingly linked to many forms of transnational networks of influence. More significantly, virtually all governments, as the principal actors in global arenas, are organized around the postulates of statist logic, including an acceptance of a system of national security based on military prowess. Furthermore, the vast discrepancies in national endowment, capability, and potential are a principal source of world order disaffection, especially to the extent that these discrepancies seem racially and regionally specific.

In essence, national political situations both *reflect* amd *shape* the international context. Wider patterns of constraint and systems of control condition national options and interfere with the achievement of national autonomy. These various interferences arise from the hegemonial structure of international politics and are discussed beneath the rubric of neocolonialism. Also the distinct forms of national governance, whether or not themselves partially caused by external factors, in turn confine the range of global policy options that appear feasible at a particular time, and in a larger sense national outlooks control the agenda, direction, and pace of global reform.

These generalizations seem relevant to any conception of world order, even if the sole objective is maximizing the stability of international relations: that is, eliminating threats of major disturbances or challenges to the international status quo. Increasingly, foreign policy for major state actors is also a managerial venture carried on within such a world order framework of concern. In this regard, such apparently normative issues as world poverty, North-South adjustment, East-West relations, human rights, and arms control are handled by reference to this generalized understanding of what will keep the international system from economic, military, or ecological breakdown. But sensitivity to domestic constituencies, bureaucratic pressures, and national interests of a short-term variety severely limits the discretion of even enlightened national leaders (that is, those with a longer term vision of national well-being based on the evolution of an acceptable form of world—one perceived as fair, as well as stable). And besides, enlightened leaders are a rarity in powerful states because political processes, whether liberal or authoritarian, produce leaders whose credibility arises from their capacity to achieve short-term goals.

These short-term goals are shaped by selfish conceptions of personal and national interests, whether measured by dollars of export sales or jobs or inflation rates. Germany cannot be induced to forgo jobs and profits from export sales of nuclear technology, no more than the Soviet Union or the United States can be induced to forgo a weapons innovation that promises some military advantage. The wider impact of state practice on human or world community well-being is largely neglected by policymakers at the national level, despite the extent to which these considerations may be acknowledged in the rhetoric of national leaders. The reality of danger is accepted in words, but the governmental means and will to do something about it are missing.

At the same time, complicating this assessment, is the positive role of Third World governments in redressing the imbalances that are embodied in the colonial heritage and that persist in a variety of newer imperial forms. Governments that protect their polity against outside intervention are acting to neutralize one source of distortion in the state system, even if such protection in some instances serves to insulate a particular repressive governance structure from humanizing pressures mounted from without. A normative balance between those considerations associated with self-determination/nonintervention on the one side and a human rights /democratic process on the other is elusive. Many human rights activists are preoccupied with mounting an interventionary strategy to liberate a particular repressed people and fail to realize the systemic consequences of their advocacy and the precedent it might set if acted upon. For progressives, it is fine to subvert fascist regimes but criminal to destabilize socialist regimes; for conservatives the opposite is true. For one group, liberation movements are positive, CIA operations are criminal; for its adversaries, the opposite is true.

Even more fundamental from a world order perspective are trends in the ideology and character of national governance structures. The main trend-line, although exhibiting some contradictory pulls, suggests an upsurge in the extent and severity of military-backed authoritarian rule in recent years, especially in the Third World. A subsidiary trend suggests the spread of bureaucratically centralized modes of authoritarian rule, whether associated with socialist or capitalist forms of economic organization. A second subsidiary trend, especially in the liberal democratic societies of the Trilateral (or OECD) sector of world society, involves the political implications of growing signs of societal decay and disturbance; these signs have prompted debate as to whether democratic polities remain governable in the North. The cumulative effect of these trends is to underscore the futility of expecting national governments to act as progressive agents of global reform. Such futility exists quite apart from the structural resistance that states as states have to making changes that reduce their relative or absolute power, authority, and prestige. At present, the energy for global reform is mainly located in the populist sector, although it is reinforced by some transnational social forces, including the network of international institutions that constitute the United Nations.

Nevertheless, the state remains by far the most important actor on the world state, and its relationship to various potential types of change is critical. A central hypothesis in this chapter is that the quality of the governance structure as it pertains to the way in which a government maintains order and promotes justice within its boundaries influences the manner in which it acts in relation to the external world. In particular, the substitution of highly coercive rule for consensual rule tends to inhibit the impact of those social forces that would move with the tides of history to build some sort of global community polity that would alone give promise that our future will not be beset by catastrophe on an unprecedented scale. For this reason, the global trend toward authoritarian rule manifest on the state level in all sectors of world society is at once significant and discouraging. The reality of this trend in the Third World is especially discouraging, as the states of Africa, Asia, and Latin America have the greatest stake in global reform. These states share a quest for a fairer international allocation of economic and psychological rewards, while at the same time emerging as principal defenders of sovereign rights both for the legitimate reason of guarding their society against neocolonial disruption and for the dubious reason of insulating their domestic rule from outside criticism. As a result, the bureaucratic base of state power is expanding in scale and efficiency. The overall international atmosphere reflects this further evolution of statism.

Part of the effort in this chapter is to portray the main variants of authoritarian rule that are currently prominent in international society. Emphasis is placed on the geographical distinction between North and South as descriptive of separate geopolitical settings. The distinction between capitalism and socialism is also emphasized as descriptive of the principal orientations toward national development and toward international economic policy.

This chapter originated in, and continues to emphasize, an inquiry into the rise of right-wing militarized regimes in key states throughout the Third World over the course of the last twenty years, as exemplified by the Brazilian experience since 1964. The foundations of authoritarian rule for Third World societies linked by choice to the capitalist world economic order and geopolitically to the United States also embraced countries that had not built up a significant modern sector comparable to what exists in Brazil. Such simpler societies, lacking a domestic industrial base, are present to different degrees in Africa, the Middle East, Latin America (especially Central America), and Asia. Therefore, the Brazilianization trend is complemented by the phenomenon of praetorianization. This type of authoritarian state is not necessarily rightist in orientation. There are instances of both left and right praetorian regimes, their identity being based on the extent to which the governing process is visibly militarized.

To focus on rightist developments alone ignores wider trends toward authoritarianism in left-wing Third World countries. Also relevant, if our concerns are global, is authoritarianism in the North. These wider trends suggest, although they do not demonstrate, that the authoritarian outcome is a reflection of the current world order system rather than a consequence of national ideology. More concretely, the global drift toward authoritarian patterns of governance seems to reflect the failure of the modern states system to assure the minimum realization of human rights on the national level. This causal hypothesis is obviously difficult to substantiate in any rigorous way. National situations are diverse and conditioned by specific circumstances. Nevertheless, the contention that global reform of a structural character is necessary to realize an agreed set of world order values rests in part on the internal failings of the state to achieve humane governance in relation to its own citizenry.[1]

An acceptable typology of the subtrends that together comprise authoritarianism seems elusive at this stage, yet, despite difficulties, some effort is worthwhile. The central distinction between capitalism and socialism, if used with caution, provides one dimension of our crude classification of authoritarian political forms. This ideological distinction is somewhat arbitrary in relation to hybrid polities (e.g., Mexico, India) and attempts no differentiation with regard to the type of socialism or capitalism. Furthermore, it ignores geopolitical alignment patterns which may cut against the grain of domestic ideological orientation.

The second dimension that seems essential is some effort at distinguishing polities by reference to their degree of modernization, as associated mainly with the size and quality of a modern (that is, an industrial) sector. Geography helps here to provide a first-order differentiation between North and South, although here too some ambiguities exist (e.g., Portugal, South Africa). On some issues—for instance, those relating to international economic policy—this geographical factor seems to shape international behavior more than anything else. A further cut is made within the South to differentiate the more industrialized countries (e.g., Brazil) from the less industrialized ones (e.g., Somalia). The ideological identity of the less industrialized countries is often astraddle the capitalist/ socialist boundary.

This effort at classification yields the following simple tables:

TABLE 4-1:

Categorization of Countries

		Capitalist	Socialist
North		V	IV
South	more industrialized	I	II
	less industrialized	III	

TABLE 4-2:

Authoritarian Tendencies

	Capitalist	Socialist
North	Trilateralization	Stalinization
South	Brazilianization Praetorianization	Leninization

Despite the existence of some borderline cases, every national society fits within one of these five boxes. Of course, there is wide diversity within each category, and national differences arranged along some particular dimension may even outweigh the similarities of political organization and ideology.

The Roman numerals in each box indicate the sequence of inquiry. Its logic is not an important element of the argument. Essentially, the most dramatic trend is that of the more industrialized Third World capitalist countries, which have not only moved toward authoritarian solutions, but toward more severe variants of authoritarian rule. Such a point of departure suggests comparing the authoritarian outcomes in capitalist

Third World countries on the basis of their economic and political relations with the capitalist countries in the North. It seems natural to wonder whether and to what extent authoritarian tendencies are being imported or domestically produced. In effect, also, it seems important to assess by what circumstances the domestic drift toward authoritarianism is being externally induced. To complete the picture it is also necessary to consider the socialist countries of the North, their corresponding linkages with socialist governments in the South, and whether their influence promotes authoritarianism.

Beyond matters of categorization and sequence lies the question of labels. What shall we call these five patterns of authoritarian tendency? Any label will be unsatisfactory to a degree, seeming either antiseptic or arbitrary. My own disposition is to accept these costs of categorization so as to highlight some key features of principal patterns. The danger of this method lies in encouraging simplistic lines of perception, lumping beneath a suggestive rubric rather distinct forms of authoritarian experience. This distinction drawn in the Third World, between Brazilianized/Leninized states that have a significant industrial sector and praetorianized states that do not, is an attempt at subcategorization among authoritarian states. And yet, of course, vast differences remain among the states clustered within a single category.

The next section of this paper contains a discussion of Brazilianization as it has evolved as a model for rightist capitalist elites in the more industrialized countries of the Third World (e.g., Iran until 1979, Indonesia, Argentina). A common feature of these polities is that they seek integration into the world trade, investment, and money markets, and are generally receptive to multinational corporations.

Attention will then be devoted to Leninization as manifest in virtually every Third World socialist society, regardless of whether it looks to Moscow, Peking, or itself for primary guidance. Why socialism has so far emerged only in these Leninized forms is an agonizing question that is raised, but not seriously discussed.

In addition to these forms of authoritarian rule, there are those that occur in conditions of relatively little industrial development. Such governance patterns can be linked with either capitalist or socialist states in the North, but are characterized more by the praetorian exercise of state power than by the ideological orientation of the regime.

A brief appraisal of authoritarianism in the socialist North will be made. Here, the central phenomenon is the persistence, despite moderating elements, of Stalinist modes of rule in the Soviet Union and its East European allies. Although Albania and Yugoslavia fall outside the Soviet orbit, and Rumania at its margin, their reliance on repressive methods and their degree of bureaucratic centralism made it tenable, at least, to include them in the broad catchment of Stalinization.

Finally, a short discussion will follow about the loss of confidence in the capacity of democratic governance to do the job in the developed countries of North America, Europe, and Japan. In this connection, it is worth noting the existence of the Trilateral Commission and its concern with the viability of democracy. Among Trilateralists the central question is how to adapt capitalism to a changing global context, especially one which requires greater "discipline" at home to achieve efficiency abroad.

After these five principal patterns have been identified, their linkage to world order prospects will be considered. Part of the analysis here will attribute trends toward authoritarian rule, and their likely continuation, to a deteriorating world order situation economically (capital shortage, terms of trade) and ecologically (energy costs and environmental/demographic overload) that generates militarized politics within and among states. There is no way to reverse or arrest these national trends without the emergence of a more cooperative and equitable system of world order at the global level. Perversely, these authoritarian trends militate against system change and are, in part, a reflection of the relative strength of system-maintaining coalitions on the national level. The policy implications are obvious in one respect—the importance of linking progressive politics at the national level to global strategies for system change—but elusive on the level of tactics. Appropriate action will depend on the possibilities and urgencies of each national situation, including its tolerance of overt forms of antiregime behavior and of transnational movements for change.

A concern with the transnational dimension of authoritarianism has to be open to the role of nonstate actors. Multinational corporations and foreign intelligence agencies may be critical elements in the causal chain that induces and sustains authoritarian solutions in a particular society. Also significant may be international financial institutions that pressure governments to adopt austerity programs, fiscal priorities that concentrate burdens of adjustment on the poor at the expense of social welfare policies. The degree of impact of interventionary agents is necessarily conjectural and provokes controversy, as in the interpretation of Allende's downfall in Chile or Egypt's turn in the late 1970s toward more repressive governance.

The main states in the world have been classified according to this five-part scheme. The results are shown in table 4-3. Some classifications are controversial, and new developments make such a table out of date before it is printed. The main purpose here is to distinguish among authoritarian patterns of rule. In addition, the geographical distribution of authoritarian regimes is shown in Map 4-1, a composite world map. (Additional maps referred to will be found at the end of this chapter.)

Brazilianization

This section focuses on escalating repression in the capitalist portion of the Third World beneath the rubric of Brazilianization. It examines, in

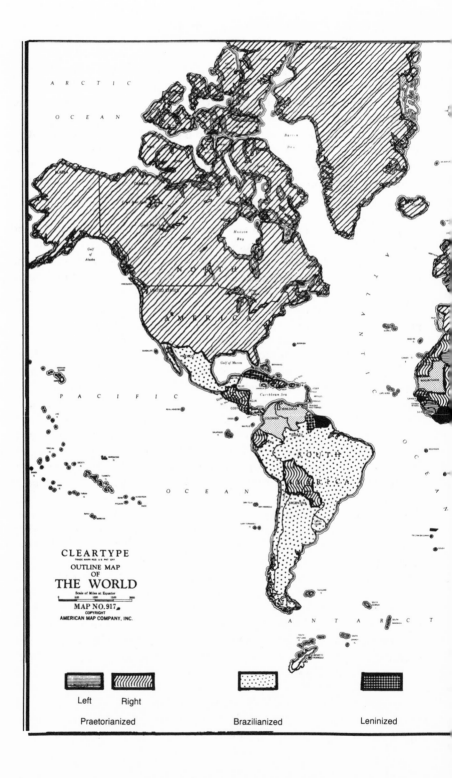

CLEARTYPE
TRADE MARK REG U.S. PAT OFF
OUTLINE MAP
OF
THE WORLD
Scale of Miles at Equator
MAP NO.917
COPYRIGHT
AMERICAN MAP COMPANY, INC.

Left   Right

Praetorianized   Brazilianized   Leninized

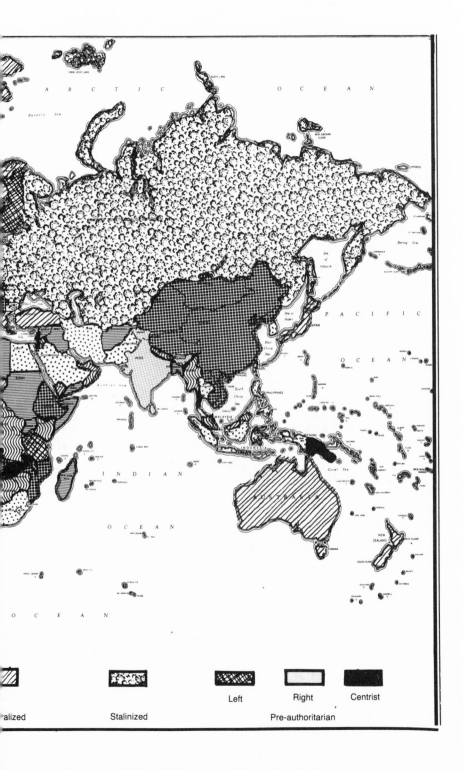

Left   Right   Centrist

alized   Stalinized   Pre-authoritarian

TABLE 4-3
Patterns of Governance

Brazilianized	Leninized	Praetorianized		Stalinized	Trilateralized	Pre-Authoritarian		
		Left	Right			Left	Centrist	Right
Argentina	Angola	Afghanistan	Bahrain	Albania	Australia	Finland	Bhutan	Bahamas
Brazil	Benin	Algeria	Bolivia	Bulgaria	Austria	Tanzania	Colombia	French Guiana
Chile	Cuba	Bangladesh	Burma	Czechoslovakia	Belgium		India	Gambia
China (Rep. of)	Ethiopia	Congo	Burundi	D.D.R.	Canada		Maldives	Grenada
Egypt	Guinea Bissau	Equatorial Guinea	Central African Empire	Hungary	Denmark		Mauritania	Israel
Indonesia	Guyana	Guinea	Costa Rica	Poland	France	Portugal	Mauritius	
Iran*	Kampuchea (Cambodia)	Iraq	Dominican Rep.	Romania	Germany (Fed. Rep. of)		Ivory Coast	Liberia
Korea (South)	Korea (North)	Libya	El Salvador	U.S.S.R.	Greece		Sao Tome & Principe	
Mexico	Laos	Madagascar	Gabon		Iceland		Venezuela	Malta
Nigeria	Mongolia	Niger	Ghana		Ireland			***
Panama	Mozambique	Seychelles	Guatemala		Italy			Surinam
Peru	Peoples Republic of China	Sierra Leone	Haiti		Japan			Trinidad
Philippines	Tibet	Somalia	Honduras		Liechtenstein			Zambia
Saudi Arabia	Vietnam	Sudan	Jordan		Luxembourg			
Singapore	Yugoslavia	Syria	Kenya		Netherlands			
South Africa		Togo	Lebanon		Norway			
Thailand		Uganda	Lesotho		Spain			
Uruguay		P.D.R. Yemen	Malawi		Sweden			
			Malaysia		Switzerland			
			Mali		Turkey			
			Namibia		United Kingdom			
			Nepal		U.S.A.			
			Nicaragua					
			Oman					
			Paraguay					
			Rhodesia					
			Rwanda					
			Senegal					
			Swaziland					
			Tunisia					
			United Arab Emirates					

*until 1979

particular, the socioeconomic setting of largely capitalist Third World countries in which repressive regimes emerge and stabilize themselves. This setting is being fundamentally shaped by a crisis in capital formation that pervades to varying degrees all but a few of the resource-rich Third World countries. For enumeration and distribution see map 4-2. The crisis is generated by a series of factors. Perhaps the most significant of these is the rigidity of class privileges and the inability of moderate political elites to maintain stability without redistributive and welfare programs to pacify the poor. If the government is reformist, it becomes impossible to sustain growth via reinvestment because of capital shortages unless the country is especially endowed with resources. There is not enough capital to go around, especially given the inhibitions on taxing and expropriating the rich. In these circumstances, attempts at compromise tend to satisfy neither end of the political spectrum. As a result, discontent, instability, and economic chaos emerge, creating a context that invites a takeover by those social forces (the military and its allies) willing and able to impose "discipline" upon the polity. This dynamic is generally played out against an ideological backdrop in which geopolitical themes, ideological images, and interventionary pressures are manipulated by the participants.

The pattern of right-wing repressive governance is exhibited in forms corresponding to the exceedingly diverse situations of Third World countries. These variations reflect differences in size, level of economic development, resource endowment, political culture, geopolitical salience. Nevertheless, despite these diversities—in fact, all the more remarkable because of them—there is an emergent form of militarized repression that shares sufficient features to justify being perceived as a pattern, although two qualifications are in order. First, the political character of each national situation is dynamic. Brazil itself continuously evolves as the governing elite shifts its leadership, seeks to accommodate crosspressures, and experiments with various tactics. Hence, "Brazilianization" refers to the essence of the Brazilian experience since 1964, without purporting to be descriptive through time. The essential point remains, however, that those political elites that align themselves with capitalist forces internal and external to their country and seek to augment the bureaucratic apparatus of state power are responding to the same set of pressures exemplified by the Brazilian case. However, if there is no modern sector in the economy, then the Brazilian case seems inapplicable. These premodern trends toward authoritarian rule will be dealt with in the next section under the label of praetorianism.

Here we set forth some of the features of Brazilianization. (See Annex 1, pp. 104–111 for discussion of the specific Brazilian experience.)

Militarized Governance

The apparatus of the state is controlled directly or indirectly by the military establishment; military officers are the key leaders and civilian institutions are subordinated, if not altogether eliminated. Typically, control of the state by the military is initially attained by extraconstitutional means, usually by a coup d'état. The coup is not, however, intended merely to obtain political leadership for a given faction within the elite; it represents a long-term commitment, more or less permanent, to restructure state power in an authoritarian direction, even though such restructuring may pass through a number of tactical phases of severity and moderation.

Rightist Ideology

Although militarized governing systems can be leftist in orientation (e.g., Libya, Ethiopia, Uganda), most are antileftist which, in contemporary terms, means anti-Marxist in rhetoric and policy, as well as linked externally to the United States, Western Europe, or Japan. This orientation is especially true for the Brazilianized category as Third World countries with a modern sector linked to the capitalist world economic order necessarily profess a rightist ideology. These rightist military and quasi-military regimes identify their countries' social-political futures with the security and prosperity of the urban upper classes working in collaboration with technocrats active in the state bureaucracy. Rightist leaders view the popular sector, or the masses, and sometimes the traditional rural elites, as potential or actual hostile social forces that must be demobilized and controlled. Internationally, such regimes are anti-Soviet, anticommunist in outlook, and look to the United States and/or its principal allies for diplomatic and economic support, as well as for arms.

Capitalist Development Strategy

The main rationalization of rightist militarization involves overcoming the obstacles to rapid national economic development when a capitalist approach is adopted, which increasingly includes relying on heavy public sector involvement. It should be understood that the capitalist impulse in the Brazilianization context tends to adopt a fascist rather than a liberal course and is influenced by neocolonialist situations of dependency. Hence, state capitalism and transnational financial influence play a strong role. The state spawns a bureaucracy which shares its own interest in expanding the role of the state, even in competition with elements of the national bourgeoisie. Similarly, the bureaucratic managers may be inclined to favor external capitalists, for reasons of either technocratic efficiency or personal corruption, at the expense of internal capitalists. In addition, the regime is often closely aligned in a dependency relationship with powerful governments in the North who exert a real influence over policy choices, sometimes even playing operational roles through a CIA-type covert presence.

The original pretext for the military takeover is normally associated with the inability of civilian leadership to maintain order sufficient to check inflation, labor unrest, political turmoil. These societal conditions allegedly destroy investor confidence and make it difficult to attract capital from abroad in the form of private investment, bank loans, or international economic assistance. The military leadership initially declares its mission to be saving the country from the chaos brought on by radical and destabilizing demands for greater "equity" and/or from corrupt or indecisive civilian-led governing arrangements. Such a role for the new military leadership presupposes the capacity and willingness of government to discipline the poor so that they will accept low wages or acquiesce in high regional and sectoral unemployment without disrupting productive processes via strikes, demonstration, and oppositional politics. The economic goal of militarization in a dependent capitalist context is a high rate of growth in gross national product, regardless of distributive consequences at least for the near-term.[2] The poor (and sometimes portions of the national bourgeoisie as well) are "squeezed" to assure revenues and stability that benefit the state bureaucracy and most, or at least some, of the traditionally privileged classes. Rightist militarization may be associated with dramatic results, at least for a time, and depending on the international economic situation with respect to economic growth; for example, Brazil had a growth rate of 9.3 percent between 1970 and 1975. These successful years were hailed as "the Brazilian miracle" and were viewed for a time as a model for governance that vindicated the functional dependence of rapid growth of the gross national product (GNP) upon authoritarian methods of rule.

Militarization along these lines typically occurs because of a perceived crisis in capital formation.[3] Civilian leaders generally seek to steer a middle course between appeasing the poor and satisfying the rich, generating frustrations on both sides that may erupt into political violence. Moderate civilian governments in the Third World generally lack the capability to reorient the economy to favor the popular sector, as bourgeois and statist elements in the government will resist such a mandate and are likely to be reinforced in their resistance by the dominant sectors of global capitalism as embodied in the rich countries of the North and reinforced by their international economic mechanisms for organizing the world economy (GATT, IMF, OECD). As a result, constitutionally based civilian leadership has appeared to lack the capacity to achieve either the efficiency of military governance or the *equity* and *participation* of left authoritarian regimes.

In this context, deepening polarization of the left and right occurs, with the balance of forces within the military being normally and intuitively aligned with the right (although not invariably) and capable of tipping the domestic balance by seizing control of the state.

Militarist "New Politics"

The leadership of Third World military establishments has for several decades been overwhelmingly trained in the North, principally in the United States, to regard their principal role as one of "internal security" —i.e., guarding the polity against leftist radical forces ready and eager to subvert the state. Such a role contrasts with the traditional domestic function of the military to act as arbiter among contending civilian forces or as temporary custodian of state power while civilian struggles for dominance are resolved; this new role for the military involves accepting a more permanent mandate to safeguard the polity and manage the modernization process. In the 1950's, and even more energetically in the early 1960s, the United States, as part of its response to the communist endorsement of "wars of national liberation," was instrumental through its aid and training programs in moving critical elements in many Third World military establishments to adopt a counterinsurgency outlook toward their own populations. This "new professionalism" of Third World military elites helps "legitimize" seizures of power at least within the military establishment itself.[4]

Ascendant Military Establishment

As might be expected, militarization along these lines tends to increase defense spending and the prestige of the military and to diminish budgets for social welfare purposes.[5] By giving the military what it wants for defense expenditure, the governing elite mutes factional disputes within the military and seeks to hold succession politics within reasonable bounds.[6] Perhaps most fundamentally, this model of militarized control produces strong state structures domestically and strengthens the capacity of a given state to participate in the world system. Statist aspirations for an enhanced status are usually associated with a dynamic military establishment. Hence, the military sector in this kind of polity is often the most dynamic, the most technologically modern, the most rapidly growing, as well as the inspirational source of continuing ideological leadership for the polity.[7]

The priority attached to a national military buildup may feed regional arms races. These are aided and abetted by the sales policies of the developed world, especially the United States. The motivations of suppliers may include the desire to earn foreign exchange with which to offset or diminish balance of payments deficits. The magnitude of North-South arms flow may thus reflect structural features of the world economy in addition to geopolitical considerations. The quantity and quality of arms sent in recent years to Iran certainly are influenced by such economic factors.[8] Arms sales have been increasing at a dramatic rate during the course of Third World militarization and have especially climbed following rising oil import costs. Tables 4-4 and 4-5 show United

TABLE 4-4

US Military Assistance for Years 1966, 1970, 1975 by Regions
(Millions of current dollars)

Regions	1966	1970	% change	1975	% change
Developing:					
Region 2 (Europe*)	281.3	295.0	+4.8	198.1	−32.8
Region 3 (Latin America)	131.4	26.4	−79.9	156.8	+493.9
Region 4 (Far East)	1179.3	2492.8	+111.3	1243.2	−50.1
Region 5 (So. Asia)	9.0	0.5	−94.9	0.6	+20.0
Region 6 (Middle East)	251.1	3.7	−98.5	104.7	+2729.0
Region 7 (Africa)	36.1	19.4	−46.2	70.5	+263.4
Developed:					
Region 1 (Canada)					
Region 2 (Europe)	49.2	0.0	−100.0	0.0	0
Region 4 (Japan)	1.7	0.0	−100.0	0.0	0
Region 6 (Israel)	90.0	30.0	−66.6	300.0	+900.0
Region 8 (Oceania)	5.0	0.0	−100.0	0.0	0

Developed countries: Canada, Japan, Israel, Australia, New Zealand, Belgium, Denmark, France, West Germany, Iceland, Italy, Luxembourg, Netherlands, Norway, United Kingdom, Czechoslovakia, Bulgaria, East Germany, Hungary, Poland, Rumania, USSR, Austria, Finland, Ireland, Sweden, Switzerland.

Source: figures for military assistance are compiled from: U.S. Overseas Loans and Grants and Assistance from International Organizatios, Obligations and Loan Authorizatios. July 1, 1945–June 30, 1975.

These European countries are considered "developing": Greece, Portugal, Turkey, Albania, Malta, Spain, Yugoslavia.

States military assistance and arms sales to the world and clearly reflect the strategic and economic interests of the United States during a given period of time. The figures for 1970 and 1975 and the percentage change between those two dates show that Latin America, the Middle East, and Africa, all areas in which militarization and repression are on the rise, have received substantially increased amounts of United States military aid, while the developed world has received no military assistance. A similar pattern is discernible for arms sales. Arms sales from the United States to all parts of the world have increased between 1970 and 1975. But the most significant increase occurred in sales to Africa, as sales to South Asia and the Middle East followed closely behind. These trends may not continue indefinitely, as thresholds of saturation may have been crossed. Also, import of ultrasophisticated weaponry builds dependency links that may conflict with nationalistic goals.

The ascendancy of the military may also produce internal strains in time. Portions of the military sector are very nationalistic, resent the

TABLE 4-5

US Arms Sales for Years 1966, 1970, 1975, by Regions
(Millions of current dollars)

Regions	1966	1970	% change	1975	% change
Region 2 (Europe*)	24.277	58.719	+141.8	322.933	+449.9
Region 3 (Latin America)	24.6	25.0	+1.6	154.7	+518.8
Region 4 (Far East)	5.8	61.3	+956.8	439.0	+616.1
Region 5 (So. Asia)	10.2	51.4	+403.9	1419.2	+2661.0
Region 6 (Middle East)	209.6	143.2	−31.6	2970.5	+1974.3
Region 7 (Africa)	7.8	7.8	0	330.0	+4130.7
Developed:					
Region 1 (Canada)	70.2	53.1	−24.3	102.1	+92.0
Region 2 (Europe)	1126.423	387.281	−65.6	2680.767	+592.2
Region 4 (Japan)	16.6	21.2	+27.7	29.6	+39.6
Region 6 (Israel)	72.1	44.9	−37.7	868.7	+1834.7
Region 8 (Oceania)	52.5	59.4	+13.1	162.7	+173.9

Developed countries: Canada, Japan, Israel, Australia, New Zealand, Belgium, Denmark, France, West Germany, Iceland, Italy, Luxembourg, Netherlands, Norway, United Kingdom, Czechoslovakia, Bulgaria, East Germany, Hungary, Poland, Rumania, USSR, Austria, Finland, Ireland, Sweden, Switzerland.

Source: figures for arms sales are computed from figures in *Foreign Military Sales and Military Assistance Facts,* November, 1975.

*These European countries are considered "developing": Greece, Portugal, Turkey, Albania, Malta, Spain, Yugoslavia.

acceptance of external control, and seek to achieve more genuine autonomy for their country. The strains may show in attitudes toward multinational corporations, international financial institutions, and even some colonial issues. Brazil, for instance, welcomed the independence of Portugal's African colonies despite their left orientation. A more telling instance of tension, although one limited in relevance to major countries, is the aspiration to become a strong world power exemplified by the quest for nuclear weaponry. Nowhere is there a clearer indication of the conflicting pulls of economic dependence and geopolitical ambition. Third World leaders view the whole web of policies embodied in the nonproliferation policies of the North with a mixture of suspicion and hostility.

Repressive Policies and Apparatus

To assure the success of militarized governance under modern conditions requires the absence of political opposition. Given the reality of right/left splits in Third World politics, ascendancy to power by either the right or the left means intense opposition by the other. Harsh means are relied upon to quell opposition. To resist under such conditions requires desperate strategies such as kidnappings, terrorism, and armed struggle.

A vicious circle of repression and resistance ensues. Successful discipline of the polity appears to require reliance on torture and official terror as staple ingredients of rule. An internal security bureaucracy that includes a network of spies and informers to penetrate all parts of society and often overseas to control exile activity emerges and grows. As with other aspects of right-wing militarization, the internal security system is developed in a modern spirit with outside (usually American) support and guidance.[9] Although militarized regimes vary considerably in their tolerance of political and cultural activity, all of them insist upon "emergency" prerogatives to remove undesirables from the scene and to impose policies designed to intimidate the population from any kind of massive protest.[10]

As the surge of oppositional activity in Iran during 1978 illustrated, modernizing forms of repressive rule may foster a wide-ranging coalition in which socially conservative groups (including those of a religious character) may unite with secular, liberalizing constitutionalists and even with radical, Marxist elements. It is not only the severity of repression and the persistence of an objectionable regime that stimulates resistance, but it is also its tendency to do cultural violence in the name of progress and modernity. Such a reality is especially true in a traditionalist society such as Iran's, where the hold of religion is strong and where a regime loses rather than achieves legitimacy by Westernizing and modernizing. In other words, the antitraditionalist character of a high technology approach to development deeply alienates certain social forces that are normally dormant and even reactionary and may transform them in certain progressive directions (e.g., to insist upon human rights).

Coalition with Technocrats

The "legitimacy" of a military takeover will generally depend on its economic performance, its capacity to provide the discipline and skill needed to increase economic and political power of the state by means of steady GNP growth, especially in the urban industrial sector. In order to assure the realization of these goals, the state must play a significant role, even overriding to a considerable extent market forces. The military will not simply protect the traditional sectors of economic privilege from the social forces whose grievances lead to pressure from below; its main objective is to stimulate, sustain, and even direct economic growth by a sophisticated mixture of fiscal and regulatory policies that make the state an important and direct participant in the economy. These tendencies toward administered capitalism antedate the assumption of direct political control by the military (for instance, in Brazil they were evident throughout the 1946–1964 period); however, with the military in power, the process accelerates dramatically. Technocrats as expert administrators are essential elements in such an economic strategy. These civil servants share with their military colleagues impatience over the "inefficiencies" of the conventional politicians who are distracted from true priorities by their search for popularity, their deference to tradition, and their tendency to support sentimental economic priorities. In the push toward modernity, the military reinforce the framework, and the technocrats supply the planning and oversight. Without the technocrats the generals would often face mounting opposition; furthermore, they would be unable to provide society with the kind of efficient and economically successful leadership that could stabilize their rule, and in time, give it a measure of legitimacy.

Public Enterprise and Investment

As suggested, the state enters the economy as principal investor in key industries, as well as presides as manager. It should be understood in the Brazilian instance that Vargas established and evolved the corporatist structure in the 1930s, and that the post-1964 developments amount to adaptations and intensifications of these earlier structures.[11] This is an important Brazilian circumstance that is not present to the same degree in other Third World countries with a modern economic sector and an authoritarian political system.

The growth-oriented ideology encourages corporatist procedures, with the state constantly expanding its economic role.[12] Many basic industries like energy production and distribution, communications, and transportation are state owned in this special form of militarization in a Third World capitalist context. The move to the right makes no attempt to establish a liberal economic order based on *laissez faire* market conceptions, nor to supplement market dynamics merely by introducing Keynesian "fixes" intended to maintain full employment at times when investment levels fall. The new focus is upon efficiency and growth of the economic aggregate, and the leaders accept high levels of unemployment and large-scale poverty for the indefinite future as unavoidable side-effects of according priority to economic viability.

In addition, management of external economic relations is often a technical matter with fundamental societal consequences. Attitudes toward external indebtedness and balance of payments deficits are directly related to the inflow of capital to a given Third World country. In recent years, the level of indebtedness, need for short-term capital credits from international markets, and payments imbalances have intensified still further the role of technocrats and have moved militarized regimes of this sort in a corporatist, state capitalist direction.

Geopolitical Links

Often, but not invariably, militarized regimes of the kind I have been describing come into being with the blessing, if not the active help, of the United States government. The precise relationship is difficult to demonstrate in most situations, although recent revelations and investigations disclose a pattern of widespread CIA support for the transition to militarized rule and its subsequent stabilization.[13] Even when links can be demonstrated to exist, their causal significance is difficult to assess. How important are precoup assurances of postcoup American diplomatic and material support? How important are different forms of advice and help at various stages of a struggle for power in a foreign society? A militarized rightest government tends to attract capital and political support both from the market economies in the industrialized world and from international lending institutions dominated by OECD perspectives. This support will not generally be reduced despite evidence of severe abuses of human rights. The Carter Administration avidly embraced a human rights diplomacy in its early months; in practice, however, it has not exerted consistent or considerable pressure on repressive regimes. Indeed, the United States has generally continued to lend its support to "friendly" governments, no matter how repressive their stance. It has, to be sure, encouraged liberalizing gestures in most circumstances. Yet even here there are notable exceptions, as for instance, Jimmy Carter's famous phone call of support to the Shah of Iran after "the bloody Friday massacre" in Jaleh Square on September 8, 1978, at which several thousand unarmed demonstrators were gunned down, some by machine guns, tanks, and even helicopter gunships.[14]

If severe abuse of human rights coincides with geopolitical antagonism, such as Amin in Uganda, then it engenders genuine opposition. Liberal sentiment reinforces assessments of material interests. And if the leader should be an anti-Western black or Arab (e.g., Qaddafi), then a racist underpinning strengthens the self-righteous demands of the West for liberalization. Regimes with equally objectionable human rights records, if important to the American-led global alliance, are entrusted with increasing regional roles as antiradical "enforcers."[15] More characteristically, the American-led Western global alliance views the principal examples of such regimes—Brazil, the Shah's Iran, Indonesia—as "junior partners" in the alliance against radicalism. In 1975–76, Iran's intervention in Oman to defeat the Dhofar uprising, Indonesia's invasion of East Timor, and Brazil's support for counterinsurgency throughout the Southern Cone (that is, Argentina, Chile, and Uruguay) illustrate these regional "peacekeeping" roles. In addition these regimes also provide the West, especially the United States, with relatively safe havens for military bases and space stations, as well as a comparatively secure and profitable setting for overseas capital and market development, including operations of multinational corporations.

Statism

Despite its geopolitical lines, the militarized governance pattern, once relatively secure in power, may impinge on investor interests as it moves strongly to realize its own statist and nationalist commitments. Its logic is to establish control and policies of its own, rather than to defer to an outside patron or "senior partner." In this respect, some militarized regimes, despite their internal reactionary policies, have actually joined in the front ranks of the struggle for a new international economic order. Part of this independent posture in international arenas appears to stem from a quest for international legitimacy on the part of governmental leadership. Experience in Brazil, India, Thailand, South Korea, and elsewhere suggests that these militarized regimes cannot count upon institutionalizing their legitimacy via the popular endorsement of official policies in elections even if they build up a record of economic successes. Unless rigged, the consistent result of "opening" the system to electoral politics, even of a restricted kind, has been the repudiation of the economic, political, and ideological approach of these militarized regimes. More recently, the principal governments that fall in the category of militarized regimes have refused to forfeit their nuclear options or to accept American leadership in the area of nonproliferation policy. Brazil, also, for instance, has been steadily diversifying its trade and investment patterns and has refused to define its diplomatic stance in the United Nations by following the American lead (e.g., Brazil voted for the anti-Zionist resolution in the General Assembly in 1975). Even on an economic plane, the drive for statist internal control has led these regimes to impose an increasingly complex web of regulatory authority around foreign investment. On another level, the growing burden of foreign indebtedness—built up to $160 billion by the end of 1976—reflects not only the extent to which these militarized politics attract outside capital, but also their degree of vulnerability; after a certain point has been reached, a government, like any large-scale debtor, must either accept external interference to sustain its credit standing or suffer the loss of credit, which might provoke a domestic economic crisis.

By describing the nature of rightist militarization in a capitalist context, I am not implying uniformity or conspiracy. I do argue that certain underlying circumstances in the Third World have generated a pattern of response in which some shared characteristics are present, although these trends are reinforced by principal imperial actors and by their close association with multinational corporations, the main bearers or agents of international capitalism in the present era. The militarized regimes established in the 1960s and 1970s are gradually being destabilized by their failures of economic performance. To the extent that these regimes do not succeed in realizing their claims to produce faster growth, control inflation, and stimulate investment, one major rationale for their oppressive existence is removed and major constituencies of support are eroded, if not lost. If, in addition, the left has been destroyed or neutralized, the other main rationale for oppression is undercut. As a consequence discontent tends to deepen and spread, and new forms of mass opposition can be expected to surface early in the 1980s.[16]

The image of falling dominoes depicted in the global trend toward militarized governance is not meant to imply that events in Brazil have had a causal impact elsewhere, except possibly to a slight extent among Southern Cone countries. Even in the Cone, domestic circumstances, abetted by international factors, have principally produced outcomes in Chile, Argentina, and Uruguay that resemble the Brazilian solution in key respects. Also there is a demonstration effect, difficult to calculate, that leads rightist policy-makers and political figures to regard the Brazilian experience as a "positive model" for their own societal situation. Daniel Patrick Moynihan, in his celebrated attack on Third World approaches to development that are infatuated with distributional priorities (which he attributed ludicrously to the Fabianism of the London School of Economics), pointed to Brazil as a healthy contrast, given its high rates of GNP growth and its emphasis on expanding the productive base of the modern sector. All those concerned with "order" as a precondition for modernization within the capitalist frame have been impressed by the degree to which counterinsurgency methods in Brazil eliminated radical politics from the scene. Note that the Brazilian case illustrated both the need to impose "discipline" on dissatisfaction, especially among workers, as well as the need to create "stability" by dealing with those who would overthrow the regime by violent means if they could. That is, not only radical, but reformist behavior must be suppressed; hence, a moderate government won't do, for only an extremist one will suppress to that degree. In South Korea this pattern of extended repression is especially clear, as the targets are often prominent religious or cultural figures boasting strong anticommunist, anti-North Korea credentials (*e.g.*, Hon Suk Han). They pose a menace because they question the fairness of the economic arrangements—especially, squeezing the poor—and object to official claims that the denial of civil liberties is necessary for the sake of national security.

They also pose a menace because Brazilianization introduces a slick, Western-evolved "international culture," symbolized by Coca-Cola, IBM, and Hilton Hotels. This cultural dimension—a spontaneous commitment to neocolonial national identity—offends deeply religious and traditional social forces and values. The anti-Shah uprisings in Iran during 1978 erupted out of this core reality of defending the indigenous culture against the disruptions of accelerated modernization.

Brazilianization is the wider pattern of political evolution in Third World countries that resembles the specific experience of Brazil since 1964. The common domestic elements are the impulse to stabilize and modernize the economy and polity without displacing privileged classes to any substantial degree and, above all, without embracing Marxist approaches or Sino-Soviet geopolitics. Put differently, the question is how to modernize to achieve GNP growth without abandoning capitalism on an international level or squeezing the rich too hard as a domestic source of capital. Part of the challenge is to concentrate capital resources in an effective, sustained way. Here, tax reform is part of the answer, as are external credit from foreign banks and international lending institutions, conditions of profitability for the MNC and for large-scale domestic enterprise (private and state), and, seemingly inevitably, large-scale corruption among the ruling elite. To pursue such a course, the popular sector must be demobilized to the extent possible and dealt with harshly to the extent necessary.

The drift of Sadat's government in Egypt during the early months of 1977 is suggestive. In order to gain external credit under IMF auspices, pressures mounted to allow the market to set food prices, but such austere if fiscally sound policies resulted in squeezing the poor beyond their levels of tolerance. As a result there were food riots, leading the regime to choose between giving way, which would jeopardize capital prospects, and imposing "discipline," which would jeopardize moderate forms of governance. Sadat has chosen the latter course, temporarily at least; his entire economic policy was based on making Egypt attractive to investors and lenders.

India's 1975 move toward "discipline" is also illustrative of the pressure in a major Third World country to couple economic stabilization with repression. It is indicative also of the unpopularity of such a strategy, despite the appearance of some temporary achievements by way of efficiency, elimination of corruption, and favoritism, and through the creation of a better business atmosphere. By calling for elections in 1977 Indira Gandhi displayed her credentials as "a pale criminal," unable or unwilling to close off the electoral channels of discontent so as to proceed with the tactics of Brazilianization. (Whoever claimed that Brazilianization was popular? The oft-quoted comment by the director of the Central Bank of Chile in the Pinochet years is indicative: "The fact that 90 percent of the people were against us proves that our economic plan is working.") It is a misunderstanding of this form of militarized governance to suppose that it can engender a popular mandate, especially to the extent that it bases its relations to the masses on the goal of political demobilization.[17] Even with good harvest years helped by favorable monsoon rains, the electoral rebuff of the "emergency" style of Mrs. Gandhi's rule was startling (as was her subsequent electoral sweep back to power in 1979), especially given the extent to which press criticism was stifled and opposition leaders jailed or isolated. However, the restoration of democratic forms does not assure the survival of moderate politics in India. Indeed, the structural crisis that made the "emergency" an attractive option in 1975 has not been resolved, and there is no prospect for the sort of socialist reforms that are needed if India is to redirect its productive and distributive resources toward the alleviation of poverty and the realization of the basic needs of its population as a whole. Indeed, the post-Gandhi governing coalition was even less inclined than its predecessor to attempt fundamental reforms in either land tenure arrangements or indigenous business entrepreneurship. As a consequence, it seems likely that the Desai government was a moderate interlude between authoritarian patterns of governance in India. We have no real understanding of how the current leadership would respond to militant demands from below that result in inflation, disorder, and a sense of anxiety among the "forces of order" in India's powerful military establishment and, more generally, among its conservative-traditionalist regional and federal governing sectors.

Leninization

The major form of militarized governance structure other than Brazilianization that emerges in the Third World builds its reality out of a reaction to capitalism. Indeed, socialist ideology proposes as its *raison d'être* the liberation of suffering humanity from the yoke of capitalist exploitation and the establishment of a socialist state. The rubric "Leninization" is not entirely satisfactory; it is used to differentiate the underlying drift toward authoritarian rule in Third World societies ruled by Marxist-Leninist elites from the pathological expression of state socialism that reached its peak in the Soviet Union under Stalin and lives on there in diluted form. Map 4-3 depicts the extent of Leninization.

The historical success of the socialist movement has reflected the wedding of a Marxist critique with a Leninist strategy for seizing and holding power. Leninism is associated with an insistence that armed struggle and the buildup of a strong socialist state are necessary preconditions to achieve sustainable socialism at the national level. The capitalist elite, with its dominance over the civil and military apparatus of state power, is never displaced by the outcome reached in electoral politics, nor will, to the extent possible, imperialist centers of power allow the spread of socialist governance structure. Examples of peaceful transition to socialism are rare and depend on a loose definition of socialism. (Does Sweden qualify as "socialist?" I tend to think not, given the persistence of a private sector and a capitalist entrepreneurial class). The failure of the Allende government of Chile in 1970–1973 to protect itself against bureaucratic harassment, internal class enemies, and external intervention appears to confirm Lenin's approach to revolutionary politics. The intervention of the United States to facilitate Allende's failure and downfall illustrates the vulnerability of a government espousing socialism if it has not secured control of the state by Leninist means.

Socialism has been sustained on a national scale only where it has been preceded by armed struggle (including the occupation of a country by the Soviet army). The darker side of the Leninist success story is that it has resulted in socialist seizures of undisputed power. The explanation for this experience in socialist countries is controversial and obscure. One explanation is to blame the arrogance of power implicit in Marxist-

Leninist thinking, especially the conviction that after the revolution the state apparatus is reconstituted as a "dictatorship" with no political space allowed for oppositional tendencies and no attention given to avoiding abuses of power by the new bureaucratic elite. A second explanation is to argue that hostile social forces internal and external to a given country generate a genuine counterrevolutionary interventionary danger that can be resisted only by mobilizing the full panoply of state power, that the danger persists, and that bureaucratic inertia of various sorts makes it difficult under such circumstances to liberalize once the danger has passed. A third line of explanation is that conditions of underdevelopment and poverty make it essential for any efficient governing structure, whether socialist or capitalist, to impose a high degree of discipline on the general population during the period of accelerating capital accumulation and industrial growth. A fourth explanation stresses the materialist failure of socialism to satisfy mass expectations or to create a genuine socialist ethos to take the place of the capitalist ethos which preceded it. That is, socialist conceptions of social and political organization remain or become unpopular with a substantial segment of the population, making it necessary to impose authority by force rather than by consent. A final explanation suggests that Third World Communist Party movements have been shaped and influenced by a Stalinized Soviet Union. Of course, in a given country, the political reality is likely to reflect some combination of these elements.

Underneath these explanations rages a vital controversy as to whether it is plausible to envision genuinely socialist states in the Third World that are viable, and yet do not move toward some form of repressive rule. Of course, the issue is one of degree, and it is misleading in the extreme to refuse to draw a distinction between the Soviet Union under Stalin, with millions of political prisoners, and under Brezhnev, with only a few thousand, or between the extent of repression present at a given time in China, Cuba, Yugoslavia, Vietnam, and the Soviet Union. Some Third World countries have embarked on various sorts of experiments with decentralization in economic, social, and political life. Despite these positive features, it remains correct that each of the socialist states has preempted most of the legitimate political, moral, and cultural space within its polity, that it has displayed virtually no toleration for even those adversaries who share socialist commitments, that it has failed to encourage popular creativity, and that it has dealt harshly and arbitrarily with its perceived opponents. Such a characterization seems applicable even for a governing process that has achieved historic results in other realms of state activity, as is the case especially with Cuba, Vietnam, and China.

There is a temptation to symmetrize the phenomena of Brazilianization and Leninization.[18] It is a dangerous temptation, because it tends to overlook the socialist advantage arising from promises about and achievements of equality, solidarity, and liberation. Socialism in some form seems like the only possible way to meet the human needs of Third World peoples in the face of the interplay between demographic and ecological pressures. And, indeed, the distributional record of socialist countries is far superior to their capitalist equivalents, although it is difficult to obtain data suitable for comparison.[19] Furthermore, since socialist governance does not entail exploitation in principle, it would seem less dependent on a coercive state to sustain itself in power.* Finally, there are many socialist political groupings in the Third World that have grown sensitive to the need for restraint of socialist state power and that seek to rule within a strict constitutional framework of accountability and competitive politics. Should these socialist elites achieve and sustain power, unless and until displaced by constitutional procedures (disproving the Leninist contentions), and should they achieve nonrepressive modes of socialist governance, then a powerful normative model for a Third World socialist state would exist. Precisely because of this prospect, I would expect strenuous efforts by Trilateralist and Stalinist centers of power (often orthodox "Communist Parties"), possibly in concert, to prevent these outcomes in the Third World, just as they appear to cooperate to avoid such political developments in Western Europe.

Having clarified the extent to which socialism is more promising than capitalism as a political solution at the national level, it is necessary to reassert the main thesis: namely, the decline in moderate possibilities deepens the left/right split, and to the extent that the left has succeeded, it has brought with it, especially in the Third World, various adaptations of Leninist forms of socialist rules. Ethiopia, Angola, and Mozambique, as well as the three countries of Indochina, illustrate this pattern, and thus contribute to the basic trend toward authoritarian rule in the Third World.

A Note on Iran's Islamic Republic

A new form of governing structure is taking shape in the aftermath of the Iranian Revolution in a country that formerly was a prime member of the Brazilianization group. It may be either a new species of authoritarian rule or one Third World model of nonauthoritarian governance.

Iran's emergent Islamic republic has promised the Iranian people democratic governance with a core commitment to social justice on behalf of the poor. If it fulfills these aspirations it will offer us a much needed Third World example of nonauthoritarian humane governance.

These positive prospects are presently clouded by a variety of disquieting signs: harshness in the application of Islamic law, reliance on secret trial procedures and summary executions to deal with those who

*For elaboration of this theme, as well as other issues related to the socialism/capitalism distinction, see Chapter V.

committed crimes against the Iranian people on behalf of the Shah's regime, intolerance toward political and cultural dissent that deviates from Shi'ia canons of propriety, and denial of group rights for religious and ethnic minorities and for women. Of course, the Iranian future is difficult to project. The situation is rapidly unfolding. Human rights never flourish in the immediate aftermath of revolution. As of the end of 1980, there seems little prospect that the Islamic republic when it takes shape will be nonauthoritarian.

If these authoritarian tendencies prevail, Iran will still not fall properly within either the Brazilianization or Leninization categories. It will, in fact, initiate a third type of authoritarian rule for Third World countries with a significant industrial sector. To associate its character with its leading element might make it convenient to classify such a polity under the heading of Islamicization. As yet, however, any classification of Iran as "authoritarian" seems premature.

Praetorianism[20]

In addition to Brazilianization and Leninization, there is a set of tendencies toward authoritarian rule that are not directly connected with late, late capitalist development. In these national situations autocratic rule is a reflection of "political underdevelopment," that is, a lack of procedures and institutions capable of legitimating governmental authority in a sustainable manner without reliance on force. In such a society, arbitrary force at the disposal of the rulers is the basic political premise, and the military or paramilitary security system is needed to secure the compliance of the population. The extent of praetorianism as of 1978 is suggested by maps 4-4, 4-5, and 4-6.

The societal structure may be closely linked in a dependent way to outside economic forces as has been the case for Central American and African countries that fall into this category. The dictator or maximal leader provides order and seeks to work out acceptable arrangements with external capitalist and geopolitical forces. Given the complexity of the world scene, such an autocratic regime may make differing alignments for distinct concerns, joining with East or West on strategic questions, insisting as a member of the South on global economic reform, and linking to the capitalist North when it comes to national developmental strategy.

In African settings this kind of autocratic rule may have either a left or right ideology. In some instances, as with Uganda, the diplomatic and ideological stance may be left, but the economic linkages may still be primarily associated with capitalist actors and markets.

The point about praetorian rule is that it involves the seizure and exercise of state power by an elite that does not rest its legitimacy on any system of political accountability to the citizenry. Furthermore, recourse to autocratic rule is not a consequence of a central economic crisis arising out of the need to deepen capitalist development or to discipline labor demands for economic shares and rights of participation. In the praetorianized instances autocratic leadership may seek to vindicate its authority externally by a claim to provide sufficient order to assure profitable investment and steady economic growth.

Unlike the Brazilianized and Leninized societies, there is little opportunity for experiments in liberalization. There is in these societies only a small number of educated individuals and no serious middle class. There is virtually no tradition of moderate political participation. Politics are polarized. Opposition to the government almost necessarily assumes the form of armed struggle.

Some Generalizations about Authoritarian Rule in the Third World

The present extent of authoritarianism in the Third World can now be considered. Here I attempt to make the basic case for a spread of repressive rule in a series of world maps beginning in 1960. (See maps 4-7 to 4-11.) On these maps I indicate those Third World countries subject to repressive rule in each five-year interval since 1960.

I distinguish degrees of repressiveness in each of the first five maps. The authoritarian pattern is far broader than the militarization of political rule and its insulation from civilian accountability. Nevertheless, the degree of such insulation gives some sense of the degree of repressiveness. Hence, we identify those states ruled by military officers, those in which martial law or state of emergency has been declared by the government, and, finally, those in which civilians rule the country but depend heavily on the military to keep them in power, disallowing a political opposition to function normally.

On the sixth map I identify left and right orientations of the repressive governments. I make this ideological classification on the basis of three criteria: attitudes toward multinationals, patterns of global alignment, and socialization of the economy. In some cases, for instance Algeria or India, the ideological profile is a confused one, and recourse is had to a "mixed" category. My attempt is to make the distinction between left and right as reasonably as possible for the most recent year in the period since 1960.

These maps, even if one objects to a particular decision as to classification, reveal clearly a trend toward rightist forms of militarization. In Latin America and Africa the shift during the period covered has been especially dramatic. As the preceding discussion of the context of militarization makes clear, it is the new character of the military outlook that creates a special concern. The ascent to power of the military or of militarized civilians is accompanied by a broadened sense of purpose for the military. The military and their civilian allies now regard their security task as mainly domestic, a matter of protecting the stability of the developmental process against antagonistic social forces. In other words, militarization is associated, whether wittingly or not, with a specific type of national politics.

In Africa and Asia trends toward militarization should be associated in part with some deferred strains arising out of the decolonization process. The postcolonial state in these regions has often expanded without generally being able to secure a mandate embracing all significant groups encompassed by state. Governance is based on imposed authority usually associated with the ascendancy of given elites, sometimes enjoying support from only certain ethnic components of the whole social order. In most Third World countries, because the military has been willing to exercise control, the strong governance option has prevailed.

In sum, the maps support the generalizations about the trends toward militarization, as well as the subtrends toward rightist variants. Such trends are vectors of change. Some exceptions exist: India's move toward militarized rule with the Emergency Decrees of 1975 was repudiated at the polls in March of 1977, and the revolutionary movement in Iran has also succeeded in eliminating one of the most militarized regimes from the world scene. Despite the current uncertainty about the future of Iran, some significant gains have already been achieved in the direction of reducing the militarized character of the relation between government and citizenry. In addition, the new leaders have emphasized their determination to cut dependent links to the outsiders and to rely much less upon a militarized approach to national security than was the case in the Pahlavi era. How far the Iranian experience will spread, and with what effects, is impossible to tell at this stage.

There are several significant implications of the cumulative trend toward repressive rule for the global community. First of all, militarization encourages the emergence of strong states in many Third World countries. Second, where state power is strong and the government sustained in power by military control, economic and political consequences are certain to result. Third, even the most repressive regimes remain vulnerable to revolutionary pressures under certain circumstances. Fourth, militarist Third World governments will not lend genuine support to global disarmament initiatives, as their links of dependency to one or the other superpower tend to be strong; this orientation works against pursuing the more natural Third World interests in denuclearization and disarmament. Fifth, the existence of a large majority of Third World governments that affirm the traditional virtues of sovereignty and statism assures the absence of any serious challenge directed at prevailing ideas about the pace and shape of global reform.

This situation creates confusion. On the one hand, militarist governments may push Third World solidarity on a wide variety of limited issues so as to secure a better relative position, especially in economic terms, for themselves in the world system. On the other hand, however, their framework of operations is bounded by traditional statism that includes endorsement of the war system and antipathy to supranationalist or pacifist lines of thinking. As such, world order values associated with peace, economic well-being, human rights, ecological balance, and positive global identity are not likely to win support from such leadership. Advocacy of a new international economic order (NIEO) is not *necessarily* associated with seeking a just and peaceful world order. And, indeed, NIEO achieved under militarist auspices would not necessarily help poor people satisfy their basic needs in the near future, even if it did help poor states improve their relative trading and development position.

In conclusion, alongside the continuing development and spread of the entire spectrum of weaponry is the expansion of militarized governance patterns. The latter augments the former in several damaging respects. While militarism in the Third World is partly a reflection of domestic factors, it is also a consequence of international factors, especially the imperial geopolitics of the United States and the capitalist domination of international economic institutions and procedures.

Reversal of this trend toward militarized authoritarianism is difficult. It depends, first of all, on a deepening domestic opposition to militarism and authoritarianism, perhaps precipitated by economic failures that extend the deprivations experienced by the poor to large sectors of the middle classes. There is some indication that the moderation of authoritarian rule in Brazil has occurred as a response to a narrowing base of political support, with prominent middle class defections especially among business and professional groups. Whether the approach to moderation will restore levels of support is likely to determine if it will persist or be superceded by more severe authoritarian tactics. In Iran, also, we observe the failure of severe authoritarian rule to sustain stability despite a plenitude of resources and capital, with an eventual falling away of support for the Shah on the part of even those urban sectors that had been the beneficiaries of his policies. In such a situation the tactical response by the rulers is either cosmetic liberalization or making authoritarian rule even more severe, or an incoherent embrace of both postures, as in Iran during 1978. None of these responses worked, as the domestic balance shifted strongly against dynastic rule while the revolutionary movement constantly broadened its popular base until in early January, the repressive regime was isolated from any base of support in the society and collapsed.

Second, overcoming militarization of domestic politics will be helped by a more "progressive" cast of politics in the leading countries of the world, and as extended to their foreign policy. Deference by the powerful to the dynamics of self-determination by the weak and restraint in arms sales and supplies would contribute to the goals of demilitarization of Third World politics. Here again the Iranian case is instructive since the revolution succeeded despite the support for the Shah given by all major outside states, including especially the United States. It remains obscure at this point whether the revolutionary success will engender similar processes elsewhere or create new counterrevolutionary pressure and tactics to avoid repetition of the Iranian Revolution in other countries. The dialectics of contradictory influence can, perhaps, be best observed in the years ahead in such countries as Egypt, Saudi Arabia, and Turkey, where Islamic movements exist in settings of capitalist development planning that is heavily dependent on outside support.

Third, reversing militarization would be encouraged by significantly reforming the lending practices of the United Nations family of economic assistance agencies like the World Bank, IMF, as well as of their regional counterparts. As present, lending by international financial institutions is closely linked with the activities of private banks, sharing virtually identical criteria of investment risk and opportunity. What Third World countries require are sources of capital that are not interventionary in socially regressive ways. One step in this direction would be for public sector lending, at least, to be tied to noneconomic criteria, such as a record of achievement by a given government with respect to income distribution or satisfaction of basic needs. As matters now stand, Third World governments are often forced to choose between securing the capital they need and pursuing policies designed for the benefit of their population as a whole, especially the bottom forty percent. Furthermore, the goals of moderate, democratic political order could be served by reliance on some kind of "clean hands" assessment of each governmental applicant for international economic assistance, a precondition that minimum standards of human rights were being observed. Such a reorientation of capital transfer policies would have to be on guard, of course, against erecting a new form of neocolonial control over Third World autonomous development in the name of human rights.

Stalinization

Socialist advanced industrial countries also suffer from rigid authoritarian rule. The phenomenon of Stalinization suggests the severity of repression during Stalin's period of rule in the Soviet Union. Stalinization, as extended to post-Stalin USSR or to East Europe, Albania, and more problematically, to Yugoslavia, refers to the pattern of dictatorial rule in a centralized socialist state in the North. (See Map 4-13.)

As is evident, Stalinization has evolved through different stages, surviving even the Khrushchev "shocks" of the XXth Congress of the Soviet Communist Party, which featured revelations of Stalin's crimes and the repudiation of his methods. The authoritarian structure remains intact, the secret police (KGB) continue to act as a principal arm of government, and oppositional activities meet with harsh responses. The Gulag mentality continues to characterize the Soviet approach to governance.

In Eastern Europe, Stalinization has taken hold to varying degrees and cannot be correlated directly with the extent of subordination to Moscow. Rumania and, even more dramatically, Albania pursue independent lines of national policy, and yet are Stalinized in their style of domestic governance. Hungary, on the other hand, is quite submissive in its international posture, and yet has evolved into a comparatively moderate polity in the years since 1956, when its heroic effort to gain liberation from Soviet domination and Stalinist rule failed.

There is little consensus or optimism about the future evolution of the Soviet system. Some "Leninists" like Roy Medvedev believe that liberalization is possible and even necessary, if for no other reason than to overcome the inefficiencies and incompetence of excessive bureaucratic centralism and administrative control.[21] Sharper lines of dissent are convinced that the structure of authority is Stalinized (or Leninized), and that nothing short of revolutionary change can end authoritarianism.

The dramatic conclusion is that we have no positive example of a socialist country in the North that has avoided the Stalinization phenomenon. Even Tito's dramatic repudiation of Soviet hegemony has not resulted in an open, nonrepressive Yugoslavia. Dissenters are repressed, and there is little political space available to those who would challenge or oppose the main lines of official policy.

The socialist experience in the North, as represented by the communist countries, seems to entail an authoritarian pattern of rule. There are variations in degrees of severity, as between countries and as between different times in a given country. There is neither an ideological tradition nor an empirical instance, as yet, of a nonauthoritarian state emerging out of the world communist movement. The potential spread of Eurocommunism in Western Europe may create a partial exception if Communist Parties gain power in Italy, Spain, or France, Even if such an eventuality should occur, it will not be accepted as a full test. For one thing, there is the view that Eurocommunists are not socialists at all, but have been co-opted through their high stake in the existing order to save capitalism from collapse in a period of crisis. Quite opposite is the equally critical view that the liberal affirmations of Eurocommunism are nothing but a fig leaf to hide the dark side of communist participation in electoral politics, that such liberalism is simply a tactic to fool voters, and that the Communist party in each of these countries remains Stalinist in its essence.

In conclusion, Stalinization seems to characterize Communist Party rule in the North; Eurocommunist liberal postures are not yet convincing either as genuinely socialist or as necessarily antiauthoritarian. The distinction between Stalinization in the North and Leninization in the South may be rather thin, especially in certain countries such as North Korea and Cuba, where the Soviet role has been significant. In addition to levels of development, the geopolitical distance of the Third World from the USSR gives the political processes of these countries relatively greater autonomy than is possible for the states of Eastern Europe.

In foreign policy, also, the Stalinized bias is apparent in Soviet behavior. Moscow is as biased toward the survival of sympathetic elites in the Third World, regardless of how repressive, as Washington. True, the Soviet group of countries so far have fewer vested economic interests in the Third World and therefore often stand to gain geopolitically from the encouragement of a liberation struggle, as in southern Africa. Once a pro-Moscow government is in power, however, no amount of severity in repressive behavior will generate Soviet criticism or disaffection (e.g., Uganda, Equatorial Guinea, Ethiopia). In this regard, the liberal strain in Western political consciousness as manifest recently, for instance, in the human rights diplomacy of the United States during 1977 and 1978 has no counterpart in Soviet behavior.

Trilateralization

It is not only the Third World and the Soviet bloc that exhibit an inability to establish satisfactory governance structures. Challenges directed at democratic practices are occurring in some of the richest, most industrialized countries in the North. (See map 4-14.) These societies are exhibiting a bewildering array of strains ranging from the prevalence of street crime, drug use, and mental disorder to the disclosure of corrupt practices by top leaders. Various forms of terrorism are rampant. Questions of governability have been raised. Can democratic societies achieve sufficent discipline to deal with the multiple challenges of the contemporary world? The Trilateral Commission has been sensitive to this weakening of the democratic fabric among capitalist members of the advanced industrial world, sponsoring a much publicized study on this theme bearing the revealing title *The Crisis of Democracy*.[22]

In effect, Trilateralists are "pessimistic" about whether values and practices associated with democratic notions of participation and dissent remain compatible with overriding priorities of disciplined behavior by the citizenry as a whole. In effect, doubts are raised as to whether the demands on government can be matched by capabilities to respond successfully to the agenda of discontent and array of disorders. One of the main authors in the Trilateral Commission project, Samuel Huntington, is of the opinion that "In the past decade, we've swung too far to the extreme of challenging authority, dismantling it, exposing all of its abuses—important and unimportant, real and imagined."[23] Part of the problem, according to the introduction of the Trilateral Commission Report, is with alienated intellectuals, "who assert their disgust with the corruption, materialism, and inefficiency of democracy and with the subservience of democratic government to 'monopoly capitalism'."[24]

Such critics are derided in the report, because they write and criticize without having to accept the burden of responsibility for practical affairs. These "value-oriented intellectuals who often devote themselves to the derogation of leadership, the challenging of authority, and the unmasking and delegitimation of established institutions . . . constitute a challenge to democratic government which is, potentially at least, as serious as those posed by the aristocratic cliques, fascist movements, and communist parties."[25] This trend is reinforced, according to the report, by counter-cultural tendencies questioning traditional beliefs in materialism, individualist gratifications, and technocratic approaches to social issues. Such tendencies "pose an additional new problem for democratic government in terms of its ability to mobilize its citizens for the achievement of social and political goals and to impose discipline and sacrifice upon its citizens in order to achieve those goals."[26] These various pressures in their cumulative effect shape the central issue for the Trilateralists: "The demands on democratic government grow, while the capacity of democratic government stagnates. This, it would appear, is the central dilemma of the governability of democracy which has manifested itself in Europe, North America, and Japan in the 1970s."[27]

This assessment of democratic prospects is striking for its failure to address the merits of the disaffection. It is a managerial inquiry that is fully consistent with the overriding concern of the Trilateral Commission with the management of threats to the international status quo. Zbigniew Brzezinski, then executive director of the commission, observes in an introductory note to the report that "The Trilateral Commission decided to undertake this project because it has felt, rightly in my view, that the vitality of our political systems is a central precondition for the shaping of a stable international order and for the fashioning of more cooperative relations among our regions."[28] And "vitality" is explained by Brzezinski as "the subtle interrelationship between liberty and responsibility." "Responsibility" is a code word for popular acquiescence and discipline, for confining demands to marginal changes. Part of this mission, according to the Trilateralist vision of the future, is to shape a *global* sequel to the uncertainties and tensions of the existing *international* order. The self-serving claim advanced is that only Trilateralist leadership of a coherent sort can accomplish this transition in an effective and beneficial fashion. The Third World is far too poor and weak, and the Soviet Union is disabled by its refusal to participate in the world economy in a regular way and by the rigidity of its bureaucratic approach to policy-making. Only a Trilateralist concert of capitalist societies possesses the mixture of material capabilities, innovative skills, and managerial disposition needed to produce a global order that could bring disruptive tendencies under control. Such a global order would also work to stabilize prevailing hierarchies of privilege and power on the national level.

Of course, Trilateralists are increasingly concerned, especially in

Europe, where economic pressures have raised the political questions in more acute form, about the challenge of Eurocommunism. This challenge, as the European section of the report makes clear, is seen as one consequence of the failure of liberal forces controlling the apparatus of state power to provide bureaucratic efficiency or to meet mass demands for social justice.[29] At stake, of course, are the capitalist economic premises of these political systems, not necessarily their democratic orientation. Indeed, the Communist Parties in Italy, France, and Spain, long stigmatized as Stalinist, have to varying degrees emphasized values of decentralization, civil liberties, and popular participation more than have their liberal adversaries, who are trapped by the technocratic centralism of the present stage of capitalist operations.

The commission report fails to examine whether "value-oriented intellectuals" might not perceive some glaring deficiencies beneath the glitter of the Trilateral world. Signs of disintegration abound everywhere—the violence-drenched "entertainment," the colossal waste, the malnutrition of overdevelopment, the rising cancer rates, the desperate search for "meaning," the apocalyptic and postapocalyptic cultural mood. These symptoms are indicative of cultural disorder, a circumstance far too deep to be handled by a shift away from democratic traditions.

The crisis of democratic societies reflects the interplay of internal and external factors. Materialist expectations "handled" by welfare state programs contribute to bureaucratic overload, mass disillusionment, and an intrusive state. The logic of national security in the nuclear age intensifies these pressures, especially in the United States, but also for NATO countries, where large standby forces ready for immediate deployment and backed up by a constant stream of technological innovations unavoidably built up a military-industrial complex and a permanent "prewar" mentality. Beyond this, economic interdependencies on many fronts require unprecedented efforts to cushion the impact of diverse national priorities, efforts made more complex by the tension between an American led ideology of free trade and a political process on the state level that is nationalistic at all times and protectionist during periods of pressure. These managerial imperatives coincide with the emerging agenda of ecological interdependencies that are, in some instances, planetary in scope (nuclear testing, ocean pollution, ozone depletion), an agenda that often squarely challenges national sovereign rights on behalf of global well-being (e.g., flag-of-convenience tanker registration, reliance on cheap pesticides). Technological developments (computerized police administration, centralized and vulnerable energy systems such as those associated with nuclear technology) also create the pretexts and instrumentalities for repressive practices.

These "structural" pressures lead progressive social forces, also, to question the capacity of Trilateral governance systems to respond adequately or to satisfy their own populations. Yet, to attribute these issues to "ungovernability," to an excess of democracy, or to the irritating influence of value-oriented intellectuals suggests a reactionary political "fix" to a series of challenges that call for a more profound process of transformation and adjustment.[30] The Trilateral Commission is busy "framing" a suspect to protect the "cover" of the real culprit— namely, an obsolete and exploitative set of social, political, and economic institutions, reinforced by self-destructive belief systems, that sustain in power transnational elites with vested interests in the existing structure of power and wealth. Unless these underlying elements of authority systems can be reconstituted in a more progressive fashion, which includes the safeguarding of precious democratic achievements, the prospects for the Trilateral world are dismal on every score. In the name of "governability" one can anticipate increasing abridgments of democratic procedures and the relegation of their operation to a formal level. In the United States the informal regimentation of the main political parties and network television effectively discourage fundamental questioning of the status quo.

One disquieting manifestation of this preauthoritarian mentality appeared in an alarming context: nuclear weapons policy. In a volume of The 1980s Project of the Council on Foreign Relations on this topic its editor notes blandly:

> In the long run, the existence of nuclear weapons could fundamentally alter government-citizen relationships. If, over time, the need of the governments to field expensive deterrent forces is not appreciated by citizens who no longer sense a real nuclear threat, popular support for the maintenance of forces could fade—and governments might feel themselves compelled to provide for deterrence without the consent of the governed.[31]

This formulation is noteworthy for the way "the need of the governments" is given objective status, whereas the popular failure of appreciation by the citizenry is regarded as nothing more than subjective sentiment, appropriately circumvented.

In sum, Trilateralist outlooks remain in ascendance throughout the noncommunist advanced industrial countries. These anxieties about governability are founded on objective realities. They confuse, however, the symptom for the disease and prescribe cures that are largely irrelevant. The Trilateralist response fails to address the need for profound economic, political, and cultural adjustments, including a transnational movement to create a just world; as such, it fails to address the intertwined challenges posed by domestic and global developments.

Assessment

Prior sections have interpreted the main patterns of authoritarian rule throughout the world. These patterns necessarily ignore special features of a given national situation. However, five crystallizations of these trends have been suggested: Brazilianization, Leninization, praetorianization, Stalinization, and Trilateralization. The pattern of repressive rule is disclosed in two different forms: first, by a table of contents, classifying each in relation to authoritarian and preauthoritarian forms of governance; second, by a series of maps that disclose trends with respect to each category of governance. Each of these broad patterns provides a general sense of political life within the national societies whose states give structure to the world political system and whose governments determine what it is realistic to expect with regard to global reform. Brazilianization is characteristically related to the dynamics of capital formation. The governing elite in a Third World country rejects the option of drastic structural reform (especially dissolving traditional classes of privilege) and chooses instead to rely upon repressive modes of structural maintenance. Brazilianization is also a consequence of the influence of transnational capital interests, especially of their relentless quest for a reliable climate for trade and investment in Third World societies. Leninization evolves out of the communist approach to the exercise of state power and to the relationship between the government and the people based on structures of bureaucratic dominance. The authoritarian tendency is also reinforced by the perceived need to defend revolutionary governments against a mixture of internal and external adversaries with counterrevolutionary designs. Praetorianization represents the imposition of order via arbitrary force in a society without evolved political institutions and traditions and without a significant modern economic sector. Stalinization has evolved out of Leninization in the Soviet Union, involving the pathological extension of Leninist attitudes toward the formation of a hard state in the postrevolutionary period and generating structures and practices of repressive rule that have not only outlived Stalin, but have persisted despite the explicit Soviet repudiation of his dictatorial methods. Stalinization has also been insinuated into Soviet hegemonic relations with East European socialist countries. Trilateralization is a preauthoritarian disposition of liberal democracies in the advanced industrial sector of the world economy, provoked by essentially the same factors as Brazilianization, but in the context of different political traditions, a more ascendant global status, and a more affluent and apathetic citizenry.

In three of these five contexts economic considerations appear to play the decisive role. Because of underdevelopment and mass poverty, Brazilianization does seem to be decisively shaped by class struggle on the domestic level that is reinforced by the geopolitics of world capitalism (i.e., state interests and MNCs). The Iran case is an anomaly to the extent that oil wealth gave the Shah's regime a special option of liberalizing rapidly without shaking up class structure. A mixture of greed and indifference, however, led the ruling group in Iran to impose tight authoritarian rule without the stimulus of any strong case of functional necessity.

Leninization may in some settings reflect the difficulty of maintaining order in the face of persisting economic austerity, an austerity often made more extreme by the hostility of the capitalist sector of the world economy; yet, on balance, authoritarian excess in Third World socialist countries reflects ideological and normative insensitivities in mainstream Marxist-Leninist thinking and practice (possibly avoidable, although as yet untested, in variants of Trotskyism), including a naive theory of the state, an undervaluation of individual rights as legally protected by independent institutions, and a failure to grasp the linkage between cultural autonomy and progressive politics.

Trilateralization is explicitly a quest for new international structures enabling separate capitalist polities to maintain their growth in the face of a variety of domestic and international challenges, and its authoritarian implications reflect the conviction that it may be necessary to police the domestic scene to overcome obstruction and disorder; capitalist activities are increasingly transnational in their critical dimensions, typified by the role of MNCs and by dependence on imported oil, but, as with Third World settings, a prerequisite to success is stability at various levels of social adjustment, a stability that contains labor demands, keeps investment profitable, and rewards the managerial elite.

It should be understood that each of these authoritarian patterns is itself in a process of constant evolution, leading to frequent shifts in tactics, style, and tone; each of these polities is beset by a variety of tensions and counterpressures that assumes its own distinctive coloration. It is characteristic for Brazil, for instance, to experiment periodically with "decompression," as its leadership maneuvers to maintain or extend its political base, which is being eroded by repressive measures that are particularly resented when economic discontent deepens or spreads. A Brazilianized regime oscillates between its central reliance on repressive violence to assure stability and its desire to gain some measure of legitimacy by way of popular support, which will alone give it longer term durability. Such an impulse for legitimacy may be augmented also by external considerations, among them outside pressures from the international community, including the United Nations; liberal American presidencies also may put pressure on their allies, as has occurred via the human rights diplomacy associated with the initial phases of the Carter Administration. As a result, a loosening of repressive policies occurs from time to time, accompanied even by promises of a return to civilian normalcy, or its cosmetic equivalent. Similarly, Leninized and Stalinized regimes zigzag in their degree of repression, depending on a variety of personality and situational factors. The 1968 Soviet invasion of Czechoslovakia to stem liberalizing tendencies disclosed an outer limit for de-

Stalinization, at least within the immediate Soviet orbit for that time period. Elsewhere the potentialities for de-Stalinization and de-Leninization have not been tested to any appreciable degree as yet, but hopeful signs are present, especially in Cuba. Trilateral polities have not yet moved across authoritarian thresholds; Europe, and possibly Japan, may evolve progressive, nonauthoritarian options in the interim, but the pressures for imposed rightist rule are mounting rapidly.

North America, with its strong democratic traditions, wealth, and power, may withstand these pressures longer than most, partly because its primacy in the Trilateral world allows it to divert some of the worst effects of these global economic pressures to its weaker, more dependent allies (e.g., the relative effects of OPEC pricing policies since 1973 on national economies). From another perspective, the United States situation is the most desperate: "When I look at this country, a modern-day Babylon that is fast approaching its twilight, and see it wallowing in decadence, corruption, immorality and banality, I am proud to realize that absolutely none of it is of my making," writes one Afro-American.[32] The most immediate vulnerability of the United States to authoritarian solutions, at present, seems connected with a mood of cultural despair, reinforced by economic and political stagnancy. In this respect, the United States manifests the imprint of repression without the existence of an authoritarian governing structure.

These drifts toward authoritarianism suggest three types of world order conclusions: (1) an inability of the state to achieve humane governance structures in any principal sector of world society; (2) a powerful set of convergent inhibitions on system change, on those transformative strategies that might establish a humane governance structure for the planet as a whole; and (3) a pattern generally unfavorable to the realization of world order values within the present structure of international society.

Each of these conclusions will be briefly discussed.

Critique of the State

Although the state remains the principal framework for the political organization of life on the planet, its performance and prospects suggest that its predominance at least in present forms is generally incapable of achieving humane patterns of governance, i.e., patterns in which basic human rights of an economic, social, political, and cultural character are upheld. Of course, comparison has to be based on whether alternative modes of political organization with a greater potential for human governance exist and whether, where, and in what respects the state is declining or increasing in its value-realizing capacities. Some general normative claims have been advanced on behalf of the state's performance; Tom Farer writes, for instance, "As for economic security, it seems plain to me that governments are doing better today than at any time in the past."[33] And certainly it should be appreciated that the state as a global phenomenon is a relatively recent development, superceding imperial modes of organization that have been dominant in most parts of the world.

Nevertheless, the negative generalization holds even in the Third World to the extent that governing coalitions must rely on authoritarian prerogatives to sustain order. Since this condition pertains so widely, the most elaborate normative claim that can be advanced on behalf of the state as a framework for national life is that it has displayed an impressive capacity to assure an increasing measure of national autonomy for the peoples of the world, especially in those areas liberated from colonial rule in the last several decades. For these societies, the state as a political actor has achieved important goals, and is regarded by all parts of the political spectrum as a positive phenomenon. Such governing elites are not ready to relinquish their sovereignty to any external actor, whatever the global rationale, nor to diminish their internal control, even on behalf of ethnic groups pressing their own claims for autonomy and self-determination.

A world order critique of the state does not entail a call for its elimination as a form of political order. It argues in favor of eroding the dominance of the state, especially in the more industrialized societies, by enhancing governance structures of both international and intranational character. This process can and should proceed initially in the countries of the North, and then gradually be extended to the Third World.

It should also be noted that authoritarian tendencies seem more inevitable in large states and in governance structures that seek to impose unified rule over ethnically, religiously, and culturally diverse and recalcitrant population groupings. At the same time, such small states as Albania, Cambodia, Chile, and Paraguay suggest that severe repression cannot be associated only with large-sized states. It is possible to imagine the rapid proliferation of small states alongside the confederalizing of large states as together satisfying national preconditions for humane polities.

Inhibitions on System Change

An attribute of authoritarian tendencies is to close off political space for innovation. By its character, such governance structures are not receptive to proposals for change that do not emerge from the supreme leader or supportive technocrats. The ruling elite, whether or not dominated by a dictatorial figure, tends to be shortsighted and mean-spirited and to assume the same for others. One effect is to accent the centrifugal features of statism. Furthermore, Brazilianized, Leninized, praetorianized, Stalinized, and Trilateralized governance structures rely on force to sustain rule, accord great influence to their respective military establishments (and their civilian allies), and develop formidable internal security bureaucracies that are exceedingly threatened by transnational goals and outlooks.

Trilateralists do, indeed, seek a systematic adjustment that depends on the development of a more integrated global economy. Such an economy would be structured to assure access to critical resources (above all, oil and gas), facilitate transnational flows of capital, and provide MNCs with assured access and stable overseas conditions for planning and the conduct of business operations. Trilateralists also emphasize the importance of controlling domestic wage pressure, inflation, and parochial distortions of the market. Given the context of Brazilianization—the principal non-Trilateral sphere of operations for international capitalism—considerations of order take precedence over the alleged concern for social justice. Labor unrest, terrorist activity or socialist policies threaten the viability of profitable overseas operations by the MNCs as well as imperil the reliability of international banking. Avoiding these outcomes is accorded priority. From this perspective, a human rights diplomacy seems either stupid (undermining primary interests), or cynical (intended to revive the Cold War, mobilize domestic support for an activist foreign policy, confuse and solicit world public opinion), or provincial (ignoring patterns of economic deprivation). The Carter Administration has virtually abandoned human rights as an explicit goal of American foreign policy, and in recent years has been busy fighting off attacks from its critics, including Henry Kissinger, that the decline of United States power was partly achieved by a human rights diplomacy. A major allegation along these lines is that Iran was "lost," in part, due to Carter's ill-advised liberalizing pressures on the Shah.

An essential conclusion is that authoritarian tendencies on a national level are not conducive to generating a climate for progressive types of global reform. Such a climate will depend on the emergence of humane governance structures on a state level that will emerge only if populist pressures and struggles to achieve such structures are successful. Authoritarianism by its nature is not humane (although it may be benevolent in certain aspects, e.g., provision of material needs), and by its logic and operation is antagonistic to populist pressures, although its policies may seek to reduce these by co-optation in various forms. Also, the preoccupations of authoritarian leaders with effective control make them ill-disposed to share power and authority with wider governance structures that cannot be controlled. Finally, the authoritarian impulse is also closely associated with centralization (to assure control). Domestic militarization of political power is, therefore, by its essential nature antithetical to downward power-sharing of the sort implied by confederalizing visions of preferred national governance structures or to outward power-sharing by way of transnational security arrangements leading toward disarmament.

World Order Values

The value implications of the various forms of authoritarianism are complicated to specify. There are, in addition, major national, regional,

cultural, ideological, and religious variations. Some very schematic cor-
relations can be discerned to suggest the patterns that underlie the five
categories of authoritarian states.

TABLE 4-7

Brazilianization and World Order Values[34]

Nonviolence	violence as central to problem-solving
and peace (V_1)	increased arms acquisition
	"security" identified with military strength
	military bias of bureaucracy
	antidisarmament perspectives
Economic	economic performance measured by growth rather
well-being (V_2)	than needs criteria
	income and regional disparities accentuated
	large proportion of labor force "marginalized"
Social and	denial of civil liberties
political	increase in repression
justice (V_3)	erosion of constitutional order (courts, legislature);
	low levels of legitimacy
Ecological	growth criteria tend to diminish concern for
quality (V_4)	conservation, pollution
	emphasis on capital intensive technology produces
	urban sprawl, decay
Participation	demobilization produces apathy, despair
and humane	statism interferes with growth of global identity,
governance (V_5)	runs counter to global cooperation, solutions

   Leninized forms of authoritarian rule do not generally have as adverse
an impact on world order values. Indeed, several Third World Leninized
societies, depending on leadership style, amplitude of resource base, and
political serenity, have remarkable records with respect to economic
well-being (V_2). In addition, the absence of a profit motive seems to have
produced a somewhat better although inconsistent record by socialist
countries on environmental issues, at least as compared to their
Brazilianized counterparts. Praetorianized polities also tend to have a
consistently adverse impact on world order values, although if left-
oriented they tend to do better on economic well-being (V_2) than their
right-oriented counterparts. Also, as compared to Brazilianized,
Leninized, Stalinized, and Trilateralized polities, those that are
praetorianized do less environmental harm (V_4), not because their value
sensitivities are more evolved but as a consequence of their lower stage of
industrial development.

   Both superpowers, leaders of the Stalinized and Trilateralized segments
of the industrial heartland of the globe, pose by far the most severe threats

to world order values through their preparations for strategic nuclear war, their arms sales policies, their drain of world resources, and their responsibility for generating much of the pressure building up in the biosphere. Citizens' movements in the Trilateral sector have been active in the environmental, health, and safety area, resulting in more environmental protection in these countries than in Stalinized countries. Although elusive, provision of jobs for everyone in socialist societies may lessen one dimension of alienation, yet neither system seems capable of providing meaningful work for much of its population.

What Can Be Done

Let us assume the basic accuracy of the preceding analysis: Authoritarian tendencies are prevalent except in the Trilateral sector, and there cultural decay and political and economic decline have created a preauthoritarian context. Trilateralists are seeking to solve the "crisis of democracy" by forging a globalist concert of capitalist economies; governing elites will generally oppose or ignore progressive and drastic demands for global reform, and will increasingly concentrate their energies and resources on arresting their own relative decline.

Despite this bleak outlook there are constructive responses available to those who believe in system change guided by world order values as posited in the prior section. The overall goal is to establish patterns of humane governance at all levels of social organization from family to planet.

Demystification

Assess trends as accurately as possible, with due weight given to structural factors, so as to reveal pressures upon democratic prospects that flow from the interplay of domestic and international sources. Especially important is a continuous critique and exposure of spurious forms of global reform such as the managerial fixes envisioned by Trilateralists. Also crucial is the exposure of the liberal fallacy that governing structures are neutral and can be moved by persuasive politics incrementally in the direction of world order values. The evidence suggests overwhelmingly that every apparent step forward is likely to involve at least one step backward, and very likely more than one. There is no other way to gain support for a given reform within a modern state bureaucracy, and without such support innovative steps are unlikely to be taken or implemented. At minimum, it is important to be on guard to notice what is bargained away within the bureaucracy to obtain the support of the military establishment (or enough of it) to achieve a given arms control initiative.

Positive Currents

Depict and support those subsidiary developments that make the over-all picture less bleak: the renewal of democratic forms in India, Spain, Greece; the successes of liberation struggles in Iran and Africa; the possibility of anti-Stalinist forms of socialist rule in Western Europe; the possibility of de-Leninization in Third World socialist countries; the growth of dissent within the Soviet Union; the salience of human rights; the fracturing of large states via various types of separatism, including the withdrawal of loyalty from central institutions; the persistence and maturation of countercultural activism, including resistance communities within the Trilateral world; the antinuclear movement; the early stages of a Third World movement linking development goals to disarmament and peace.

Actions, Activities

This means support for human rights broadly defined to encompass economic and cultural issues, and possibly expanded to include ecological subject matter. Place the emphasis on popular sovereignty with respect to human rights—asserting, namely, that rights inhere inalienably in the peoples of the world and that governing structures and leaders lose their legitimacy to the extent that they fail to uphold these rights. Lend specific support to individuals and movements of dissent and resistance, especially to those who espouse progressive goals associated with democratic forms of socialism. Take advantage of official campaigns for human rights launched for propaganda purposes, but also expose the negative side-effects (e.g., reviving the Cold War, mobilizing domestic support for interventionary diplomacy, distracting attention from repressive features of imperialist global roles).

Support, similarly, demilitarizing initiatives in all contexts. Link disarmament agenda with other world order values, especially initiating the process of demilitarization of domestic societies in the North, possibly by slowing down the arms race, and later on reversing it.

Underlying a specific agenda is the reshaping of political consciousness. Above all, we need a growing number of influential individuals and groups who will think, feel, and act like planetary citizens, as well as fulfill traditional roles as loyal participants in local and national community processes. Possibly, too, the United Nations can be weaned gradually away from the state system and begin to serve the cause of humanity as a whole, not naively, but rather fulfilling a mandate from a war-weary world to protect the planet from the adverse effects of antagonistic sovereign national wills and gradually incubating the growth and strengthening of world community structures and sentiments.

Annex 1
A Note on the Brazilian Experience

Brazil is, of course, the exemplary case of Brazilianization. The broad analytic contours can be reinforced now by a brief sketch of the Brazilian experience to date. (The link between Brazilianization and world order values is summarized in Table 4-7.)

Brazil, long perceived as the sleeping giant of Latin America, has in actuality been awakening since the Vargas period. Somewhat misleadingly, the rest of the world has associated the Brazilian awakening almost exclusively with the move toward militarization initiated by a coup on March 31, 1964. In key respects, of course, the story of Brazil underlies the phenomenon of "Brazilianization": First, the decisive impetus toward militarization came from an internal developmental crisis, involving an inflationary spiral, labor and student unrest, economic stagnancy, and an uncertain investment climate; second, the seizure of power by the military on behalf of capitalist interests was necessary to head off a popular drift toward radicalization and socialism.

Of course, the Brazilian story is complex, and interpreters do not agree on all critical points. There is general agreement that João Goulart's government in the 1962–1964 period was being moved to the left in response to increasing demands for policies more favorable to workers and the rural poor. It is also true that the labor challenge was widely held to be responsible for producing instability, via strikes and demonstrations, and that continuing wage demands were helping to generate an inflationary spiral and were threatening the position and prospects of the Brazilian upper and middle classes. In actuality, real wage levels had been declining, and the struggle of labor had the conservative goal of holding its relative position in the social structure. An atmosphere of uncertainty about the future prevailed, discouraging savings and investment. Economic growth was slackening in this period, and this led to a radicalization of popular sector politics, calling into question the viability of capitalism as a means of equitable development. Such a dynamic led entrenched classes to be frightened, especially at a time when the regional mood was dominated by Castro's victory and expansive claims, and helped set the stage for the 1964 coup.[35]

The military coup of 1964 was an ideal situation for the right, as the demand for order seemed to emanate from large segments of the population. It is thus generally accurate to contend that the overthrow of Goulart was not just a military coup but was endorsed by the overall climate of political opinion, enjoying the active support and leadership of significant sectors of Brazilian society. The great majority of the people seemed confused and passive, and were easy to neutralize. Even liberal political groupings were ambivalent. The response to the coup by the centrist PSD was reticent, and even segments of the syndicalist-influenced PTB welcomed the military takeover. When they fell, President João Goulart and his supporters were isolated and defeated men, not only in military but above all in political terms.[36]

The Brazilian left (and possibly also the military) was unrealistic about its own power base. Many of the poorest among the urban squatters of *Favelados,* contrary to expectations, actually gave their support to the 1964 coup at first.[37] Outside of organized labor—and even labor was split and its degree of autonomy from the state vastly exaggerated—there were no strongly mobilized social forces ready to defend the constitutional order. The Brazilian military leaders who took power in 1964 were under constant pressure in subsequent years from their own supporters to go further in a repressive direction. There were demands from elements of the military that steps should be taken to neutralize individuals or social forces that might otherwise mount a movement of political opposition. Although never fully claiming the legitimate right to rule, the military rulers have stayed on, and give every indication of holding tightly the reins of power.

The role of the military was more expansive than seizing power; it was to secure favorable linkage to the world economy so as to enable rapid economic growth based on modernization. Such goals required "stability," which, in turn, produced "discipline" and "demobilization" of the popular sector. The main policies used to achieve "discipline" involved getting a reliable labor force that would not press "unreasonable" wage demands, nor resort to strikes or demonstrations. Part of this process of achieving discipline was to perpetuate and enlist the corporalist labor structures that had been created during the Vargas period (1930–1945) on the model of fascist Italy and had remained intact up through 1964; Goulart's mobilization of labor had depended partly on moving outside the semiofficial state-dominated labor bureaucracy and partly on putting more progressive labor officials in key positions within the bureaucracy. This socially conscious element of labor leadership was quickly purged after 1964 and a state-controlled movement put in its place.

Instead of bargaining wage increases, the process of wage adjustment was entrusted to technocrats who "computed" the appropriate raise, given the overall economic policy of the country. The regressive results are well known. For instance, as Mericle note, "Between 1964 and 1966, reduction of the real minimum wage was an important component of the stabilization program. In the eight-year period from March 1966 to April 1974 (during which real per capita GNP increased substantially), the real value of the minimum wage averaged only 68.2 percent of its average and real value in the period from July 1954 to December 1962."[39] Regressive redistribution of income also occurred in this period, accentuating a pre-existing situation of gross disparity of income: "The top 5 percent of income earners increased their share of total income from 27.4 to 36.3, while the share of the lower 80 percent fell from 45.5 to 36.8 percent."[40]

Phillipe Schmitter, writing in the early 1970s, believes that the stabilization policies may have led to "a decline in worker purchasing power in the
major industrial center of the country of 64.5 percent since 1958."[41] Other
sectors among the poor have done even worse. Robert McNamara in 1973
described the Brazilian growth pattern in similar terms: "In the last
decade Brazil's GNP per capita, in real terms, grew by 2.5 percent per
year, and yet the share of the national income received by the poorest 40
percent of the population declined from 10 percent in 1960 to 8 percent in
1970, whereas the share of the richest 5 percent grew from 29 percent to
38 percent during the same period." Income redistribution occurred, but
in a regressive direction. Under these conditions, especially given the prior
rise of political consciousness, there would be a strong movement of
resistance in the absence of an effective system for preventing labor
unrest and challenge.

Another feature of Brazil's economic program was to sustain the
concentration of investment on the urban industrial sectors, thereby
accentuating preexisting urban-rural and regional disparities. The situation of the Brazilian Northeast is especially relevant, given the extent of
its abject poverty. Schmitter reports figures that show that the Northeast
proportion of gross domestic income declined slightly from 14.78 percent
in 1960 to 14.52 percent in 1968, while the Southeast (including Rio, Sao
Paulo) increased its share from 62.77 percent in 1960 to 63.20 percent in
1968. Schmitter's intraregional data on income distribution even suggest a
regressive tendency. For instance, in the city of Recife the percentage of
total income going to the lowest 40 percent declined from 16.5 percent to
11.5 percent in the period from 1960 to 1967. Schmitter reports that "In
only one of the eight cities did real per capita income rise for this
oppressed sector of the population in this oppressed region of the country."[42] These trends, amid general prosperity for the upper 20 percent,
suggest the insensitivity of the Brazilian regime in this period to the needs
of the very poor.

The essence of Brazil's technocratic strategy was to extend state
control over the economy, continuing the Vargas heritage of a steadily
increasing share of public expenditure in relation to the gross development product (GDP). The government initially tried to improve the
relationship between spending and revenue, hoping to cut inflation and
restore confidence. The so-called 1964 revolutionaries had pledged a
return to "sanity" with regard to the economy, as well as an end to
"corruption." One of the major policy reforms was to make the tax
system generate increased revenues for the government. Here, too,
although the picture is complicated, it seems clear that the rich were
required to actually pay taxes and that the poor were burdened to a
greater degree even than previously. Schmitter writes accurately: "The
highly touted 'squeezing' of the rich must be placed in context—the poor
have been squeezed even harder."[43] One of the means of squeezing "the

poor" has been indirect taxes that are more regressive in effect than are direct taxes. It is important to note that, despite the original enthusiasm for the regime on the part of those espousing *laissez faire* economics, the Brazilian experience since 1964 has been frustrating. State control and foreign penetration of the economy has been increasing vis-à-vis the private sector, by means of regulation and by the expansion of state-owned enterprise. The logic of economic technocrats in the government bureaucracy has produced a steady consolidation of economic power under state auspices rather than lending stimulus to a competitive market propelled by classical liberal notions. Indeed, the priorities of the technocrats tend to favor "scale" and capital intensity that seem to work against indigenous private capital as compared to either international capital or state capital.

One further feature of the post-1964 situation in Brazil is the increase in spending for national security (defense, police) purposes and a corresponding decrease in health and welfare spending (educational expenditures remain stable). As Schmitter notes, there is a natural tendency in such a regime to do what is necessary to have "a satisfied and unified military," as well as a perceived need to build up "a large internal police apparatus for informational and security purposes."[44] From 1964 to 1971, defense spending increased from 14 to 20.4 percent of federal expenditures, including a high point of 25.1 percent in 1967. During this period public health spending declined from 2.5 to 1.3 percent and social welfare from 3.0 to .9 percent. The priorities of the Brazilian leadership are clear.

The success of the "Brazilian miracle" is largely a matter of having devised for a time a series of policies that resulted in the combination of contained inflation and sustained economic growth. The following updated version of Schmitter's table summarizes this record.

It is important to appreciate that despite the difficult period in the Goulart years, Brazil had enjoyed a more extended period of impressive economic expansion than that associated with the period since the coup of 1964. Norman Gall reports that "recent calculations indicate that the economy grew in real terms at an annual average rate of 6.1 percent for the entire forty-two year period from 1933 to 1974."[46] A considerable spur for this growth was a combination of natural resource wealth and cheap energy. Gall suggests that "Brazil may be the first large country in history to rely almost entirely on the internal combustion engine to develop its economy and to tie together its territory." In recent decades, ". . . the automobile, the truck, the tractor, and the helicopter have done for Brazil what the railroad and the reaper did for the United States a century ago."[47] In the period between 1950 and 1975, auto registrations in Brazil increased from 236,000 to more than 4,000,000. In the years between 1970 and 1974, Brazil doubled its car production and has since become the first Third World country producing one million vehicles a year. Tractors have been extensively relied upon to develop mechanized agriculture along the

TABLE 4-6

Overall Economic Performance in Brazil, 1960–1976[45]

	1960	1961	1962	1963	1964	1965	1966	1967
Annual rate of gross economic growth	9.7	10.3	5.3	1.5	2.9	2.7	5.1	4.8
Annual rate of industrial growth	9.6	10.6	7.8	0.2	5.2	−4.7	11.7	3.0
Annual rate of gross fixed capital formation	17.1	17.3	18.1	17.7	16.6	14.8	15.4	14.6
Annual rate of inflation in cost of living	29.3	33.2	51.5	70.8	91.4	65.9	41.3	30.5
Total foreign debt in $US millions	3910	3773	4025	3986	3874	4759	5196	3197
Balance of foreign trade (in $US millions)	−24	111	−90	112	344	655	438	213

aDash indicates no data available.

Sources: Inter-American Development Bank, Annual Reports 1960–1977; U.S. Department of Commerce, International Economic Indicators, Sept., 1977 and June 1978; International Financial Statistics; International Monetary Fund Direction of Trade.

Brazilian frontier, both to produce enough food for the burgeoning domestic population and possibly enough for export as well. Helicopter resource surveys have been used to identify large iron and bauxite deposits in remote jungle regions.

Such a development dynamic was heavily dependent on imported oil, and so Brazil was hit especially hard by the multiple increases in oil prices since 1974. Since then foreign indebtedness has grown, developmental projects have been receiving budget cuts, some inflationary pressures have re-emerged (50 percent in 1976), and there is some hesitation among capital suppliers. Brazil's development depends on huge investments of capital to open up its frontiers and to develop a domestic nuclear and hydroelectric energy base. Given global economic recession and the high cost of oil imports, it seems likely that more "austerity" is in the offing for the Brazilian population. At the same time, the Brazilian technocrats have

1968	1969	1970	1971	1972	1973	1974	1975	1976
8.4	9.0	9.5	11.3	10.4	11.4	9.6	11.8	9.2
13.2	10.8	11.1	11.2	—a	—	—	—	—
16.8	16.6	—	—	—	—	—	—	—
22.3	22.0	20.9	13.7	19.6	13.6	34.1	30.8	44.8
3677	4079.1	5080	5823.2	7759.8	9557	12,023	14,143	18,094
26	26	232	−363	−215.9	−60.8	−4706.6	−3511.5	—

been quite successful in overcoming oil-based trade deficits by taking measures to stimulate Brazilian exports and by substituting barter for currency transactions through the purchasing policies of Interfrás, the global subsidiary of Brazil's huge public energy company, Petrobras.

A concomitant to this course of economic development has been a reliance on repression. Civil liberties have been infringed to a serious degree; labor unions, universities, and political parties have been principal targets. Torture has been systematically employed, especially in the period after 1968 when student demonstrations and some left terrorism created an atmosphere where the hard-line view among the military took precedence. Commenting on these tactics, a Brazilian editor writes, "The months that followed were perhaps the most somber in the political history of the country; a series of kidnappings and terrorists' attacks justified the build-up of a police state and the abolition of civil guarantees, at the same time increasing the importance of the organs of repression and security within the dominant military system."[48]

The American role in bringing about this Brazilian solution has been analyzed at some length.[49] The official claim was most vividly stated by Lincoln Gordon (United States ambassador to Brazil, 1961–1966), who contended to the Senate in February 1966 that "the movement which overthrew President Goulart was a purely, 100 percent—not 99.44 percent—but 100 percent purely Brazilian movement.'' Gordon has recently acknowledged that the embassy knew a coup was in the offing in 1964, but not exactly when, nor did it have any role in planning its execution. At the same time, recently disclosed documents show that a United States task force consisting of an aircraft carrier, six destroyers, and four petroleum tankers was dispatched to Brazilian waters on March 31, but ordered to turn back on April 2. Lincoln Gordon has recently written that nothing comparable to the Dominican intervention was contemplated by such a maneuver, as the forces sent "would have been totally inadequate for any such purpose."[50] But when Gordon explains their role, he virtually concedes the position of those who claim that the Americans, at the very least, stood behind the coup leaders:

> The task force was intended to make possible a limited form of American action in a particular hypothetical contingency, a civil war with Brazil divided on geographic lines, the forces evenly matched, and with one side recognized by us. In that hypothesis, the task force would have had three purposes: (a) to provide logistical support, especially in petroleum products, to the side we believed to represent moderation and democracy; (b) to discourage the opposing side through the showing of the American flag on a powerful vessel; and (c) to assist if necessary in the evacuation of American citizens from regions involved in civil combat.[51]

As Gordon acknowledges that at the time "no effort was made to disguise our relief at Goulart's departure," it seems clear which side the United States would have taken had a confrontation developed. Note also that "moderation and democracy" are associated in the official American mind with a group of anticommunist generals rather than with a constitutionally elected civilian government.

The American pattern of overt diplomatic and economic support once the Castelo Branco military regime ascended to power in 1964 is well known: immediate diplomatic recognition, economic assistance, encouragement of foreign investment. Since the political change-over in 1964; the Brazilian assets of United States multinational corporations have multiplied sixfold and are now valued at four billion dollars.[52] American support for the Brazilian developmental pattern has been unflagging, even during the worst interludes of repressive rule. Brazil has been invoked as a model for "healthy" patterns of Third World development. And Brazil has been increasingly viewed as a junior partner of the American-led global imperial partnership. Kissinger's visit in 1975 promised the Brazilians "a special relationship" that included a consultative role in the formation of global policy.

At the same time some unexpected developments have occurred, undermining the extent of United States influence over Brazilian behavior. Brazil's expansion has led it to diversify its trading patterns. As the United States has become proportionately less important, Japan and

Europe have become more so. The same pattern is evident in relation to arms supplies. More striking is Brazil's emphasis on good relations with OPEC and with the Third World. The dependence of the Brazilian economy on imported oil is undoubtedly a major factor in this evolving "pragmatic ecumenicism," but also evident is a commitment to nationalist goals of autonomy. American diplomatic leadership has endured several "shocks" from Brazilian independence on foreign policy—support for self-determination in Angola and Mozambique, insistence on the enormous nuclear deal with West Germany over American objections, support in the United Nations for the anti-Zionist resolution.

In turn, Carter's human rights emphasis has led Brazil to renounce fifty million dollars in credits it had been granted to facilitate military purchases in fiscal year 1978.[53] It seems evident that the "subimperial" role of Brazil is real to the extent of serving to oppose Latin American radicalism and to encourage militarized governance associated with state capitalism, but it is simplistic to assume that this role is coincident with American global interests in other settings. The Brazilian leadership has made clear its own quite separate ambitions that extend to regional superpower status that could eventually seek to banish the United States from South America. In these respects, Brazilianization as it evolves threatens the American dream of a liberal internationalist economic and political order centered in Washington. Even American business interests recently report being "puzzled" by the confusing paradox of Brazilian foreign economic policy, which seeks developmental capital from overseas and yet imposes heavy regulatory constraints on foreign investors. In essence, the imperial intention does not always translate into an adequate imperial solution, especially in an era when nationalist tendencies run strong, regardless of ideological outlook.

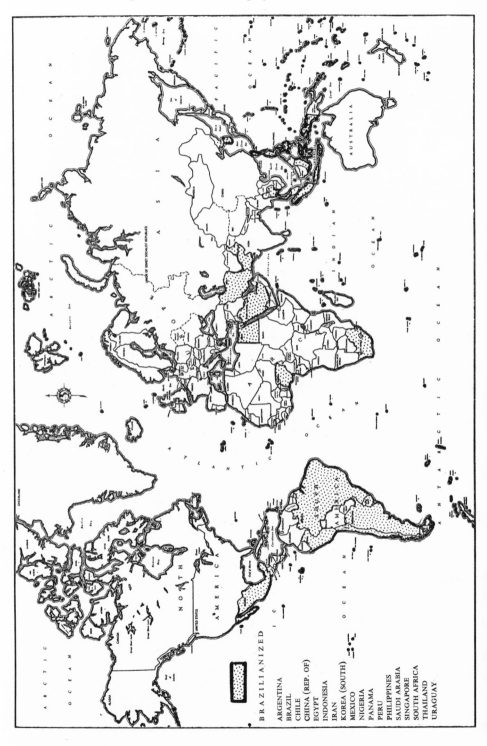

BRAZILIANIZED

ARGENTINA
BRAZIL
CHILE
CHINA (REP. OF)
EGYPT
INDONESIA
IRAN
KOREA (SOUTH)
MEXICO
NIGERIA
PANAMA
PERU
PHILIPPINES
SAUDI ARABIA
SINGAPORE
SOUTH AFRICA
THAILAND
URAGUAY

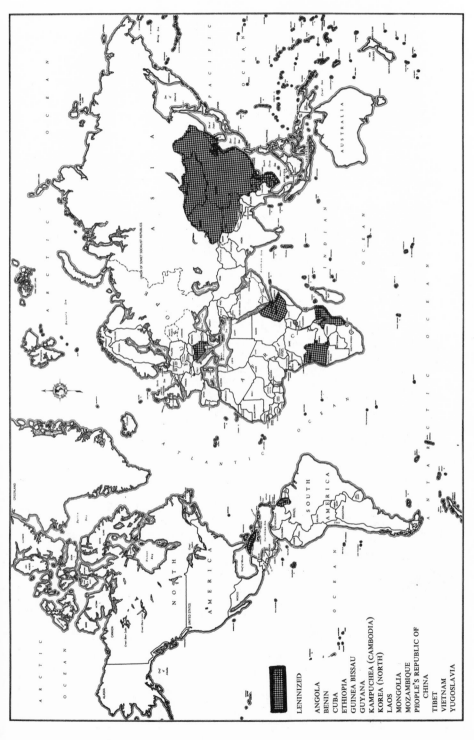

MAP 4-3   *Leninization*

LENINIZED

ANGOLA
BENIN
CUBA
ETHIOPIA
GUINEA BISSAU
GUYANA
KAMPUCHEA (CAMBODIA)
KOREA (NORTH)
LAOS
MONGOLIA
MOZAMBIQUE
PEOPLE'S REPUBLIC OF
    CHINA
TIBET
VIETNAM
YUGOSLAVIA

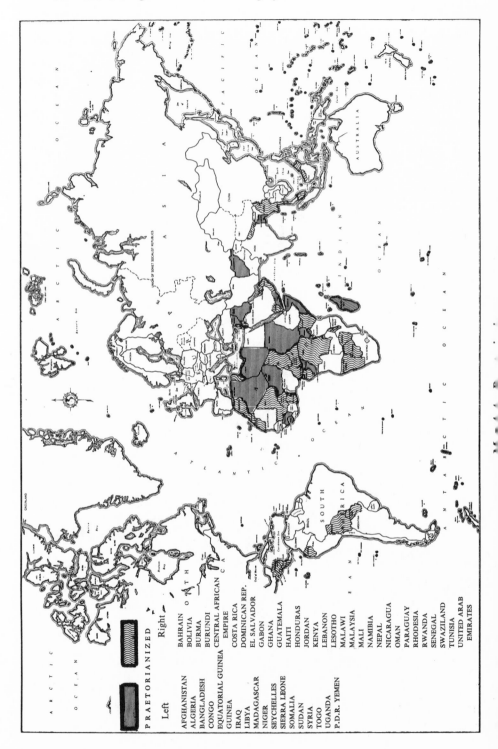

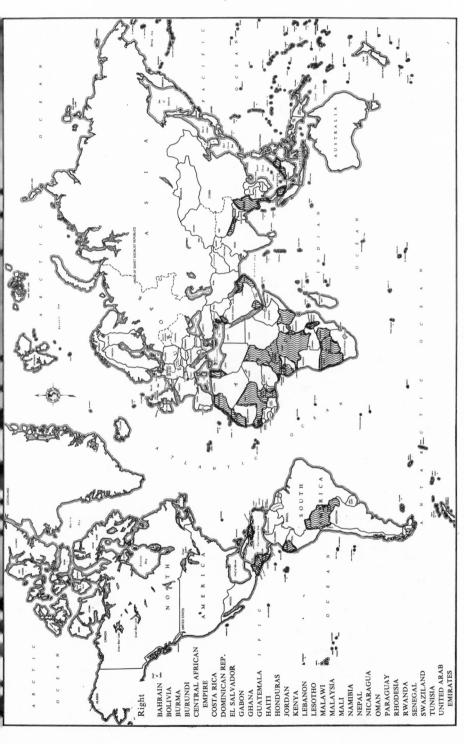

MAP 4–5   *Right Praetorianism*

Right

BAHRAIN
BOLIVIA
BURMA
BURUNDI
CENTRAL AFRICAN
  EMPIRE
COSTA RICA
DOMINICAN REP.
EL SALVADOR
GABON
GHANA
GUATEMALA
HAITI
HONDURAS
JORDAN
KENYA
LEBANON
LESOTHO
MALAWI
MALAYSIA
MALI
NAMIBIA
NEPAL
NICARAGUA
OMAN
PARAGUAY
RHODESIA
RWANDA
SENEGAL
SWAZILAND
TUNISIA
UNITED ARAB
  EMIRATES

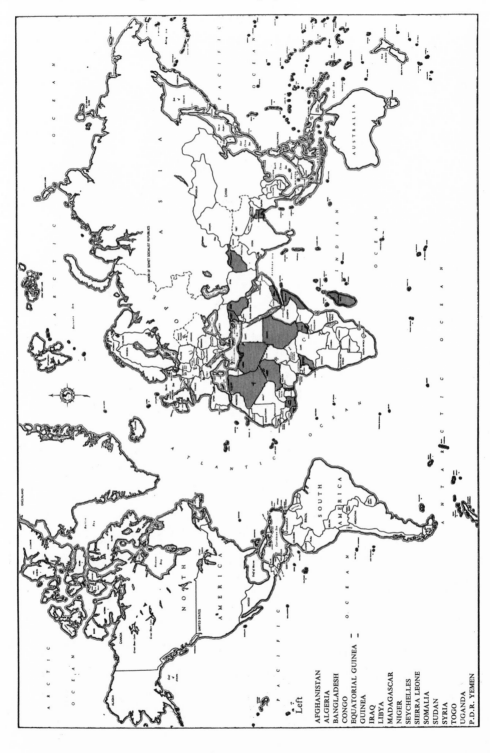

Left

AFGHANISTAN
ALGERIA
BANGLADESH
CONGO
EQUATORIAL GUINEA
GUINEA
IRAQ
LIBYA
MADAGASCAR
NIGER
SEYCHELLES
SIERRA LEONE
SOMALIA
SUDAN
SYRIA
TOGO
UGANDA
P.D.R. YEMEN

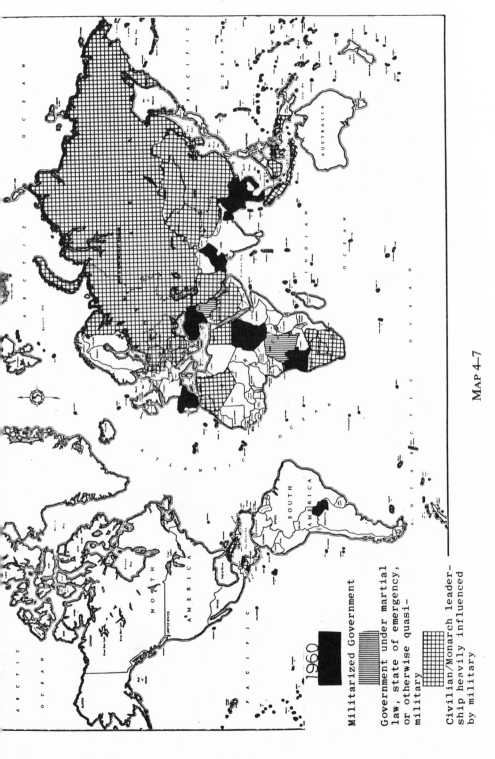

1960

Militarized Government

Government under martial
law, state of emergency,
or otherwise quasi-
military

Civilian/Monarch leader-
ship heavily influenced
by military

MAP 4–7

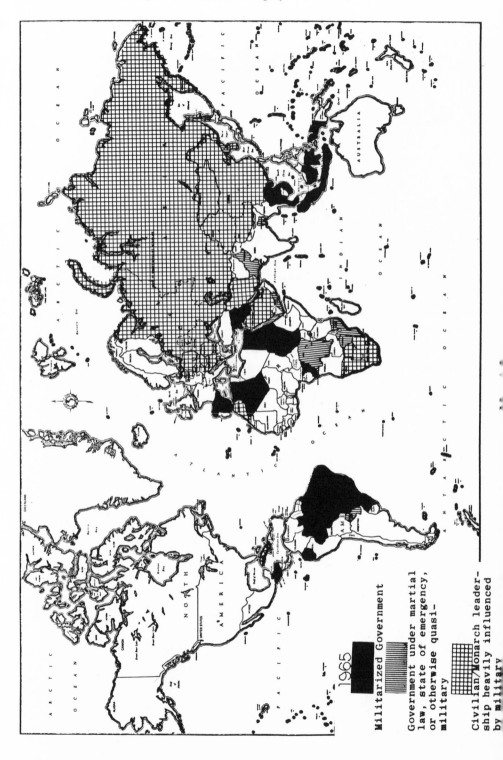

1965

Militarized Government

Government under martial
law, state of emergency,
or otherwise quasi-
military

Civilian/Monarch leader-
ship heavily influenced
by military

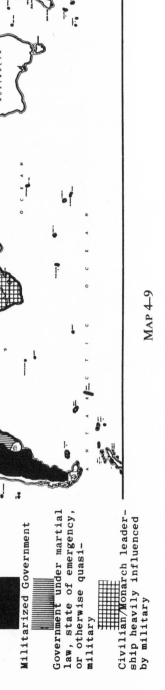

MAP 4–9

1970

Militarized Government

Government under martial law, state of emergency, or otherwise quasi-military

Civilian/Monarch leadership heavily influenced by military

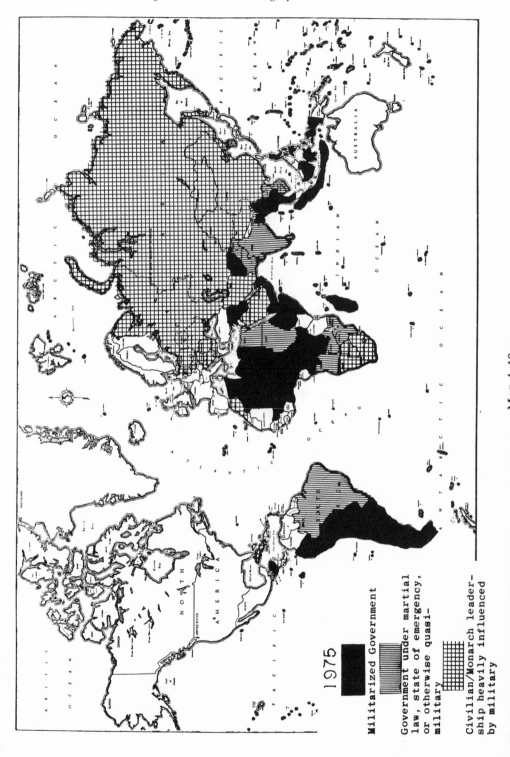

1975

Militarized Government

Government under martial law, state of emergency, or otherwise quasi-military

Civilian/Monarch leadership heavily influenced by military

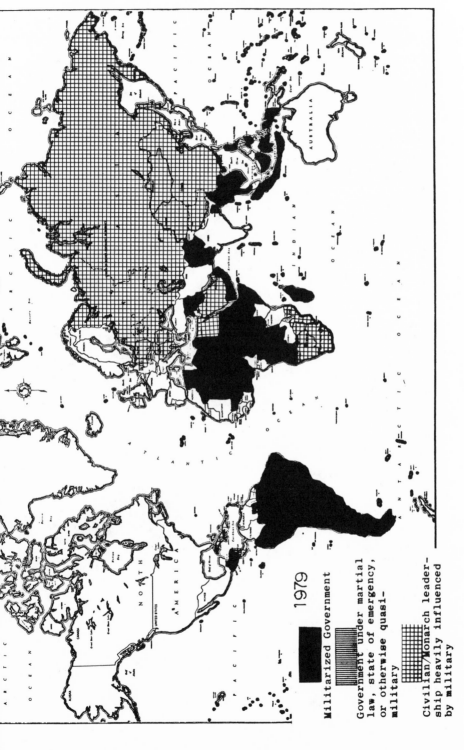

1979

Militarized Government

Government under martial
law, state of emergency,
or otherwise quasi-
military

Civilian/Monarch leader-
ship heavily influenced
by military

MAP 4–11

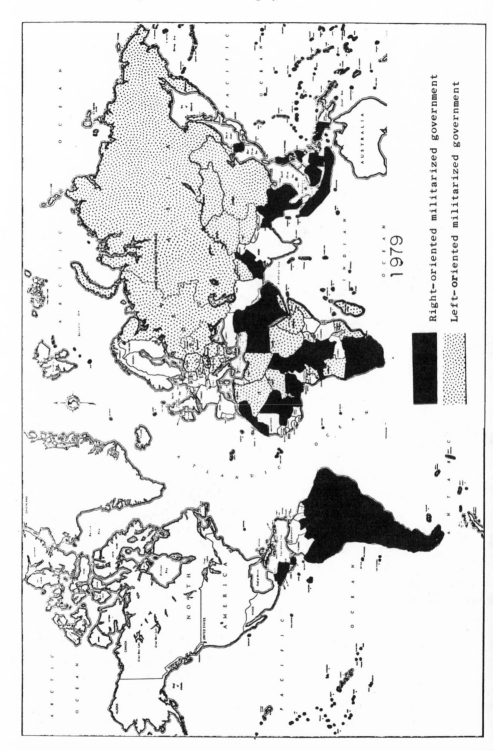

Right—oriented militarized government

Left—oriented militarized government

1979

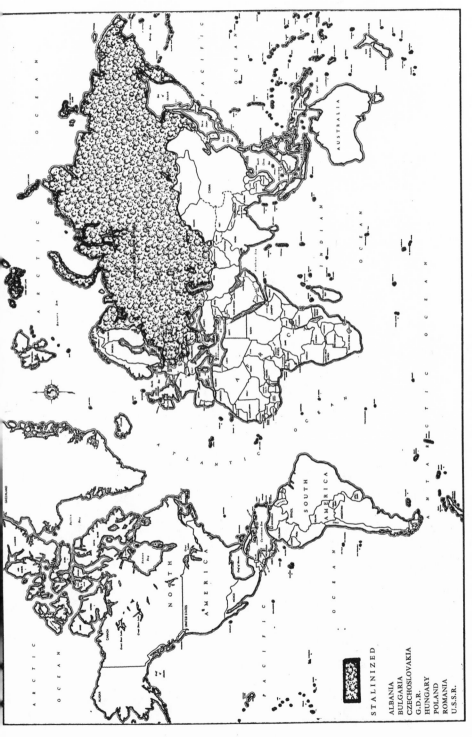

MAP 4–13   *Stalinization*

STALINIZED

ALBANIA
BULGARIA
CZECHOSLOVAKIA
G.D.R.
HUNGARY
POLAND
ROMANIA
U.S.S.R.

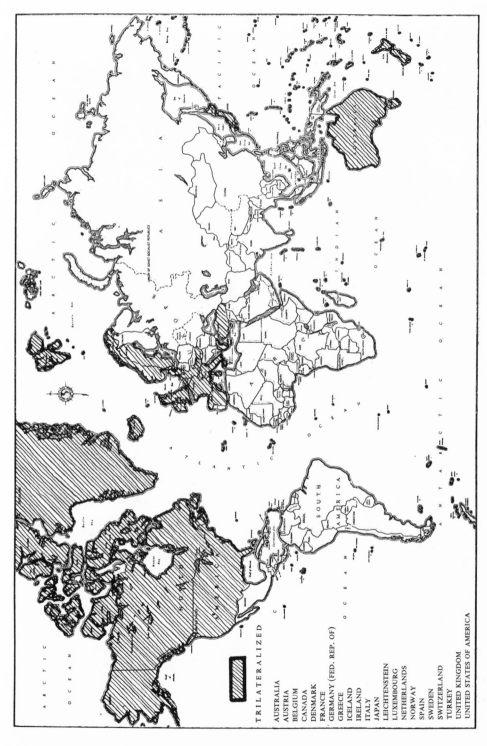

MAP 4-14   Trilateralization

———————V———————

Comparative Protection of Human Rights in Capitalist and Socialist Third World Countries

> In the economic policies of the government, one finds not only the explanation for its repressive crimes, but also a greater atrocity which punishes millions of human beings with carefully planned misery. . . .
>
> *Open letter by Rodolfo Walsh to the Argentinian junta*

With colonialism gone, the separate states of Africa and Asia have moved in diverse directions. The states of Latin America, despite some notable differences in terms of formal status, ethnic identity of ruling elites, and resource endowments, share sufficiently their national challenge and international difficulties to deserve to be joined with the states of Africa and Asia in a single inquiry into the Third World. Formal independence has not, in many of these instances, brought the blessings expected. New forms of external control and influence have emerged, both more subtle and, possibly, more disruptive, perceived collectively under the vague label of neocolonialism. Perhaps more disturbing is the degree to which Third World peoples, in this period celebrated for the collapse of colonialism, have found themselves yoked to new forms of internal oppression, in some instances far more terrifying and comprehensive than anything they had experienced at the hands of foreign masters.

Another source of disappointment was the American role in the decolonialization process. The United States, with its own war of independence and liberal tradition, might have exerted a benign influence on the transition to independence. Instead, geopolitics intruded to place the United States on the colonial side of the struggle, and afterwards, in the postcolonial settings of Asia and Africa and in Latin America, the United States engaged in interventionary diplomacy generally on behalf of authoritarian political solutions that were, in many instances, more inconsistent with the realization of human rights than other plausible options.

This trend toward oppressive rulership is evident in all parts of the

Third World. Its perception is usually interpreted, by way of an ideological filter, as "socialist" (or "communist") or "capitalist." In both sets of cases the realities of oppression are evident, as is the characteristic tendency to enlarge the role of military influence and technique in the administration of power. Militarized politics is the most characteristic expression of oppressive rule in the Third World.

A focus on human rights represents an attempt to specify the standards of nonoppressive rule as an entitlement of all peoples, whatever their stage of development, cultural heritage, ideological persuasion, or resource base. In effect, the claims embodied in human rights take precedence over the prerogatives of state sovereignty, and acknowledge the oneness of the human family as a normative premise.

The developmental crunch in the Third World has generated a wide array of authoritarian political solutions. These solutions invariably violate prevailing conceptions of human rights, although to different degrees. The central argument of this chapter is that the economic premises of authoritarian solutions are an important, although not necessarily in each instance a decisive, determinant of the degree of authoritarian severity. Socialism and capitalism, although each is manifest in a variety of forms, provide the ideological underpinnings for the principal choice between developmental options. Comparing the record of socialism and capitalism with respect to the protection of human rights seems like a useful way to consider whether there are any systemic regularities that flow from a given ideological orientation.

The choice of ideological labels raises some difficulties. It would be possible to categorize regimes by the simple "left"/"right" distinction. However, the ideological leanings of these regimes are better understood if directly identified with attitudes toward economic policy, the role of the market, of private enterprise, and of developmental priorities. Here, the affinities of Third World regimes are generally clearly drawn from "Marxist-Leninist" roots or from some adaptation of capitalism, although the latter orientation is not generally proclaimed as such. It is sometimes contended that the term "fascist" covers one or another form of authoritarian rules.[1] Some Third World governments that possess a capitalist attitude toward development disguise it for public relations reasons beneath a socialist rhetoric. Some Western ideologues prefer to call these "left" regimes "communist" rather than "socialist." The issue of nomenclature should be faced in a rigorous fashion at some point, but it is not important for the analysis that follows here.

On balance, "socialism" and "capitalism" seem like the most convenient noninflammatory ways to emphasize the links between authoritarian and development choices in the Third World.

The position taken here is that there are distinct virtues and vices attributable to capitalism and socialism in the context of Third World countries. The relative importance of these virtues and vices is difficult to assess—how does one rate, for instance, the greater economic equity of socialist systems against the greater cultural openness of capitalist systems? There is no satisfactory way to objectify such analyses. I arrive at the uncomfortable conclusion that the human rights records of both socialism and capitalism are so poor in the Third World at this point that it is quite unconvincing to insist that one approach is generically preferable to the other. This conclusion is so uncomfortable because it seems clear that only socialism has the capacity to deal with mass poverty in the short run, and surely economic deprivation is a key element of human rights. However, the transition costs of moving to socialism have turned out to be so heavy, the absence of any tradition of checks and balances or pluralist politics and culture have made the administration of power in socialist states so totalitarian, and the effectiveness of control has been so great as to make popular control over a socialist state so difficult to exert that we cannot conclude, with confidence, that a given Third World society is better off "socialist." In effect, my position is that socialism *as applied* to date in the Third World deprives it of the moral advantage associated with socialism *as theory* or as an ideological perspective.

Surely, capitalism is not attractive, in general, from a human rights viewpoint for a Third World country. Its capital-intensive approach to development does not generally improve the relative or absolute poverty of the masses. The productive process, oriented around profits and foreign exchange earnings, tends to satisfy the cravings of the rich rather than the needs of the poor. In addition, when the masses are poor and excluded from the gains of the economy, as is the case in Third World capitalist economies (with some minor exceptions having special explanations), then a *structural* tendency to repress exists. There is no way to assure long-term stability in such a societal setting except by intimidating and repressing those who are victimized by it. Thus, while socialism cannot be preferred, given its record, capitalism is a recipe for doom, unless the country is exceptionally endowed with resources, including skills and leadership abilities, and even then, as the case of Iran illustrates, the results of a capitalist orientation may be national disaster.

In effect, from an ideological perspective, socialism is the preferred system for a Third World country, but its record in practice is too poor at present to support the preference. From the viewpoint of human rights the prescriptive challenge is to reconstruct socialist practice so as to achieve greater overall protection of human rights, or alternatively, to comprehend at the level of theory the consistent betrayal in practice of socialist ideals.

Even without the developmental crunch, we would expect to encounter widespread repression in the Third World. Indeed, the integration of society by the bureaucratic state is itself coercive to a degree. In the circumstances of many Third World countries, lacking a recent tradition of political competition, the mere structure of state power creates a strong disposition toward repression, especially given the diversity of antagonistic ethnic elements contained within many Third World state boundaries. And yet, the whole point of the socialism/capitalism debate is the contention that some forms of repression are better than others in terms of the stakes, as well as the identity and proportion of winners and losers. The deep structure of oppression is important to appreciate, if only to undergird an inquiry into reasonable expectations for human rights goals. Other structural explanations of repression will be mentioned, as well. "Intermediate" structural explanations place weight on the international system, making the propensity to repress at the state level a consequence of patterns of transnational domination (e.g., imperialism, neocolonialism) at the global level. Finally, manifest structural explanations of repression place weight on the pathological makeup of those who emerge as the primary leaders of a modern state, given the competitive struggle for dominance within political elites.

This chapter proceeds as follows. It considers, first, the structural explanations of repression associated with statism, and refers briefly to those associated with imperialism and personal pathology. Second, it seeks to put the Third World human rights situation in the context of the debate between socialism and capitalism. Third, it tries to identify a conception of human rights that follows from this concern, as well as from a diagnosis of Third World priorities and trends. And fourth, it briefly illustrates the distinctive patterns of human rights failure appropriately associated with socialism and capitalism.

Deep Structure

Simone Weil notes, "What is surprising is not that oppression should make its appearance only after higher forms of economy have been reached, but that it should always accompany them."[2] In particular, socialism and capitalism, as the dominant modes by which "higher forms of economy" are organized, have, in this most fundamental sense, been oppressive. As Weil argues in her essay, oppression is associated with the organization of any complex social order, both through its dependence on leadership and bureaucracy to administer an unequal division of labor and by its necessary sponsorship of a dynamic of power by which only a privileged few exert control over the masses, ultimately by reliance on armed might. In this regard, the crystallization of power in the coercive state assures the persistence of oppression in this fundamental sense, and seeks to endow oppression with legitimacy. As Stanley Diamond, Marvin Harris, and Simone Weil each contend, the only instances of nonoppressive social orders are primitive forms of social organization that do not depend upon or lend themselves easily to coordination of effort and status differentiation. It is significant to note that there is virtually no support in the Third World for a destructuring of state power so as to achieve nonoppressive social orders. Gandhi's original vision of India after independence came closest, perhaps, and yet it never had much of a chance, given the overriding drive to build a modern state that could respond to domestic expectations of economic growth and modernization, as well as protect the autonomy of India against a hostile and unpredictable outside world. At this time, the deep structure of oppression is accepted by most advocates of human rights as an inevitable ingredient of modernism.

Marx clearly perceived the incompatibility between statist organization and liberation, as is evident in his celebrated prediction that the state would wither away in a communist society. However, the failure to address seriously or even to understand the tremendous resistances to the dissolution of the state in the socialist phase of societal evolution has restricted the usefulness of his deeper insight. There is an odd dichotomy in Marxist thought: in the distant postrevolutionary future we have a theory of the nonstate; in the immediate postrevolutionary future we are saddled with a theory of the superstate, that is, with a legitimated dictatorship that is regarded as necessarily coercive, operates in a political vacuum, and so is not even ideologically insulated against its own intoxication with power. In country after country during this century, Marxism-Leninism in practice has led to systematic abuse of power, ossified in a variety of bureaucratic centralist governmental forms. In fairness, the ferocity of capitalist responses to socialist triumphs created an unanticipated priority for national security that inevitably hardened the state, and lent credibility to the preoccupation with internal and external enemies.

More modest than Marx, nineteenth-century liberal philosophers who set forth the creed that dominated the bourgeois state of northern Europe and North America were content with the notion of setting up a balance between different parts of government and between the state and its citizenry. Market mechanisms, as well as the sanctity of private property, were intended to create a private realm relatively secure against encroachment by government; the minimum state, rationalized by *laissez faire* economics and morality, as well as by a skeptical account of human nature, was conceived to provide sufficient guidance and security for the polity without endangering the autonomy of its citizenry. Here again, however, the prescriptive vision gave way to social forces that have witnessed a steady accretion of state power as vast bureaucratic establishments have arisen, partly to assume the welfare tasks accepted by the political leadership of capitalist societies as the necessary alternative to a revolution from below. Built into the capitalist ethos is an acceptance of inequality, exploitation, and hierarchy, as well as the continuous struggle for power within and among states, necessitating a police system within the state and a war system within the global realm, realities consistent with the maintenance of oppressive structures at all levels of social intercourse.

Doing away with oppression in these fundamental senses seems tantamount to an insistence on modifying capitalism and socialism as basic historic modes of social, economic, and political organization. Each of these ideological traditions has been compellingly challenged by antagonistic subtraditions that condemn the corruption of what exists in the name of capitalism and socialism as a betrayal of an underlying libertarian promise. These libertarian critiques (ultraindividualism on the one side, anarchism on the other) call for revolutionary dissolutions of state power. As critiques of the prevailing order, they are generally dismissed with scorn by mainstream opinion. They are said to lack political credibility and to have no capacity to maintain even minimum order in the wider and complex social settings of the modern world. Nevertheless, the popular appeal of these radical countertraditions abides, especially in the affluent postindustrial sectors of world society, where it is increasingly understood that the reality of the modern state makes oppression inevitable.

In many African and Asian countries the challenge of state-building after formal independence unleashed dangerous ethnic antagonisms that had been bottled up or used as a divisive tactic during the colonial period. These antagonisms, combined with the drive of ruling groups to build strong states capable of standing on their own, helped produce an authoritarian "fix" in many countries. This "fix" was virtually inevitable in those states where one ethnic group captured all or most state power at the expense of others. Thus, even without the developmental crunch some strong reasons for the spread of authoritarian rule exist.

"Deep structure" also relates to the special overlapping claims of self-determination in which rival nationalities appear to seek exclusive, or at least dominant rights, within a given territorial state. The rival claims of Israeli and Palestinian self-determination, or of white and black claims in South Africa, illustrate this underlying structural situation. In such a situation, the dominant claimant must repress the subordinate or revisionist claimant so as to sustain the structure. The severity of repression reflects the actual and perceived relation of forces, as well as tactical judgments of elites as to the effects of differing techniques for exerting control. The structural basis of repression is reinforced by prevailing Hobbesian views of order that premise effectiveness on physical force and control. As a result, efforts at compromise are generally not made voluntarily, but only under pressures generated by violence. A closed loop of escalating violence is created by the action/reaction dynamics of antagonistic claimants, perhaps broken over time by exhaustion and disillusionment.

In the interim, the dominant elite is faced with a security dilemma. If it softens its approach, it makes itself feel (and quite become) more vulnerable to the destructive impulses of its rivals. If it remains hard, it unwittingly encourages its rivals to rely on brutal means and to seek total victory for itself. The structural quest for state sovereignty at the expense of an alien people seems inconsistent, at once, with either compromise or nonrepressive forms of political order.

In addition to "deep" structure there is an "intermediate" structure of transnational influences that tips the exercise of power at the state level in a repressive direction. The role of multinational corporations, arms sales and training programs, and covert operations all exert an antidemocratic interventionary influence. This feature of politics can be best understood in terms of "spheres of influence," "neocolonialism," and "imperialism," various names for patterns of domination by which rich and powerful elites in the North exert control over political life in the South. The direction of this influence is repressive in the sense that the external elites seek to maintain stability and to keep their dependable friends in power, as well as to assure access to resources, markets, and base rights. Only a dependent national elite or one isolated from nationalist consciousness would accept such an arrangement; its stability depends not so much on legitimacy as on its coercive capabilities to intimidate.

Finally, there is a structural bias toward repressive rule associated with leadership. The struggle to be primary leader in the intense political life of most Third World states seems to emphasize a commitment to nonmoderate forms of competition. The personality type that prevails in such competition tends to be acutely sensitive to the threat of displacement by others who might be equally unscrupulous. Hence, there is little toleration of oppositional activities or dissent. The leader may carry such intolerance to pathological extremes, but it is a pathology that is partially induced by the nature of the power chase in Third World polities.

These elements of deep structure are aggravated in the contemporary period by the character of military technology. The Third World, in particular, is victimized by the dangers of nuclear technology over which it has no control. Superpowers use space and oceans to establish their earth-girdling security systems, and expose the planet as a whole to enormous risks. Also, global patterns of industrialization result in disproportionate claims on energy and other earth resources by non-Third World societies. As well, dangerous environmental hazards result and are "exported" to Third World pollution sanctuaries or are "externalized" to inflict various degrees of harm on the planet as a whole. In addition, the shifting economics of productive enterprise is inducing shifts to more dangerous technologies (e.g., nuclear power). The Third World is a passive participant in the process of technological and lifestyle choice going on in the North and yet will suffer the consequences. To wit, repression as an international structure is real, even if not fully perceived.

At the same time, although deep structure conditions political prospects, it does not preclude certain forms of progress with regard to human rights.

Ideological Affiliations in the Third World

The specific identity of a national political system can only be provisionally established by whether it is classified as "socialist" or "capitalist." Such labels may be more or less descriptive of actual patterns of organization and underlying approach to governance. Many governments in the Third World have evolved distinctive economic programs, allowing private economic initiative in some sectors, while reserving others for state ownership. Others have opted for hybrid ideological and political approaches. The declaration of Nigeria's Olusegun Obasanjo that "[n]o African country is about to embrace communism any more than we are willing to embrace capitalism" is also part of the picture.[3] Regardless of their internal development strategy, most Third World governments seek to project an international image of nonalignment so as to safeguard their political independence and discourage meddling by the superpowers. Third World leaders of almost every persuasion are eager to avoid getting caught in the maelstroms of geopolitics; this preoccupation undoubtedly lay behind General Obasanjo's remark and, more widely, explains the widespread controversy in the Third World over Cuba's African presence, because whatever else, Cuba *is* aligned. Nevertheless, ideological orientation as capitalist or socialist does seem to have a significant bearing on the degree to which the economy and development strategy of a given society will accord priority to meeting the basic needs of its population as a whole. Despite the immense pressure from the United States, recent studies support the view that Cuba under Castro has done exceptionally well by needs criteria, even as compared to Mexico, and despite a series of economic setbacks and obstacles.[4]

I draw a fundamental distinction in this chapter between doing away with repression and securing respect for human rights. Neither capitalism nor socialism is responsive to the fundamental challenge of the repressive state, but the enterprise of human rights is more modest, less ambitious in its goals, far less drastic in its diagnosis. The satisfaction of human rights claims does not purport to challenge the legitimacy of statist modes of organization, and in fact is endorsed by governments of all ideological persuasions. Therefore, human rights can, in principle, be realized in any state, whether rich or poor, whether organized along socialist or capitalist lines.[5] Recently, specialists in human rights, sensitive to ideological dualism in our world, have been striving to identify a set of core rights that reflect the professed values of both socialism and capitalism as operative global ideologies and avoid giving priority to what one, but not the other, ideology regards as important.[6] Such a search for what is mutually compatible does not mean identifying the lowest common denominator acceptable to both ideologies. As "human rights" were formulated initially as a dimension of liberal, capitalist ideology, what has been required is the elimination of those aspects of human rights that pertain *only* to capitalism (e.g., rights to property) while adding those rights that have been protected heretofore only in socialist conceptions (e.g., rights to basic human needs).

Not only must the conception of human rights be broadened to take account of socialist perspectives, it must also be deepened to include international structural issues. The attempts to achieve a new international economic order are part of the struggle for human rights in the present world setting. Even the notion of "basic needs" can be regressive unless associated with the international, collective expression of economic rights (for countries, as well as for the poor in countries) prefigured in the United Nations Charter of the Economic Rights and Duties of States. Surely part of the squeeze on Third World societies comes from "neocolonial" patterns, as well as from distortions of international economic relationships reflecting longer term differentials of power, wealth, prestige.

It is also increasingly unacceptable to overreact to the socialist critique of Western liberalism by going to the opposite extreme of associating human rights exclusively with basic needs or economic rights, conceived of as the material bases of minimum human existence. In the development debate going on in the Third World there was a widespread tendency some years ago to repudiate the political side of the human rights agenda as formal Western liberalism that is a dispensable political luxury for most Third World societies, and to claim that the only test of satisfactory government performance is a materialistic one. On the one side are the claims of official technocrats that growth measured in terms of GNP is what counts, and on the other side are the claims of disenfranchised intellectuals that satisfaction of basic needs is the proper measure. An extension of this argument contends that human rights in the noneconomic sense are limited in their applicability to the liberal democracies of the advanced industrial countries in the North. The argument is sometimes coupled with the assertion that Third World countries have always been authoritarian, that repression is virtually predetermined by political culture, or that conditions are not yet ripe for the introduction of more moderate governing strategies. A recent leader of Bolivia, General Juan Pereda Asbún, announced that he would rule over "a Bolivian-style democracy in which the armed forces ratified the popular decisions." He justified this assertion by saying that a poor country, filled with illiterate peasants, could not "have the same kind of democracy as that experienced by industrialized countries."[9] Similarly, the Shah of Iran often said, in effect, that when the people of Iran began to act like the people of Sweden, then he would begin to rule like the King of Sweden. In more recent years, as the severity of repression has increased throughout the Third World, the claim is increasingly accepted by Third World observers that nonmaterial issues relating to measures of repression are crucial to assessing a government's performance, and even its legitimacy.

Now, oddly enough, it is only the capitalist exploiters who intimate the nonapplicability of noneconomic human rights criteria to their national situations.

The Cocoyoc Declaration of 1975, an important expression of recent Third World outlook, declares itself clearly:

> Development should not be limited to the satisfaction of basic needs. There are other needs, other goals, and other values. Development includes freedom of expression and impression, the right to give and receive ideas and stimulus. There is a deep social need to participate in shaping the basis of one's own existence, and to make some contribution to the fashioning of the world's future. Above all, development includes the right to work, by which we mean not simply having a job but finding self-realization in work, the right not to be alienated through production processes that use human beings simply as tools.[10]

Even China, which in the 1960s and early 1970s was virtually exempt from criticism except from avid anticommunists, is being evaluated more skeptically recently as a consequence of taking into account human rights criteria additional to those associated with its programs to eradicate deep poverty and gross inequality.[11]

It would seem that socialism is *structurally* better adapted to the realization of fundamental human rights than is capitalism, especially in the setting of the Third World. In a world of resource and environmental constraint, of population pressures, and mass poverty amid rising material expectations and dissolving traditional bonds, the adoption of a socialist model of development appears to be a necessary precondition for the realization of human rights, although it is not of course sufficient. Without socialism there is no prospect of rapidly eliminating poverty, achieving relative economic equality, and imposing limited consumption on the rich. Capitalist models of development necessarily produce a privileged elite that appropriates a large proportion of the capital surplus not allocated for further development, and a substantial fraction of that elite may not even be resident in the country. Furthermore, socialist models tend to be based on national economic autonomy to a far greater extent than do capitalist models, as the roles of multinational corporations and international financial institutions are much smaller and more selective, if they exist at all. Especially in Third World country settings where securing the fruits of formal independence against outside encroachment invariably has the status of a fundamental human right of a collective character, a capitalist orientation seems disadvantageous.

Of course, in practice a given socialist Third World country (say, Cambodia) may compile a worse human rights record than a given capitalist country (say, the Ivory Coast). One political scientist indicted "liberal journals like the *New York Times*" for spreading the view "that any group calling itself 'socialist' must be an improvement over the 'corrupt' Lon Nol, Souvanna Phouma, and Nguyen Van Thieu." In fact, Professor Lande contends, "How relatively benign they appear in retrospect."[12] Nevertheless, the structural argument (in both its national and international aspects) holds. A capitalist-oriented polity cannot begin to achieve human rights (as these will be formulated below) unless the country happens to be endowed with exceptional wealth relative to its population, and even then the record may well be deplorable (e.g., Iran, Singapore). Of course, there are those who dispute this structural argument. Daniel Patrick Moynihan, for instance, argues that capitalist Third World regimes "commit abominations in practice; the Communist countries commit abomination in principle." He goes on: "Anyone who cares about human rights will know what type of abomination is the more destructive of those rights."[13]

Mao Zedong, is an important speech outlining an approach to democratic centralism, argued that the problems facing the Chinese government arose from only that four to five percent of the population drawn from "landlords, rich peasants, counter-revolutionaries, bad elements, and anti-Communist rightists."[14] The rest of the Chinese population, Mao went on to contend, were on the side of socialism. Of course, socialist rulers have, in practice, alienated a far greater proportion of most socialist societies, although precisely how large a proportion is difficult to assess. Nevertheless, there is, I believe, a deep insight in Mao's assertion that bears on the relative capacity of socialist and capitalist polities to realize human rights in Third World countries. There seems to be little doubt that the domestic component of "the growth dividend" in capitalist Third World countries goes predominantly to the upper ten to twenty percent of the population (as well as to external elites), widening rich/poor gaps, and in most cases deteriorating the real income of the bottom forty percent at least for a period of some decades.[15] In effect, the mass of the population suffers as the result of a capitalist orientation toward development. This orientation can no longer be successfully legitimated by resting the claim of the rich and powerful on some traditional ground of privilege (e.g., caste, vested property rights), or by invoking "trickle down," "expanded pie" imagery. Only repression works. It is functional for a capitalist Third World country, and it generally assumes an acute form because of the depth of poverty, as well as the high ratio of poor to rich in the overall stratification of the population. For this reason, the extent of coercive authority and its duration and severity do not seem as integral for a socialist approach as for a capitalist approach in a Third World country. However, as I shall note later on, the costs of the transition to socialism seem higher in practice than those of the persistence of a capitalist social order, thereby offsetting to a significant extent the humanitarian structural advantage of socialism.

In essence, both socialism and capitalism will be repressive in most Third World contexts because of the developmental squeeze, requiring capital formation to persist under conditions of mass poverty combined with popular expectations of higher living standards. The distributional priorities of socialist states, as well as the absence of any need to produce "profits," make the squeeze, other factors being equal, both less severe and less exploitative. Again the appeal of a clean generalization gives way to some complicating realities. The capital squeeze in socialist Third World societies, although more equitably distributed in its effects, may be more severe than in capitalist societies because of the greater tendency toward self-reliance and the high priority attached to collective goals (e.g., heavy industry, defense capability).

And there is another factor. Capitalist Third World countries display a far lower capacity than do their socialist counterparts to provide jobs for their populations. The crisis of unemployment and underemployment, intensified by the introduction of profit-maximizing, discipline-minimizing capital-intensive technology, constitutes a pervasive failure on the part of capitalist Third World countries for which no relief is in sight. Even a country as relatively prosperous as Mexico now is able to provide jobs for only about half of the six hundred thousand Mexicans added each year to its work force, and this situation is not atypical for capitalist Third World countries.[16] The severity of the employment crisis is hidden to some extent by not counting the grossly underemployed (i.e., the person holding a superfluous part-time job at a tiny salary) in the ranks of the unemployed.[17] If statistics were recalculated to count underemployed, the ranks of the unemployed in Third World capitalist countries would rise to levels between thirty and sixty percent.

There are some factors pointing in the opposite direction. Capitalist polities maintain certain realms of private freedom to a greater extent than do socialist polities. The ethos of the market, the class affinities of intellectuals and bureaucrats, the importance of sustaining ties to the liberal West all tend toward preserving, by and large, some space for cultural freedom and creativity in otherwise repressive Third World societies. Also, capitalist rulers have so far been somewhat less successful in stabilizing their repressive systems of rule than their socialist counterparts, making it easier to sustain some opposition patterns of behavior.

On balance, it still seems appropriate to argue that, except in very unusual domestic circumstances, socialism is a precondition for human rights in the Third World, whereas capitalism assures their massive denial. At the same time, in practice the shift to socialism may entail severe transition costs that outweigh its greater equity of operation once established, and its successful domination of political and cultural space may make it virtually impossible to overcome deformations of socialism once they occur in a given concrete instance.

The international dimension of the comparison is also relevant. International capitalism as a mode of organizing the dominant global market makes its own independent, significant contributions to authoritarianism. The role of the United States as the leading imperial actor in the world system uses coercive power to advance capitalist interests, which include biasing developmental patterns in a capitalist direction, by interventionary means if necessary.[18] The Soviet imperial role in Eastern Europe reveals an analogous control process, but the Soviet role in the Third World has, up to this point, been less widely detrimental to the pursuit of human rights than has the American role. This is partly a consequence of the historical circumstance which made the protection of investment, markets, and access to raw materials a vital vested interest for the capitalist West, as exemplified by American leadership, throughout the Third World, and a rallying point of Soviet opposition.

It is possible to draw some preliminary conclusions:

1. Human rights as a focus of normative concern do not extend their reach to the wider structures of repression allegedly inherent in state power or flowing from irreconcilable claims for security and self-determination, nor do they extend to the internal effects of imperialism or of authoritarian personality types to prevail in struggles for political leadership at the state level;

2. Human rights, as a set of limits on the exercise of state power, possess historical origins associated with Western liberal ideology, including the ethos of *laissez faire* capitalism, and, as such, generate an appeal that is often suspect in the Third World, although decreasingly so;

3. Reformulations of human rights are seeking to achieve sufficient universality of tone and content to engender respect and legitimacy in all parts of the world, regardless of cultural heritage or ideological orientation;

4. An acceptable reformulation of human rights in these universal terms will necessarily be eclectic, and will include a synthesis of the equity preoccupations of socialist systems with the liberty preoccupation of capitalist systems (note that capitalist Third World dictatorships tend to preserve some kind of private economic sphere for business enterprise);

5. Nevertheless, the ideological situation is not symmetrical in the Third World, as the objective conditions of mass poverty, aroused expectations, and resource constraints make the adoption of a socialist program of development a virtual necessity except in a few isolated "special cases" (Israel, Kuwait, Taiwan, Venezuela) where affluence or external capital accumulation makes it possible (although not assured) that both the material and nonmaterial elements of fundamental human rights can be realized; in general, capitalist systems of development seem incapable of a positive performance across the board of human rights concerns, although their performance relative to each other can be compared;

6. Furthermore, neocolonialist patterns associated with superpower diplomacy, multinational corporations, and international financial institutions reinforce repressive tendencies in Third World capitalist countries to a significantly greater extent than do certain analogous international patterns associated with "socialist imperialism";

7. No clear lines of normative preference can be persuasively drawn. On

the domestic scene, transition and termination costs of socialist forms of development may seem, on balance, more severe for the population as a whole, than do the maintenance costs of capitalist forms; in the end, we are left with the requirement of assessing, at a given point in time, the foreseeable costs of alternative paths of development in the concrete circumstances of each country.

Fundamental Human Rights

Having specified some ground rules, we can now clarify the content of human rights that will serve as the criteria for assessing the performance of particular governments. The most obvious starting point of inquiry is the substantial body of international law on the subject. Leaving aside the thorny question of whether and to what extent human rights norms are binding on various governments (including the extent to which the obligations imposed depend on expressions of formal sovereign consent), can we rely on the Universal Declaration of Human Rights (along with more detailed, specialized, and treatylike instruments such as the International Covenants on Economic, Social, and Cultural Rights and on Civil and Political Rights) as an adequate description of what is to be encompassed by "human rights"? After all, the Universal Declaration is the product of intergovernmental negotiation, it has been widely endorsed and invoked as authoritative in all parts of the world, and it is an eclectic instrument that seems reasonably sensitive to the concerns of both socialist and capitalist systems. The same generalizations apply, to a lesser extent, to the subsequent international human rights treaties. There are several difficulties, however, with these "authoriative" formulations that rest on international law:

1. The type of eclecticism embodied in the documents of international law includes whatever is *vital to either ideology* rather than what is *fundamental to both;* for instance, Article 17 of the Universal Declaration upholds the right of property, obviously inimical to socialist systems, whereas Article 23(1) affirms the right of everyone to work at a job of his or her choice, obviously inconsistent with the operational codes of capitalist systems;

2. The rights endorsed include those that can be realized only through the dissolution of the coercive sovereign state and the abolition of the war system; for example, Article 28 of the Universal Declaration states: "Everyone is entitled to a social and international order in which the rights and freedoms set forth in this Declaration can be fully realized";

3. The corpus of international human rights law is too diffuse in coverage to permit a focus on the most serious, pressing, or correctible violations;

4. Some important "fundamental" human rights are omitted, for example, rights to survival associated with ecological balance and threats to use weapons of mass destruction;

5. The normative foundations of human rights are entrusted too exclusively

to mechanisms of negotiability and implementation among governments of sovereign states; the legitimacy of naturalist, communitarian, and populist assertions should also be incorporated into the basic conception;

6. The ideological "bias" embodied in international human rights law is somewhat slanted toward the liberal ideas of capitalist society rather than toward the ideas and ideals of socialism, thereby reflecting the relevant weight of the two ideologies in the negotiating setting, and such law offers no proposals for rectifying the international economic order.

The Carter Administration has proposed a more focused conception of human rights, loosely connected with the international legal norms mentioned above, but incorporating also features of a new global consensus that brings vital or basic needs explicitly into the orbit of human rights.[19] This conception of human rights was authoritatively set forth by the American secretary of state, Cyrus Vance, in his 1977 Law Day address at the University of Georgia. Vance proposed the separation of human rights into three categories:

> First, there is the right to be free from governmental violation of the integrity of the person. Such violations include torture; cruel, inhuman, or degrading treatment or punishment; and arbitrary arrest or imprisonment. And they include denial of public trial and invasion of the home.
>
> Second, there is the right to the fulfillment of such vital needs as food, shelter, health care, and education. We recognize that the fulfillment of this right will depend, in part, upon the stage of a nation's economic development. But we also know that this right can be violated by a government's action or inaction—for example through corrupt official processes which divert resources to an elite at the expense of the needy or through indifference to the plight of the poor.
>
> Third, there is the right to enjoy civil and political liberties: freedom of thought, of religion, of assembly; freedom of speech; freedom of movement both within and outside one's own country; freedom to take part in government.[20]

As Vance observed, these rights "are all recognized" in the Universal Declaration, and yet his formulation of the American approach provides a selective focus. In actuality, the potential suspension of foreign military assistance is correlated with "gross violations of internationally recognized human rights" by legislative enactment. "Gross violations . . ." are defined as "torture or cruel, inhuman, or degrading treatment or punishment, prolonged detention without charges and trial, and other flagrant denial of the right to life, liberty, or security of the person." The Carter Administration in 1977 actually reduced aid to only three (Argentina, Uruguay, and Ethiopia) of the fifty-seven countries found guilty of gross violations.[21] It is a selective approach, omitting any reference to the Article 23 affirmation of rights associated with work or the Article 27 affirmation of rights connected with cultural and scientific activity. It provides an appealing compromise between a comprehensive approach and an emphasis on a few items that capture popular imagination at the moment. The Carter Administration has consistently employed Vance's categorization in discussing human rights and has organized its annual edition of country reports (as required by congressional legislation) around this conception. As a shorthand, considered from a purely intellectual point of view, this conception facilitates communication, understanding, and mobilization, and it aptly confines its goals to the human rights enterprise of reform within the state system.

Nevertheless, the Vance conception has disadvantages. First, its formulation by American officials limits its international authoritativeness, especially in certain sectors of world society where the United States is seen as a principal violator of human rights. Second, it leaves out of account, as does the Universal Declaration, critical rights pertaining to ecological balance and freedom from threats of mass destruction. Third, the application of the Carter approach is slanted by anticommunist domestic pressures and by the overriding geopolitical rivalry with the Soviet Union. This impression is confirmed by the concrete application of the Carter approach; for instance, Carter instructed his representatives in international financial institutions last year to vote against loans to Cuba, Cambodia, Laos, Vietnam, Angola, Mozambique, and Uganda, and other "gross violators" of human rights.[22] Fourth, the Carter approach, as would be expected, is statist in character, resting its claims of right on what governments do.

A quite different approach to human rights is staked out by the Universal Declaration of the Rights of Peoples, adopted in Algiers on July 4, 1976 (called hereafter "the Algiers Declaration"). This declaration was the outgrowth of efforts by the Lelio Basso Foundation for the Rights of People (an Italian private institute) working in cooperation with especially qualified individuals in a large number of countries, including representatives of National Liberation Movements.[23] The Algiers Declaration affirms the positive activity of the United Nations General Assembly, singling out the Universal Declaration of Human Rights and the Charter on the Economic Rights and Duties of States. The Algiers preamble makes a partisan diagnosis, attributing central responsibility for the denial of human rights to "new forms of imperialism" that have emerged in the postcolonial period "to oppress and exploit the peoples of the world":

> Imperialism, using vicious methods, with the complicity of governments that it has itself often installed, continues to dominate a part of the world. Through direct or indirect intervention, through multinational enterprises, through the manipulation of corrupt local politicians, with the assistance of military regimes based on police repression, tortures and physical extermination of opponents, through a set of practices that has become known as neo-colonialism, imperialism extends its stranglehold over many countries.

And to make its position even clearer the preamble goes on:

May all those who, throughout the world, are fighting the great battle, at times through armed struggle, for the freedom of all peoples, find in this Declaration the assurance of the legitimacy of their struggle.[24]

The operative provisions emphasize the rights of "peoples" as distinct from "individuals"; there is a greater stress on economic liberation and on cultural autonomy. In the background of the Algiers Declaration is a preoccupation with those transnational structures of domination (and their domestic collaborators) that preclude genuine political, economic, and cultural autonomy on a national level, and that have been identified above as "intermediate" structure. The Algiers Declaration is distinctive among human rights documents by the degree of emphasis it accords to international structural factors as explanatory of violations of human rights. Article 27 of the Algiers Declaration also declares that "[t]he gravest violations of the fundamental rights of peoples, especially of their right to existence, constitute international crimes for which their perpetrators shall carry personal penal liability." Rights of resistance against internal oppression are also affirmed, including the right "in the last resort" to use force as specified in Article 28. This emphasis on criminal accountability of repressive leaders and on rights of popular resistance is also distinctive in the human rights context.

The Algiers Declaration has several advantages over the Universal Declaration or the Carter approach. First, it extends the coverage of human rights from individuals to peoples and movements. Second, its diagnosis and prescriptions pointedly reflect the actual content of Third World concerns, and its promulgation at Algiers gives its existence a more genuine Third World flavor, which is appropriate given the preponderance of peoples and countries in the Third World and their minimal role in earlier formulations of human rights law. Third, it posits a claim that rights can be authoritatively formulated by populist initiative and do not depend upon governmental actions. Fourth, it assesses the landscape of repression and assigns primary responsibility to the interplay between neocolonialism and struggles for control internal to the Third World, thereby linking up denial of human rights with capitalist dynamics. Fifth, it introduces ideas of popular rights of resistance and enforcement, and of criminal responsibility, into the corpus of human rights law.

The Algiers Declaration also has several disadvantages or, more aptly, limitations. First, it is incomplete without incorporation of the traditional corpus of human rights, and yet it never sufficiently clarifies its connections with it. Second, the legitimacy of a populist norm-generating procedure is highly controversial, and its claims are ignored or dismissed by most governments and many private groups. Third, the content of analysis and prescription is unbalanced to the extent that it virtually overlooks abuses to the rights of peoples emanating from socialist origins. Fourth, as with other approaches considered, it fails to depict rights relating to environment and to threats of mass extermination.[25] Fifth, the auspices of the Algiers Declaration are relatively obscure, and funds at its disposal sparse, as compared to principal governments or even the United Nations, and therefore its position on human rights remains relatively unknown.

Various attempts have been made by individuals to focus the human rights struggle by proposing specific formulations. Moynihan, in the course of attacking Carter's approach to human rights for its tendency to avoid the central ideological struggle, argues on behalf of an antitotalitarian focus as the priority element in any adequate conception of human rights. Partisanship is the hallmark of Moynihan's approach, and he resents Carter's attempt to equate the pursuit of economic goals with antitotalitarian ones. Moynihan believes that the socialist countries, led by Soviet armed might, "are the most powerful opponents of liberty on earth," professing "the only major political doctrine that challenges human rights *in principle.*" For this reason, Moynihan believes that overriding attention should be given to the plight of the "billion-and-a-half" persons who "live in totalitarian Marxist states."[26] Moynihan regards the struggle against socialist forms of totalitarianism as being a matter of survival rather than moral preference: *"Human rights has nothing to do with our innocence or guilt as a civilization. It has to do with our survival."* He views the Vietnam defeat in this light, as a setback in the struggle to halt the expansion of totalitarianism: ". . . it did not end the expansion of totalitarianism, nor yet the need to resist. If anything, it added enormously to the importance of ideological resistance, and this precisely is the role of 'Human Rights in Foreign Policy.' "For this reason, he connects the American response to the Third World with the willingness of specific governments to join in on the correct side of this struggle: *"The new nations must be made to understand that our commitment to them depends on their ceasing to be agents of the totalitarian attack on democracy."*[27]

Moynihan's approach, although substantively almost opposite from that taken in this chapter, is notable in at least one respect. It links the conception of human rights to a value-oriented, explicit politics that is appropriately centered on the ideological tension between capitalism and socialism.

However, such a politicized approach has serious drawbacks. First of all, it chooses sides on a basis that is unconvincing, especially with respect to the well-being of Third World people; it overlooks the achievement of socialist societies in reducing dramatically the incidence of poverty and gross income disparities. Second, by mobilizing human rights constituencies around an avowedly anti-Soviet interpretation of the central global struggle, it tends to increase international tensions, thereby contributing to an arms race mentality and quite possibly increasing the risk of general warfare without doing anything appreciable to help human rights in the target societies. Third, Moynihan's approach is completely insensitive about the degree to which American initiatives, direct and covert, have contributed to the rise of totalitarianism in the Third World, or about the seriousness of human rights violations at home or elsewhere in the capitalist First World. Fourth, this self-righteous, militantly anticommunist emphasis is extremely unpopular with public opinion in most parts of the world and, thereby, does not possess any capacity to mobilize wider international support for human rights concerns.

Another quite different approach has been advocated by Peter Berger. Berger argues strongly that much of the debate on human rights is flawed by its failure to draw a clear distinction between ethnocentric and "fundamental" human rights; only the latter are sufficiently legitimated by underlying cultural values to support an international stature. It is necessary, Berger argues, to reject those claims of right that owe their origins to Western values, and, in effect, to ignore even those rights incorporated in international legal instruments that cannot pass the test of cultural resonance. Therefore, Berger excludes from the fundamental category of human rights those associated with either "political democracy" or "economic rights," contending that these are distinctively Western. Berger restricts the scope of human rights as international claims to those "grossest cases" of abuse that infringe the minimal views of decency embodied in every major world cultural tradition:

> Genocide; the massacre of large numbers of innocent people by their own government or by alien conquerors; the deliberate abandonment of entire sections of a population to starvation; the systematic use of terror (including torture) as government policy; the expulsion of large numbers of people from their homes; enslavement through various forms of forced labor; the forced separation of families (including the taking away of children from their parents by actions of government); the deliberate desecration of religious symbols and persecution of those adhering to them; the destruction of institutions that embody ethnic identity.

According to Berger, "in condemning *these* as violations of human rights, we can call upon a consensus far wider than that of Western civilization. That consensus emerges from all the major world cultures—especially in their religious foundations."[28]

Peter Berger's approach has several attractions. First, it anchors the international affirmation of human rights in a universal consensus that allegedly has identifiable indigenous roots in each principal world culture. Second, rooting human rights in values rather than norms premises the basis for collective international action on more promising grounds when it comes to mobilizing genuine support. Third, the concreteness of Berger's list of specific abuses has a mobilizing potential that the more abstract designations each lack, and yet it appears to lack the partisanship that mars Moynihan's approach.

Berger's approach is not, however, on balance, very appealing. First, by placing an overriding emphasis on tradition-based cultural values, Berger's "consensus" seems to reject critical elements of an operational consensus emergent in the Third World outlook, especially its emphasis on basic needs, on economic rights and duties of states, and on the campaign against apartheid; as a consequence, contrary to what Berger claims, his approach *appears* to stress only those concerns that currently agitate the West, and possesses the very partisan character it is so preoccupied with avoiding. Second, the Berger list omits some critical universal dangers, including those associated with threats of mass destruction and ecological decay, that seem important to include in a contemporary conception of human rights, regardless of whether they pass the cultural resonance test. Third, the Berger list of fundamental human rights makes no assessment of responsibility as between socialism and capitalism for their abridgment, purporting to rest human rights on a basis that transcends this central, ideological fissure, and therefore deprives the domain of human rights of a principal moral and political rationale; in this regard, cultural consensus as the central tenet of legitimated human rights is insensitive to their potential role on behalf of reformist claims in the international political system. Fourth, Berger's approach overlooks international factors (e.g., "neocolonialism," interventionary diplomacy) that cause, or at least reinforce, various repressive tendencies, and therefore avoids making structural prescriptions as human rights correctives.

A quite different attempt at a human rights focus is that of Fouad Ajami. He orients his analysis toward the debate about human rights initiated by Carter's approach. He contends that "flawed concepts of human rights" allow the United States to be a human rights champion while at the same time opposing "the New International Economic Order and Third World demands for a fairer distribution of global wealth."[29] Ajami also criticizes Third World leaders who ". . . speak the language of egalitarianism abroad, while they defend systems of acute inequalities within their own boundaries." He regards militarized politics at home as almost invariably leading to severe denials of humane politics, a characterization, he contends, that holds for " 'leftist' Ethiopian soldiers as well as for 'rightist' Brazilian officers."[30] In the spirit of the Algiers Declaration, yet with less partisanship, Ajami's approach to human rights seeks to attribute responsibility for their decline to an interlocked series of domestic and international factors. As a consequence, the political roots of repressive rule give direction to Ajami's views as to what needs to be done.

Perhaps the most original, challenging features of Ajami's approach is that it places emphasis on the link between the war system and human rights. He argues that matters of survival (rather than liberty, or even equity) provide the "domain" within which "the fate of human rights will be determined"; "the nexus of the war system and technology is our principal trap.'' Against this background Ajami affirms an eclectic conception of human rights that seeks to encompass principal sensitivities involving liberty, equity, and survival, without enumerating a long shopping list of human rights issues. Ajami emphasizes four sets of concerns that embody "the maximum feasible consensus at this time":

1. The right to survive; hence the concern with the war system and nuclear weaponry.

2. The right not to be subjected to torture.

3. The condemnation of apartheid; it is accepted that other societies violate racial equality but that South Africa's blatant, officially sanctioned and codified racism is particularly intolerable.

4. The right to food.[31]

The Ajami approach is attractive for several reasons. First, it is encompassing and universalistic, yet focused. Second, it is sensitive to the main areas of perceived abuse and danger. Third, it stakes out a progressive position, and yet criticizes all sectors of international society without seeking refuge in legalism or moralism. Fourth, it regards militarization, nuclear weaponry, and threats of mass destruction as core human rights issues. Fifth, it formulates human rights issues in language that can be translated into political action and goals.

Although these positive features seem generally persuasive, I have a few reservations about the Ajami approach. First, there is no effort to ground its proposals in the Universal Declaration and other legitimating instruments, although this could easily be done. Second, the approach does not focus directly on the link between neocolonial features of the international system and national development impacts on the national level, although the stress on the New International Economic Order (NIEO) could be so interpreted. Third, it doesn't relate the struggle between capitalist and socialist models of development to the prospects for human rights, especially in relation to the rapid alleviation of mass misery in the poor societies of the Third World. Fourth, its short list of four human rights goals places too insufficient an emphasis on restraining state power to allow it to have a wide appeal at this time.

Jorge Dominguez has attempted to combine the focus of a short list with the coverage of a comprehensive conception. He grounds the content of human rights in the norms of the Universal Declaration on Human Rights, yet he offers an orientation that identifies the most serious violations: "At the top of the hierarchy I would place concern for any identifiable government action that reduces a people's right to life and health. Attention would be focused not only on political massacres, arbitrary action by governments, but also on governments whose identifiable actions aggravate famines and epidemics."[32] The Dominguez image of priority rights is much less crystallized than is the Ajami short list; as such, it leaves more room for interpretative differences. It does encourage an observer to concentrate on specific accomplishments and failures in a given country and, as such, is far more amenable to social science observations or to acceptance by human rights nongovernmental organizations than is the Ajami list. Ajami's list, on the other hand, is more useful for mobilizing change-oriented constituencies, as it is much more responsive to political agendas that dominate international policy-making arenas.

My purpose is intermediate between those of Dominguez and Ajami. I seek a theoretically sound framework for comparison, yet one that yields an understanding that can relate easily to policy debates. At the core of my approach, as has been outlined above, is the conviction that socialism and capitalism are the fundamental approaches to Third World actualities, and that these actualities center on choices of developmental strategy. In the background of developmental choices are some wider issues of world order that also should be brought into the human rights framework, including those relating to cultural autonomy, the war system, and over-burdening of the environment.

The content of human rights is obviously controversial. My proposal of five categories draws inspiration from the approaches discussed here. It does not restrict its image of human rights to norms legitimated by intergovernmental consent or, even, by United Nations consensus. Populist initiatives (e.g., the Algiers Declaration) can also achieve legitimacy. To focus inquiry, reflection, and policy recommendation, five categories of rights are set forth as a proposal to delimit the subject matter of human rights:

1. *Basic human needs:* the rights of individuals and groups to food, housing, health, and education; the duty of governments to satisfy these rights, taking into account resource constraints and natural disasters (e.g., drought, flood);

2. *Basic decencies:* the rights of individuals and groups to be protected against genocide, torture, arbitrary arrest, detention, and execution, or their threat; the duty of peoples and governments and their officials to establish an atmosphere wherein these rights can be securely realized, including the protection of the society against paragovernmental violence of various kinds (e.g., "death squads"), taking into account constraints on governmental capabilities and the threats and tactics relied upon by enemies of the state;

3. *Participatory rights:* the rights of individuals and groups to participate in the processes that control their lives, including choice of political leadership, of job, of place of residence, of cultural activity and orientation; the duty of peoples and governments to uphold these rights in ways that provide individuals and groups with opportunities to lead meaningful lives, including the freedom to participate in procedures for the shaping and execution of norms;

4. *Security rights:* the rights of individuals and groups (including those of unborn generations) to be reasonably secure about their prospects of minimal physical well-being and survival; the duty of governments and peoples to

uphold this right by working to achieve sustainable forms of national and ecological security;

5. *Humane governance:* the rights of individuals and groups to live in societies and a world that realizes the rights depicted in 1–4; the duty of individuals, groups, governments, and institutions to work toward this end.

Categories 1–3 are fairly standard. Category 4 speaks to the special circumstances created by nuclear weaponry and other military technology, as well as to the situation created by the scale and character of global industrialization; these concerns are mainly a consequence of what has taken place in non-Third World sectors of world society, yet its effects on the Third World are potentially massive. Category 5 is a kind of world order imperative that implies an inability to achieve human rights in 1–4 without transforming the political order that now exists; as such, it extends the boundaries of human rights beyond those set by the state system with its operative code of sovereignty, which limits attention to carefully depicted national territorial limits.

This approach does not purport to achieve a rigorous conception of what is a "right," how "rights" inhere in unborn individuals or in relation to protection from policies that risk nuclear war or environmental harm. A theory of right that rests upon the emerging reality of planetary citizenship needs to be developed as an intellectual foundation for the approach advocated here.

Such an approach loses the specificity of a more legally grounded conception of human rights that assesses whether a claim is a right by whether it is potentially justiciable according to some constituted judicial or administrative procedure. The broader approach is less directed at issues of enforceability than of appraisal, the standards relevant for assessment of how far a given polity realizes the elements, as set forth, of humane governance.

It is also important, especially given the focus of socialism versus capitalism, to have some way of capturing phases of the cycle of political development. To simplify matters, three phases seem crucial: initiation, maintenance, and termination. These phases direct attention at essential aspects of ideologically diverse developmental experiences.

Initiation Phase

The inception of a political system as socialist or capitalist, and its secure establishment as the stable, dominant order can be appraised from a human rights perspective. In general, the initiation costs tend to vary with the degree of societal discontinuity, as well as with the relation of internal forces. Capitalist developmental forms are more continuous with colonialist or dependent status than are socialist forms. Soviet and Chinese initiation costs entailed millions of casualties. The initiation phase may also include a period of civil strife that can involve great suffering and loss of life. The Indochina War, carried on against the

French and then against the Americans, should be understood, in part, as a struggle between socialist and capitalist developmental orientations. Outside capitalist forces greatly magnified the transition costs to socialism in Indochina.

At the same time, the initiation costs in Cambodia, relatively more severe than in either Vietnam or Laos, suggest that factors other than ideological orientation broadly conceived can be significant. The prevailing attitude about the construction of socialism in the aftermath of a devastating internal war is a significant variable in the initiation phase. The behavior of outsiders, especially their adherence to norms of nonintervention, is likely to exert a strong influence on the construction of human rights in the initiation phase. Also significant is the "openness" of the society, its readiness to engage in diplomatic, economic, and cultural contacts with outsiders across ideological battle lines. In this regard, Vietnam seems particularly "open," possibly because it seeks to avoid being squeezed between rival socialist superpowers.

If capitalist developmental forms are reestablished, even after interludes of "soft" socialism, as in Indonesia (1965) or Chile (1973), the initiation costs are also likely to be quite severe, suggesting that the degree of discontinuity may be more telling than ideological identity.

Initiation costs are sometimes minimized by allowing "enemies" to emigrate, especially if their destination is distant. However, if exile communities continue an armed opposition, under the protective cover of a foreign state, then the initiation costs can be high and the phase extended for a longer period. Cuba experienced this pattern, being confronted by enemy exiles given encouragement, protection, resources, military training, and equipment, and by the political presence of a hostile neighboring superpower, the United States. Naturally, such a climate hardened internal security requirements in Cuba, and may have helped generate an internal security apparatus that would otherwise have evolved differently and played a lesser role. Also, we must assume that the extent of Stalinization of Cuban socialism reflected to some degree the extent of the Soviet presence, which was itself largely a reaction against American antisocialist hostility.

Thus, we can say that socialist orientations are generally more discontinuous with the socioeconomic structure of a given country, and hence most likely to stimulate an all-or-nothing struggle. This discontinuity is reinforced by the greater tendency of foreign capitalist states, especially the United States, to support the internal capitalist faction by funds, arms, and advice. As a consequence, heavy start-up or initiation costs are associated with the transition to socialism, although most of these costs may be incurred during the armed struggle phase, which included an anticolonial rationale. Once socialism is established, the reestablishment of capitalism will also tend to induce heavy costs during its initiation phase.

Comparing initiation costs of the new order with the maintenance costs associated with the old one is difficult. One observer, for instance, reports thirty thousand deaths in connection with the initiation costs of the Ethiopian socialist regime as of mid-1977, whereas maintenance costs for its predecessor included two hundred thousand victims of the 1972 famine, many of whom might have survived if the ruling elite at the time had acknowledged and competently responded to the problem.[33]

Maintenance Phase

The maintenance of a stable socialist or capitalist order after it has secured control over the apparatus of state power can also be assessed. Here, no issue of discontinuity is present, although a given political form, whether socialist or capitalist, evolves along a broadly varied path. In this regard, even ultrastable political systems are experimental, especially in their efforts to generate satisfactory economic policy. Also, political elites factionalize and struggle, at least within limits, for dominance, especially at times of economic crisis and of leadership succession.

In general, after the initiation phase, socialist systems seem stable in the maintenance phase. The programmatic commitments to equity and the elimination of poverty, as well as the capacity to find jobs for virtually everyone and to orient productive output around needs, lead to a condition of mass acquiescence (or subservience). Extreme self-reliance (Cambodia during famine, China after earthquake) suggests that socialist governments may not acknowledge disasters even sufficiently to receive outside help that could mitigate the suffering.

Capitalist maintenance is more problematic. The capitalist approach necessarily slights the well-being of the masses and runs contrary to the Marxist economic and ethical consensus dominant among intellectuals and students in the Third World. Because capitalism emerged often with the help and support of ''liberal'' Western outlooks, extreme repression was not undertaken, meaning that an opposition persists, and is likely to grow, in the maintenance stage. For these reasons, governments like those in South Korea, Iran, and the Philippines have to sustain high levels of active repression throughout the course of their existence. The class politics of capitalist development means that the masses must be kept actively disorganized and their leaders intimidated.

At the same time, the pluralist character of a capitalist system, with its private business and cultural sphere, its nominal consumer and intellectual diversity, makes it easier for an opposition to stay alive and flourish. The totalness of socialist control makes repression less necessary, yet the control itself is a form of repression. Cuba and Yugoslavia have shown some limited capacity, especially at certain stages, to combine cultural pluralism with a socialist approach to development.

In general, socialism seems to do better in the maintenance phase with economic rights and with those human rights concerned with the avoidance of extreme abuse of the person, while capitalism seems to do better with respect to preserving some cultural and political space for oppositional tendencies and general creativity.

Termination Phase

The termination period during which a political system is discarded and replaced by another in the final object of assessment. The termination phase is analogous to the initiation phase, calling attention to the dynamics of a transition. Whereas "initiation" is located in time as postcolonial (or post-1945), "termination" is viewed as a subsequent phenomenon in which socialism replaces capitalism or vice versa. Also, initiation refers to the birth process, once a particular elite is established in power, while termination refers to the death throes of a particular system.

The essence of termination is the process of getting rid of an abusive or weak regime. We assume that withdrawal of popular consent, via electoral politics, is rarely sufficient, especially in the case of a socialist governing elite. Experience suggests that it is virtually impossible to get rid of socialist regimes once they have managed to get into the maintenance phase and have adopted a "hard" orientattion toward the retention of state power. Outside intervention, as in Iran (1953) or Guatemala (1954), can topple a "soft" socialist or socialist-inclined government rather easily.

Similarly, "soft" capitalist governments cannot survive, and have been steadily superseded by harder ones. The evolution of capitalist governance in South Korea, the Philippines, and Iran is exemplary. With the elaboration of bureaucratic structure, internal security systems, and a militarized form of politics, the "hard" capitalist regimes are also becoming very difficult to terminate, even when exceedingly unpopular.

What is true, however, is that oppositional forces remain active and coherent in struggle in capitalist instances of authoritarian rule. Enough "space" is maintained because of pluralist pretensions and realities; degrees of factional disagreement of reduced repression. Unlike a socialist conception of total control by the state as integral to class rule, the capitalist conception relates repressive rule more closely to functional necessity; as such, it is more reactive, although its bureaucratic structures have a life of their own.

As yet, we have no experience with the termination of "hard" socialist regimes. The attempts of Eastern European governments to evolve in moderate directions and to break away from Soviet domination suggest the phenomenon. The perception is blurred by the heavy element of Soviet imperial presence, blocking termination initiatives. Also, the Soviet imperial issue establishes a legitimated basis for oppositional tendencies except in the most Stalinized of socialist systems.

The approach advocated, then, would suggest the following matrix:

A given government could, then, on the basis of available data be rated on a scale of 1–5 for each category in each phase; lack of data would be indicated by the notation "i.d." (insufficient data); nonapplicability of instance by notation "n.a." (not applicable).

Some Remarks on Appraisal

Of course, the criteria set forth are difficult to apply. Requisite data are either unavailable or uneven. What data exist are difficult to use in any systematic and objective way. It is an immense task, requiring a staff of specialists, to make a careful appraisal for all Third World countries. At the same time, one of the purposes of the framework is to propose an orientation for data collection and evaluation projects.

Obviously, a comparison of countries should be as objective as possible, making it desirable to operationalize criteria of appraisal. At the same time, qualitative considerations are often decisive. For instance, a human rights comparison that overlooked Kathleen Gough's finding that workers in a Vietnamese community are far more satisfied with their lives than workers in an Indian community at a similar socioeconomic level would be deficient.[34] So would one that did not assess the relative degree of cultural vitality operative in a given polity.

Phases of governance / Categories of human rights	Initiating Phase	Maintenance Phase	Termination Phase
Basic human needs			
Basic decencies			
Participatory rights			
Security rights			
Humane governance			

At this stage, the evidence available enables only crude forms of comparison with respect to the relative achievement of human rights in particular states at particular times. It heightens sensitivity about broad Third World patterns and trends. One way to proceed is to try out exemplary case studies of national profiles of ideological prototypes: for instance, to describe Brazil, Iran, and South Korea for capitalist variants, and to describe China, Cuba, and North Korea for socialist variants. The hypothesis is that these cases would reveal, in addition to their critical, distinctive features, a patterning of developmental dynamics and human rights that would be more or less played out in other country examples. Such a hypothesis is central to the view that ideological orientation is associated with certain structural patterns. This hypothesis need not be deterministic: variations would emerge (due to resources, quality of leadership), pressures may vary (due to mass consciousness, safety valves for opponents, geographical position, attitudes by external governments), policies may reflect diverse antecedent conditions (due to land tenure arrangements, ethnic diversity and structure, prior degree of industrialization, reliance on foreign skills and capital). Nevertheless, the fundamental argument remains: Authoritarian solutions seem virtually unavoidable in most Third World countries over the period of the next decade or so, although their degree and form of severity will vary greatly. In general, socialist forms of authoritarianism are to be preferred to their capitalist counterparts because of a combination of domestic and international factors that have been indicated above, but not unreservedly.

─────VI─────

Responding to Severe Violations

Any serious violation of human rights represents some debasement of political process, as well as a deprivation for those whose rights are abridged. When violation of human rights becomes part of a systematic pattern of governance, it undermines the prospect of humane relations between government and citizenry. At present, in a large number of states the systematic and deliberate violation of human rights is an integral part of the governing process. Indicative of this disturbing feature of the modern world is the 1977 Amnesty International annual report, which concludes that serious human rights violations appear to be occurring in at least 116 countries.[1]

There are many reasons to be skeptical about how much can be done to improve this lamentable situation. Violations of human rights generally arise from the way a government treats individuals and groups within its territory. Territorial sovereignty is the basic characteristic of international relations, has become even more so in recent years as a result of decolonizalization, and is likely to remain so through the 1980s. Almost every state is jealous of its sovereign rights and places the highest premium on the protection of its polity against various forms of encroachment. Generally, political leaders also recognize that their own claim to sovereign rights depends on respecting comparable rights of other states. Even the most powerful states are exceedingly touchy about any outside pressures that can be construed as "interventionary." The sanctity of state sovereignty is one of the most insistent demands of strong, as well as of weak states. At the same time, the reality of interventionary statecraft is associated with the impositions of the strong upon the weak. In the present period of international history virtually all governments, however weak and dependent they may be, want to appear as sovereign as possible, and thereby make a rallying cry of norms of nonintervention. The priority accorded the nonintervention concept as the basic juridical guideline of international behavior is also expressed by the extreme reluctance of most governments to endorse intervention in foreign societies, even if under international or regional auspices or in response to what is generally condemned as an extreme abuse of human rights. Governments seem wary that the sword used against others today could be turned against them tomorrow. Hence, there is reluctance about any undertaking that could be generalized beyond a particular situation and turned into a precedent. In this regard, antiapartheid intervention gathers widespread support because the situation in South Africa seems *sui generis,* whereas anti-Amin intervention was impossible to organize because it would have created a precedent perceived as dangerous.

Underneath support for the nonintervention norm is a generalized anxiety that creating exceptions for humanitarian purposes will open up additional possibilities for the strong to impose their will on the weak.[2] John Vincent, perhaps the most authoritative modern interpreter of interventionary practice, can discover only the French intervention in Syria in 1860 to save Christian Maronite tribes from abuse by Moslem Druses as an instance of pure humanitarianism. The record of statecraft is the story of self-interested uses of power, and this makes it especially problematic to lend approval to any generalized right of intervention, regardless of alleged motives. Aside from states that are neighbors and may have a common interest in a given situation, the impulse to intervene is largely associated with the most powerful states active in a particular period of international history. But the motives and interests of these states make them least trustworthy as custodians of international morality.[4]

Also, within international society there is no consistently authoritative way to determine the existence of human rights abuses. Regional organizations often function more like alliances than community organizations; aside from the European setting, regional actors are very deferential to sovereign rights except in cases of a regional pariah—e.g., Cuba versus the Organization of American States (OAS), Israel versus the Arab League, South Africa versus the Organization of African Unity (OAU). It is difficult, therefore, to maintain that judgment at the regional level of when humanitarian intervention is appropriate is likely to be more objective than the judgment made by the governments of the largest states.

The United Nations is a body more representative of principal international tendencies, and hence has never singled out Cuba, in the manner of the OAS, as an appropriate target of community pressure because of its adherence to Marxism-Leninism. Nevertheless, the United Nations can be an intensely partisan arena in which a fair consideration of the realities is unlikely to occur. For this reason the political organs of the United Nations are increasingly regarded as more likely to reflect arbitrary crosscurrents of international politics than to provide an arena for their transcendence.

The severity of an abuse of human rights is not enough to generate a serious effort to do something about it. For instance, although criticism may be directed in a variety of directions, no real consideration is ever given to organizing coercive responses to human rights violations occurring in large states. Also, in the case of smaller states that are closely aligned with a large one, a prudent forebearance dissipates serious attention at the global level to their human rights violations.

For these reasons, nongovernmental organizations (NGOs) in the human rights area have played an increasingly important role recently in identifying and documenting human rights violations. However, these organizations can operate only to the extent that they are tolerated by territorial sovereigns. Furthermore, they are dependent on private funding, the character of which may introduce elements of bias. The liberal democracies provide the main base of operations for NGOs in the human rights area: government policy in these countries can make it more or less likely that such organizations can operate independently and successfully. One of the solid gains of former President Jimmy Carter's stress on human rights was to raise, at least temporarily, the stature of these NGOs and to encourage government officials to support their activities in countless ways through informal cooperation.

In addition, the legal situation pertaining to human rights, although it is evolving rapidly, remains ambiguous. The generalized norms of international law as set forth in the main legal instruments on human rights are either "declaratory" in stature (as is the case with the Universal Declaration), nonbinding because not widely enough ratified (as is the case with two international covenants covering the gamut of human rights), or simply discounted because they are perceived as "soft" law.[5]

Part of the difficulty, here, is a product of an overgeneralized debate on human rights. Especially in the United States there has been a cycle of high hopes and disillusionment. In idealistic statements by Woodrow Wilson, Franklin Roosevelt, John F. Kennedy, and most recently by Jimmy Carter in the early period of his presidency, there have been periodic ardent endorsements of human rights as the foundation of world peace. At such times, the norms of human rights are proclaimed as universal, applicable to friend and foe alike. Conservatives tend to regard this posture as pompous and foolish. They regard the serious concern over human rights by foreign policymakers as misguided and self-righteous intrusions in matters that are essentially the domestic concern of each state; they believe that such a stance is bad foreign policy to the extent that it weakens bonds that hold geopolitical allies together in a world of conflict. The split in world politics between communist and anticommunist societies accentuates the domestic debate as to whether the promotion of human rights should be based on universal standards or should focus on the shortcomings of the other side.

At the bottom of this debate are different conceptions of human nature and international society. Those who believe in the universal promotion of human rights are generally optimistic about eliminating aggressive behavior through reform and believe that in time a harmonious human community can, will, and must emerge; they also tend to believe that democratically and humanely governed political systems are more stable, and that therefore it is practical to encourage allies, as well as adversaries, to uphold human rights. Those who are skeptical of universalism believe that conflict is endemic in the world and that it is best to look after one's own interests without entertaining the illusion that the world can be made into a more humane place; they tend to believe that human rights and democratic procedures are ill suited for poorer countries and non-Western cultures, and that it is a mistake to insist upon universal standards of application.

The dynamics of the state system seem to lend greater support to the more skeptical position on human rights. Governments rarely shape their foreign policy according to moral considerations. As has often been argued, perhaps most influentially by Machiavelli in *The Prince,* a statesman's main task is to advance the security and interests of his own polity. To expend resources or endanger friendships for the sake of reforming a foreign society or the world as a whole is, in this view, dangerous and sentimental. It is dangerous because it can be provocative, and it is sentimental because it ignores the wellspring of statecraft. All the norms and indignation in the world are powerless against a determined government with the repressive apparatus required to control its own population. And the upsurge of partisanship and propagandizing on human rights issues in the United Nations, often the work of spokespeople for some of the more reprehensible regimes, does nothing to discount this skeptical assessment.

Yet there is a healthy refusal on the part of many to accept this kind of cynical realism as definitive. Despite the larger context of constraint, some possibilities exist to cope with human rights violations. The modern consciousness of global interdependence makes it virtually impossible to seek humane goals for one's own society while ignoring the extreme sufferings of others. For the sake of our own self-esteem and dignity, a concern for human rights is one element in the recognition of the unity of the human race. This sense of unity is being formed, slowly and indistinctly, in part as a by-product of the space age, which has allowed us to see the planet as a whole. This sense of wholeness carries with it the implication that political boundaries are artificial, that if we care about hungry people in Appalachia and the South Bronx, we also will care about them in the Sahel or Calcutta.

Also, so-called realists often overstate their case by underestimating idealistic elements in human experience. The existence of widely supported legal norms can have mobilizing effects in the domestic arenas that are the scene of violation. This seems to have been the case with Soviet dissenters, who frequently ground their actions in an appeal to international human rights instruments that have been endorsed by their own government. Some violations of human rights may be curtailed by making foreign political leaders believe that without reform other serious interests of their state will suffer; these modifications may turn out to be more "cosmetic" than "structural," but, even if this is the case, particular individuals may be freed, torture may be eliminated or reduced, and the degree of repression may be diminished.

Finally, there are certain situations in which a global consensus can be achieved. In the present period, the campaign against official racism in South Africa is the best illustration. Whether sincere or not, all major governments have joined in denouncing the racist features of South Africa. The common cause against apartheid is premised on the importance of eliminating severe abuses of human rights. It is partly a moral reaction to the indecency of extreme and official racism. But it is also in part pragmatic, representing a concern that unless something is done on behalf of the victims, a race war is likely to ensue that would present unacceptable choices, especially for the white industrial governments of the West.

What "doing something" involves is a subject of intense debate. The moderate position is to induce the ruling elites to make a series of voluntary reforms; the more radical position is to insist that a new elite representing the victims achieve power, by armed struggle if necessary. The tactical controversy is due in part to a discrepancy in assumptions about change that occurs in societal relations. This issue will be considered later.

The main thesis of this chapter is that the state system imposes drastic limits on what can be done at the international level to improve respect for human rights, but with an awareness of these limits in mind it is still possible to imagine some useful international responses to severe violations. It should be understood that severe violations usually express either pathological or structural realities, and are, therefore, particularly resistant to outside pressures that appeal to the rationality or good will of the violator.[6] This type of pressure does not enter in the cost-benefit calculus of the government violating rights except in the tactical sense that a target regime will deal with the pressures in such a way as to minimize their impact. Thus those who seek change must necessarily employ *coercive* strategies. Somehow, the regime violating human rights must be toppled or its leaders induced to make fundamental changes. This can be done either through domestic struggle, outside intervention, or a mixture of the two. Coercion can be applied internationally through psychological and diplomatic pressure, economic sanctions, embargoes on exports, boycotts on imports, and the resort to military force.

Before considering the narrow circumstances under which it is possible to respond effectively to severe violations of human rights by coercive means, it seems important to consider the types of severe violations of human rights that it would be desirable to do something about and the kinds of governments or leaders that engage in these violations.

Types of Severe Violations

We are assuming that a government and its officials are normally responsible for violations of human rights that occur within their borders. Usually this connection is an active one, that is, they either engage in the objectionable behavior as a matter of policy, rely on state resources and personnel, or deputize others to act on their behalf. Occasionally, the connection may be more passive, for example when certain individuals are not protected from destructive and unjust forms of private or semiprivate action. It is also conceivable that the situation giving rise to concern is beyond the control of the territorial sovereign, as when certain terrorist groups operate in weak states, when civil strife leads to the commission of atrocities, or when corruption brings about severe abuse of rights. The Lebanese Civil War of 1976–1977 illustrates several dimensions of the assault upon human values that can result from the breakdown of domestic order.

Defining a pattern of behavior as a severe human rights violation depends on several interrelated standards of appraisal. First and foremost are self-evident convictions about right and wrong. These require neither proof nor assent to be authoritative. For example, whether or not there is a prohibitive norm, the practice of torture or genocide seems "criminal" to the ordinary person. In effect, we affirm a natural law position. That is, certain patterns of behavior are forbidden and subject to corrective action whether or not a government sanctions prohibitive norms and independent of condemnation by the organized international community. Therefore, although the norms of international law are indicative of the standards of natural law, they are neither exhaustive nor are they all essential. That is, international treaties and customs incorporate most standards of behavior implicit in natural law, but their bindingness rests more on the fundamental foundation of international morality than on formal consent and codification. In recent years, despite its shortcomings as a politicized arena, the General Assembly of the United Nations has helped articulate this human rights core of international relations.

Second, we can identify offenses as severe by their incompatibility with widely endorsed standards of behavior. The endorsement can be formalized in binding international treaties or inferred from informal agreements. For instance, widespread assent to a nonbinding resolution of the United Nations General Assembly can be relied upon as evidence of what is regarded as forbidden behavior in the human rights field. There are two elements operative: the *consent* of particular governments and widespread *agreement* within the international community on the content of minimum human rights.

Third, we can assess offenses as severe by reference to the amount of harm and pain that they inflict. A situation can very persuasively be judged as severe when large numbers of people are harmed. It makes a difference in evaluating the Indo-Pakistan War or in assessing Idi Amin's rule in Uganda whether there were many victims or just a few. Although each victim's circumstance deserves concern and protection, there is a quantitative threshold that places domestic activities in the international arena for the protection of human rights. There is no way to supply numbers that establish these thresholds. Each situation needs to be assessed in context to determine whether the number of victims qualifies the offense as severe. Given, for instance, the small numbers of Aché Indians living in Paraguay, it seems plausible to regard them as victims of genocide even if the number of verified killings is small.[7]

Fourth, the continuing character of the violations is also important. If the objectionable behavior has ended, then the humanitarian impulse and the case for intervention is gravely weakened. A punitive mission would remain possible, but given the difficulty of doing anything effective about ongoing abuses in the first place, it would seem foolish to concentrate on such a cause. Of course, if the harm done was of especially grave character or the government was expected to renew its violations, then it might make sense to take action.

According to these standards of appraisal, the following categories of human rights offenses seem severe:

Type A: Genocide
Type B: Official racism
Type C: Large-scale official terrorism
Type D: Totalitarian governance
Type E: Deliberate refusal to satisfy basic human needs
Type F: Ecocide
Type G: War crimes

The 1980s will probably witness governments that commit violations in each of these categories. Because of the prevailing influence of nonintervention logic and in the absence of effective supranational capabilities, most of these violations will be impossible to do anything about—beyond improving the capacity to take notice. Only exceptional violations will provoke significant response. Before considering the possibilities for response, it seems useful to describe each type of human rights offense.

Type A: Genocide

The intentional killing, mutilation, or humiliation of a distinct ethnic group within a society is an extreme and self-evident abuse of human rights. Hitler's infamous "final solution" for Jews (and other disfavored groups) constitutes a paradigm for "severity" in the violation of human rights. After World War II, this assessment was given a formal legal character in the Nuremberg Judgment, the Nuremberg Principles endorsed by the United Nations General Assembly, and the Genocide Convention of 1950.

Despite the moral and legal status of genocide, it is often difficult to generate international concern unless victims have a powerful transnational constituency. For instance, considerable evidence of genocidal killing of tribal adversaries (Tutsis and Hutu) as a matter of official policy in both Rwanda (1964) and Burundi (1972) was treated with virtual indifference by governments and institutions in international society. Still greater neglect, extending to the media, was accorded the substantial allegations of genocidal behavior on the part of the Indian government in the course of its counterinsurgency war against the Naga and Mizo peoples in the period 1956–1964. In recent years, a series of large-scale genocidal campaigns has been waged against tribal populations in Africa and Latin America. Some individuals have tried to report on these instances of genocide, but it has been difficult to mobilize effective response because of the unwillingness of governments to become involved. In certain situations, adverse publicity discourages genocide to some extent. Often, genocidal policies are motivated by a mixture of economic and ethnic motives, and do not necessarily reflect a formal policy of the government to commit genocide per se; genocide, in such a situation, is an unintended by-product, but one for which there is responsibility, as it is the natural consequence of policies deliberately pursued. For instance, the destruction of American Indian peoples throughout the Western hemisphere is most centrally associated with seizing land or devoting it to more profitable uses.[8] Such activity, since it is now marginal to the development of the dominant society, has some prospect of being inhibited by publicity and a private campaign of censure designed to discredit the regime in world public opinion. These issues, despite their seriousness for the people involved, rarely engage the formal attention of foreign governments or the organized international community. The former tend to be uninterested because of the absence of any specific national interest, whereas the latter is deterred by nonintervention considerations and by the absence of any outside state or group of states that is deeply engaged on behalf of the victims.

Uganda and Pakistan stand as partial exceptions. The pursuit of genocidal policies via widespread killings directed at minority tribes in Uganda has been coupled with inflammatory instances of terror directed at Christian leaders and Westerners.[9] Amin has also taunted Western sensibilities in a variety of respects, adding a posture of defiance to the abuse of rights and giving the objectionable domestic behavior an international character. These elements in addition to genocide have generated relatively serious international concern, although it is centered in Great Britain and the United States.

The brutal repression of Bengali nationalism in 1971 by the West Pakistani Army possessed a genocidal character. Unarmed civilians with any leadership potential were systematically killed and as many as one million deaths (some estimates run as high as three million) resulted. Another ten million Bengalis fled across the border to India. Numerous horrifying crimes against humanity were reported and authenticated.[10] This chain of events did provoke military intervention by India. It was an effective operation, leading to the birth of the separate sovereign state of Bangladesh in what had been formerly East Pakistan, under the initial leadership of Sheik Mujibur Rahman, whose popular movement for regional autonomy had brought on the initial repression. India's motives for intervening were undoubtedly a complex mixture of geopolitical opportunism and humanitarian concern.

Some national situations exhibit genocidal features, for example, in Equatorial Guinea or Cambodia, but are better treated as instances of large-scale terror because the ethnic identity of the victims is not the essence of the crime. Also, official policies often erode the cultural identity of a people and thereby inflict "genocidal damage" without actually threatening individuals with physical death.[11] A typical example is the Canadian intention to build a pipeline along the Mackenzie Valley that would disrupt the traditional tribal lands of the Dene Indians.[12] These deprivations of human rights can cause irreversible damage for the group in question and should be considered severe if the internationally recognized territorial government does not establish its own procedures for protection. At the same time, given the problems associated with humanitarian intervention on behalf of such victims, it is inconceivable that anything more coercive than fact-finding and criticism would be undertaken by outside governments or intergovernmental groups. Nongovernmental organizations may go further and propose a variety of economic measures, especially a privately enforced boycott on exports, although normally NGO's ability to mobilize coercive responses is very limited.

Type B: Official Racism

When a government endorses racial discrimination by official laws and practices, it flagrantly violates widely accepted norms of racial equality. The salience of such patterns of racism will depend on how extreme the discriminatory policies are, as well as on the degree of humiliation associated with belonging to the subordinated race(s). It will also depend significantly on the degree to which outsiders identify with the fate of the victims, and their ability to do something about it.

Apartheid in South Africa is currently the prime instance of official racism, which is perceived as a severe challenge to human rights.[13] In South Africa racism is buttressed by brutal repression directed against even moderate opponents of the present situation. From the massacre of unarmed demonstrators at Sharpville in 1960 to the apparent murder of Steven Biko in 1977 by prison officials, there exists a chain of unmistakable evidence that the South African government and its officials will stop at nothing to prevent any challenge of the racist structure of the state.

The apartheid context is distinctive because it combines a series of elements. Black political leaders in surrounding countries identify directly with the victims of apartheid. Also, the economic, social, and cultural stratification of South Africa is both a precursor and a legacy of the colonial period. The retention of a white-dominated bastion of power and wealth on the African continent has further antagonized black African governments and the Third World generally. The United States, with its own domestic struggle to move from slavery to racial equity, and the Soviet Union, with a clear anticolonial, anti-Western line on African issues, are united in opposing apartheid. A virtually universal consensus has formed in opposition to apartheid, but, as I shall discuss later, there is still much disagreement on what to do about it. The consensus has been reinforced by a steady stream of actions in the United Nations and other international forums, especially those organized by Third World countries. The Convention on the Elimination of Racial Discrimination, drafted in 1965, embodies this minimum consensus on opposition to apartheid in a widely endorsed legal form.

It is fair to wonder whether or not this consensus is opportunistic, making South Africa, in effect, a scapegoat. Is it fair to single out South Africa when racial discrimination has been rampant in other societies in the world? For instance, Asians in East Africa, especially in Uganda, have been deprived of their wealth and livelihood after generations of residency and in some cases have been forced to emigrate. Victims of genocide, as in Burundi or East Pakistan, have received very little attention from outsiders even though their fate has been worse than the victims of apartheid.

Such arguments are valid, and yet largely irrelevant from a descriptive and normative point of view. First, objective observers agree that apartheid involves a deprivation of basic rights and dignities that qualifies as a severe offense. But second, the racism associated with apartheid is not a minor and trivial case of racism. In sum, the classification of a human rights violation as severe appropriately draws on political factors, including perceptions, priorities, and the willingness to act. For these reasons apartheid deserves to be treated as a continuing, severe violation of human rights; and the fact that it mobilizes and unites the international community creates a greater opportunity to act. That is, while the emphasis on apartheid may be arbitrary in relation to other forms of racism, it helps establish a situation where it might be possible to do something.

Type C: Large-Scale, Official Terrorism

When a government systematically engages in terror to maintain its political control or intimidate its opposition, this activity can be defined as large-scale official terrorism. It differs from genocide in that it is a means of directly exerting authority rather than a campaign of persecution directed against ethnically distinct elements. Of course, as in Hitler's

Germany or Amin's Uganda, there may be a generalized terrorist style of rule that complements official genocide.

Official terror can take many forms. Its essential character has to do with killing, maiming, and torturing members of the society without due process of law. It may be carried out by elements of the state apparatus—e.g., the former National Security Information and Security Organization in Iran, known in the Shah era as the SAVAK, or the Korean Central Intelligence Agency (KCIA) in South Korea—or by paragovernmental "death squads"—e.g., in Argentina during the period of General Videla's rule. Official terror may also occur in the brutal repression of peaceful labor and student activity or other citizen demonstrations—e.g., Thailand in 1975.

The scale and persistence of official terror are significant. A regime that relies on continual terror places itself in a special subcategory of aggravated offender. For instance, Amin in Uganda, Masie Nguema Biyogo in Equatorial Guinea, or Somoza in Nicaragua relied on persistent terror as an ongoing feature of their regimes. In certain crisis situations, a government may resort temporarily to large-scale terror, as Cambodia did in 1975 when it resettled its urban population in the countryside. The events in Cambodia remain obscure and controversial, although in recent months the scale and scope of terror seem to have diminished, if not altogether disappeared. In contrast, Stalin's regime became cumulatively more and more terroristic. Sometimes official terror is associated with a regime in which a single individual dominates the government for an indefinite period of time. However, the generals who have run Brazil since 1964 have relied on the periodic use of terror whenever such tactics seemed relevant to the maintenance of their political authority.

Private terror directed against the civilian population is also a severe violation if its perpetration can be reasonably attributed to a political entity, such as a government or liberation movement. If the conduct occurs in a situation of war, then it also belongs to type G: large-scale war crimes, which will be discussed later. Certainly several of the Palestinian liberation factions and their leaders are guilty of terrorism against civilians. Governments that support terroristic activities—by granting asylum and lending support to perpetrators—join in the violation as accessories. Qaddafi in Libya has played such a role in the mid-1970s, especially in relation to Palestinian terrorism.

Another type of accessory is a state that grants terrorist organizations a base of operations. This may occur in a strong state eager to cause trouble elsewhere; the auspices and encouragement given to anti-Castro operations of the Cuban exiles by the United States during the 1960s illustrate this pattern. It may also occur in a state too weak to assert full sovereign control over its territory, as has arguably been the case in Jordan and Lebanon in relation to the Palestinian Liberation Organization (PLO) at various stages of the Arab-Israeli conflict. The point here is that governmental encouragement or inability to exercise control may produce a de facto situation of large-scale official terrorism that would qualify as a severe violation of human rights.

This category of severe offenses also includes governmental policies that support various domestic groups. The evidence suggests that elements within the Argentinian government have encouraged right-wing ultras to pursue "leftists" by terroristic means, including kidnapping and murder, with the assurance that such acts will be ignored by the police. If the pattern is widespread, and in Argentina hundreds of deaths and disappearances appear to have resulted from such means, the large-scale official terror can be said to occur even though it is not directly committed by government operatives.

Type D: Totalitarian Governance

The special feature of totalitarian rule is the comprehensiveness of governmental interference in the full range of civil, political, and cultural rights. Totalitarian rule does not have to extend to large-scale terrorism or genocide, as it did in Hitler's Germany and Stalin's Russia. It may involve merely an efficient bureaucratic apparatus that rigidly constrains freedoms of thought and action, the sort of polity so vividly portrayed in George Orwell's *1984*.

Totalitarian governance can mean centralization of authority that does not necessarily imply a dictator. With modernization comes the expansion of the state role. In the process most governments become more efficient and almost automatically acquire a totalitarian potential, that is, the means and rationale to stifle dissent and opposition. If pressures from below on consensual and moderate government continue to grow, as the outbursts of terrorism seem to suggest, then we can expect many currently democratic polities to become vulnerable to what Jean-François Revel has recently described as "the totalitarian temptation."[14]

Some Eastern European countries (e.g., Albania, Bulgaria, and East Germany) appear to be administered in a totalitarian fashion. Whether it is appropriate to characterize the Soviet Union as totalitarian in the Brezhnev era is a matter of controversy among experts. Surely it has totalitarian features, including the bureaucratic insistence on regulating virtually all features of society, on refusing to open channels for dissent, and on employing extralegal forms of mistreatment against political prisoners. However, moderating trends are visible, including less harsh repressive tactics and greater toleration of grass-roots autonomy in civic and regional affairs.

In a totalitarian state the pattern of rule is difficult to transform from within or without, especially if the regime can solve the succession problem. As post-Franco Spain and post-fascist Portugal suggest, it is sometimes possible to end patterns of highly authoritarian rule rather bloodlessly, but the bureaucratic apparatus of repression never fully penetrated several major domains of activity within the Spanish and Portuguese societies. Also, it must be admitted that the threat of a recurrence of repressive rule has not been fully removed, especially in Portugal.

Type E: Deliberate Refusal to Satisfy Basic Human Needs

Unlike types A through D, the deliberate refusal to satisfy minimum human needs is a category of human rights offense that is not yet generally accepted or fully understood as a violation. To contend that individuals are entitled, as a matter of human rights, to have their basic human needs satisfied is tantamount to insisting that governments—and the international community—are legally and morally compelled to perform, at least to a minimum degree, as a "welfare state."

An obligation like this is nowhere spelled out. However, the constituent rights are endorsed in the Universal Declaration, and further specified in the International Covenant on Economic, Social, and Cultural Rights. In Article 23(1) of the Universal Declaration, for instance, "the right to work" is affirmed, and Article 25(1) details "the right to a standard of living adequate for the health and well-being of himself and of his family, including food, clothing, housing, medical care and necessary social services, and the right to security in the event of unemployment, sickness, disability, widowhood, old age or other lack of livelihood in circumstances beyond his control." Article 24 even affirms "the right to rest and leisure."[15] Whether or not they are embodied in a formally binding legal instrument, it seems correct as a matter of customary international law and of international morality to regard such prescriptions as emergent authoritative norms.[16]

The satisfaction of basic human needs is beginning to be seen as a realizable goal. It is possible to view the agitation around the new international economic order as a movement to assure that individual governments are provided with the capabilities to satisfy the basic needs of their citizens. The emphasis of the World Bank and other international aid and lending efforts in recent years has been upon policies designed to help the poorer countries and the poorest strata in these countries. Furthermore, on practical and moral grounds, leaders of rich countries have acknowledged the obligation to work toward the rapid elimination of world poverty. Recent research strongly suggests that most Third World countries possess the resources to eliminate poverty and satisfy basic human needs if their policy makers were so inclined.[17]

To speak of basic needs as human rights refers to the minimum requirements for sustaining physical life, that is, health, food, housing, clothing, work, literacy. Broader conceptions of basic needs are often affirmed, but I think it would be difficult to ascribe authoritative status to them as "rights."[18] These minimum requirements of physical and social well-being can be regarded as "rights" at this stage, and the deliberate failure of a government to satisfy these minima, especially when it is in a position to do so, is a severe violation. Such patterns of violation are widespread, and can be discerned in a preliminary way by the disparities between GNP and the innovative Overseas Development Council's Physical Quality of Life Index (PQLI). The PQLI is based on calculating relative achievement in life expectancy, infant mortality, and literacy.[19] Johan Galtung and others have described official policies that lead to mass misery and short life expectancy as "structural violence" to accentuate the severe character of the governmental practices.[20]

In effect, then, a government that maintains an economic situation in which a small proportion of the population gains most of the wealth while a large majority subsists at or below the poverty line is guilty of violating this category of human rights. Furthermore, as governments are increasingly expected to meet the basic needs of their citizens, there is a tendency to demand results in militant terms. To neutralize such demands and also mobilize the society for growth-oriented development can lead governments to employ repressive techniques.[21] On the other side, meeting basic human needs may also lead a government to rely on terrorism to achieve its goals. A revolutionary elite may feel it must engage in large-scale terror to achieve the transition to a needs-oriented society. In the early years of Mao's rule in China, for instance, many dispossessed landlords, merchants, and privileged elements from the prior social order were killed.[22]

The deprivation of basic human needs can be used to achieve explicit political ends, such as the denial of food in settling an ethnic conflict. Characteristically, the central government may deprive an ethnically distinct antagonistic component of its population of food so as to starve it into submission, as has been alleged in several African interethnic conflicts—the Ibos in Nigeria and the Somalis and Eritreans in Ethiopia. If this deprivation results in the decimation of the target group, it amounts to genocide. Given the prevalence of ethnic conflict, it is important in the context of human rights to become more attentive to those national situations where a government deliberately deprives an ethnic group of basic needs in order to impose its will.

Although it is possible to identify a basic human needs violation by reference to "waste" or a highly disproportionate income distribution, there is no consensus yet on the proper economic and social policies for a given society to adopt. Some commentators have argued that only socialism can meet mass needs in a nonindustrialized country that is experiencing rapid population growth.[23] Others have endorsed capitalist approaches based on order, growth, and a corporative state to assure the well-being of all societal sectors. It should also be appreciated that Hitler's Germany and Mussolini's Italy did well by needs criteria as compared to their more moderate predecessors—e.g., standard of living of workers improved in both countries.[24] At this time, the choice of *means* to achieve basic needs is a matter of national discretion, as long as the policies do not violate other standards of human rights.

Type F: Ecocide

The protection of the environment is understood increasingly to be vital for human well-being, if not survival. The Stockholm Conference of 1972 on the Human Environment formulated a Declaration of Principles that was endorsed with some modification by the United Nations General Assembly. The protective principles of this declaration are an emergent area of international law, mainly perceived at this time as a series of declaratory duties imposed on governments. Human dependence on environmental quality is becoming so evident that it seems assured that it will begin to be treated as a dimension of human rights in the 1980s.

Suppose a government carries on atmospheric tests of nuclear devices despite the evidence that harm results to foreign societies, or continues to permit use of aerosol sprays despite indication of global ozone depletion, or licenses unseaworthy tankers, or orbits unspaceworthy satellites, or disposes of toxic wastes in the oceans. These "offenses" are not traditionally dealt with in human rights instruments, but they involve official conduct that seriously endangers the life, health, and serenity of current and future generations. The notion of human rights is incomplete to the extent that it fails to encompass those forms of deliberate behavior that produce serious environmental damage.

This set of concerns is not an exotic or marginal category. In an increasingly interdependent global setting, where elaborate technology is used and where even higher levels of industrialization are contemplated, environmental quality is a critical dimension of human dignity that may have a significant impact on development, and even survival, of mankind. At minimum, this reality should be acknowledged in the strongest possible normative terms.

Type G: War Crimes

As with Type F, it is not yet usual to consider war crimes as a violation of human rights.[25] However, it is an artificial exclusion. Michael Walzer, in his recent comprehensive book on war crimes, grounds his concern with justice in wartime on a human rights argument.[26] The obligation of states to refrain from aggression and abhorrent practices in war arises from the concept of the sanctity of innocent life. Rules against causing unnecessary suffering and using cruel tactics and weapons are based on a human rights rationale that regards even combatants as protected persons under certain conditions.

The last rationale can be most vividly observed, perhaps, in relation to legal, moral, and political efforts to safeguard prisoners of war. The reality of this concern was dramatically expressed on behalf of the several hundred American pilots held captive by North Vietnam during the

Vietnam War. The treatment of these prisoners became a major issue of domestic politics and influenced the peace negotiations.[27]

A government that initiates war for aggressive purposes, that subjects a civilian population to inhumane treatment and that wages war without regard for legal norms is guilty of severe violations of human rights. "Aggression" is difficult to define objectively, as are the facts surrounding war policies. The notion of "military necessity," as well as the behavior of other belligerents, may also complicate the task of assessing whether a severe pattern of violation has occurred.

In the backgrounds is the status of modern strategic doctrine, particularly as associated with nuclear deterrence. The deterrent posture is based on a threat to inflict indiscriminate devastation on enemy populations, with deaths numbering in the tens of millions in the event of general nuclear war. It also implies causing collateral damage through radioactive fallout on the peoples and environments of nonbelligerent third countries. In the 1980s the question may well be posed as to whether or not governments that base their military security on threats to use nuclear weapons violate fundamental human rights.

What Can Be Done about Severe Violations?

Because an intervenor may not be trustworthy, because the effects of intervention may be damaging to the people of the target society, and because interventionary precedents once set are likely to be extended to more dubious instances, it is plain that interventionary approaches to human rights violations, however severe, should be recommended with extreme caution. This caution is reinforced by the structure and history of international relations. In addition to these concerns about the *wisdom* of intervention are the problems connected with its *feasibility*. However severe the violation of human rights, there is no reason on that basis alone to expect responsive action at the international level. The fundamental limits of action are set by the realization that it would normally require a significant mobilization of capabilities to intervene effectively from outside, that successful intervention would often require military means and include the establishment of new governments, and that geopolitical interests often insulate the violator from pressure. In effect, there are three sets of inhibitions:

1. Insufficient motivation to devote the resources required for successful intervention
2. Unwillingness to protect human rights through coercive intervention in internal affairs
3. Mixed geopolitical interests that preclude the formation of an enforcement consensus

In addition, intervention is a problematic remedy. If it is nonmilitary, for example in the form of sanctions, then it generally seems ineffectual. If it takes military forms, then it amounts to a virtual declaration of war against the target state. Even unpopular regimes can mobilize against outside intervention, and hence the costs of intervention may be large and its effects may be indefinite. For this reason, interventionary response confined to the territory of the human rights violator seems implausible no matter how severe the outrage. If there is an active domestic resistance to the violator, or if the government is very small and within the sphere of influence of a large state, then a humanitarian intervention may occasionally occur. An example of the latter is the official American impulse to encourage, or at least acquiesce, in plans for the assassination of General Trujillo, the leader of the Dominican Republic from 1930 to 1961.[28]

Responses to Genocide, Racism, Terrorism, and Totalitarianism

Several considerations always bear on the possibility of doing something about a severe pattern of human rights violation:

1. *Prudence.* Does the response seriously endanger more valued policy goals, including world peace, the integrity of alliance relations, and the protection of foreign economic interests?

2. *Motivation.* Do some important government(s) favor taking coercive action designed to put pressure on the violative regime? If so, that usually presupposes either a strong domestic constituency that identifies directly with the victims or strong geopolitical grounds for eliminating the regime and its leaders.

3. *Leverage.* Is the target polity relatively weak, small, and especially vulnerable to nonmilitary coercive measures (e.g., boycotts, embargoes directed at particular products, discontinuance of outside aid)?

4. *Mandate.* Do the coercive measures have the support and authorization of the world community as a whole as well as the backing of most governments in the region? Have the facts of the case been verified by independent and objective sources, especially by respected NGOs in the human rights field? Has the target regime any significant transnational support?

5. *Legitimacy.* Do the claims advanced have the backing of widely accepted norms of international law and morality? Has a reasonable effort been made over a sufficient period of time to induce compliance by persuasive means?

To cross the hurdles above is very difficult. Indeed, it is difficult to identify a real world situation in which these various conditions have been generally satisfied. Only in conjunction with other elements can one imagine that severe violations of human rights will be removed by international action:

● *Independent provocation.* Has the violator also infringed vital interests of foreign states by seizing territory, withholding critical raw materials, confiscating foreign investments, repudiating debts, interfering with international navigation:

• *Alien victims.* Do the persons harmed owe allegiance to or have juristic and emotional ties with powerful outside states (e.g., execution or torture of foreign nationals)?

In these special sets of circumstances the basis for coercive action may exist even if the conditions set forth above are not entirely satisfied. At best, the parallel rationale of human rights violations helps shape the cover story, although it does not account for the real interventionary motivation. The struggle against Nazism and fascism during World War II was mainly geopolitical in character, and only incidentally did the Allied victory result in ending patterns of severe violations of human rights on the part of the defeated countries. Although it is true that as the extent of Nazi crimes became known in the course of the war, the human rights motivation seemed to grow more integral to the war effort as well as help to shape postwar arrangements. The nuclear dimension of post-1945 world politics greatly reinforces prudence in foreign policy and makes it even more difficult to organize coercive action to overcome human rights deprivations.

Nevertheless, even in the current international setting, there are several situations of severe deprivation in which international interventionary responses are relevent. To illustrate the approach, consider in schematic form the impulses and the inhibitions toward intervention in the Ugandan (Amin) and South African (apartheid) cases. The fact that Amin was overthrown in 1979 as a consequence of a Tanzanian invasion does not invalidate the analysis of factors relevant to forming a policy toward a tyrant of this sort. Other such tyrannies exist, and some of the same considerations apply.

The Ugandan Case

The challenge: genocidal elimination of specific tribal elements from positions of influence and a more generalized reign of terror that had been associated with the regime of Idi Amin Dada.

The following is an assessment of whether conditions existed prior to Amin's overthrow to support coercive measures, and if so, at what level of coerciveness:

• *Prudence.* There was no reason to suppose that coercive measures to topple the Amin regime would have endangered world peace, although they might have raised East-West and North-South tensions if the intervention had been an American military initiative or otherwise predominantly conceived, staffed, and supported by NATO countries. There might, in other words, have been geopolitical costs of short duration. Less coercive measures, such as a boycott of Uganda's coffee crop, although of smaller magnitude, might have had a similar impact.

If there was no reasonable vision of how intervention would have improved the overall situation in Uganda, it would have been imprudent to intervene. Suppose intervention had been likely to unleash a civil war or resulted in Amin being replaced by a military leader who embarked on a new campaign of large-scale terror. Prudence involves having reasonable assurance that a positive precedent will emerge, both in relation to the form of intervention and its effect on the target society.

• *Motivation.* The United States and Western European governments seemed shocked and outraged by Amin's actions, which in part was a response to the antiwhite, anti-Christian, and antiforeign animus of his regime. Some African governments were critical, and Tanzania and Kenya gave varying degrees of support to anti-Amin plots. By and large, the Soviet and Arab blocs maintained normal and friendly relations with Amin, including providing some economic and military assistance.

• *Leverage.* Uganda is still a relatively small and weak country, but it had, under Amin, a considerable army with modern equipment for an African country of its size. It was economically shaky and allegedly vulnerable to boycotts, especially by purchasers of its coffee crop, a principal source of export earnings. Some speculated that even a unilateral boycott by the United States, buying one-third of Uganda's export crop, might have exerted significant pressure.[29]

• *Mandate.* There was no reasonable prospect for an explicit authorization of coercive measures by either the OAU or the United Nations. Offsetting this, however, was abundant, uncontradicted verification by human rights NGOs and respected individuals of the large-scale descent into barbarism that occurred during Amin's rule. Also, the hostility of Uganda's East African neighbors needs to be taken into account.

• *Legitimacy.* The documentation that provided the mandate also established a persistent pattern of transgressions in relation to the most basic and universal norms of international law and morality. There was also a long record of attempts to moderate Amin's policies through negotiation and persuasion. Therefore, even "aggression" by another state could easily be presented as "humanitarian intervention," and, as the Tanzanian invasion shows, other states and the world community as a whole were unlikely to treat Uganda as "a victim" of aggression.

• *Resistance.* It is difficult to assess the degree of organized resistance to Amin's regime. Several coup attempts had failed since his assumption of power, and there was firm evidence of widespread latent opposition. But there was also considerable intimidation on the part of Amin's regime. It seems necessary to conclude that there was no significant resistance movement operating within the country. Although opposition in the military sector could possibly have succeeded with a coup, without the support of popular resistance it can be argued that no significant intervention was possible short of the outright military invasion undertaken by Tanzania. Paradoxically, if there had been significant popular resistance, a coup would not have been necessary. This situation suggests that there must be evidence of a viable alternative to the present regime before outside intervention can accomplish its goals.

• *Performance.* With respect to development goals, Uganda's progress under Amin was poor—whether development is measured in conventional terms or by reference to satisfying the basic needs of the population as a whole. There were also reports of widespread corruption, stagnation, and a deteriorating international credit situation, although these elements did not distinguish Uganda from a large number of other Third World countries.

It seems evident that some of the conditions for international action were satisfied, but not all, and that no decisive inhibitions or coercieve measures were present. Therefore, the Uganda challenge fell into a gray area where no significant action against Amin was likely to occur without developments independent of the existing barbarism. That is, intervention was more likely if Uganda became involved in large-scale warfare with neighboring countries, especially if it could have been plausibly cast in the "aggressor" role, or if Amin had unleashed terror directed at the several hundred aliens still residing in Uganda, or if he had lent support to terrorism in foreign socities.

The South African Case

The challenge: systematic, official racism administered in brutal fashion by a government of the minority white race, involving economic, social, cultural, and political discrimination carried out in a harsh and humiliating manner. The severity of the racism entails the commission of other violations: genocide, terrorism, and totalitarian rule.

Do conditions exist to support coercive measures, and if so, what kind of coerciveness?

● *Prudence.* There is no reason to suppose that coercive measures would provoke a wider war, although there is every reason to expect South Africa's modern military and paramilitary forces to put up a ferocious fight. Given the advanced weaponry at South Africa's disposal and the sequestration of the African population in easily contained urban townships, a direct interventionary effort to topple the white regime would produce a major war and a great loss of life. There is also the possibility of conflict spilling over into neighboring countries. If armed intervention proceeded with wide backing, this would be a major step in cooperative human rights enforcement, although its execution might produce sharp competition among participants over shaping the orientation of the black successor regime. As time passes, the conditions for coercive measures may ripen, but the reluctance to intervene will increase if it is believed that South Africa possesses even a small arsenal of nuclear weapons. South Africa is a major supplier of uranium, and it might withhold this critical nuclear fuel from states that join in mounting a coercive movement.[30] However, South Africa, despite a large stockpile of emergency reserves, is relatively vulnerable to an oil embargo. The uncertainty of the effects of intervention in this case are also inhibiting: it is often claimed that the main victims of outside intervention would be the supposed beneficiaries—namely, the black majority. Also, insufficient coercion might result in intensifying repression or unleashing a prolonged period of civil strife and chaos.

● *Motivation.* The African countries are united in their hatred of apartheid, although several regional governments carry on normal trade relations with South Africa because their geographical position and extreme poverty create the practical necessity or because of opportunism. Third World countries, in general, dislike the South African system because it appears to be a white legacy of the colonial era and an alien presence within the Third World. The Soviet bloc and China dislike apartheid and its accompanying political and economic system because it is so avidly anti-Communist and closely linked to the United States and the United Kingdom in economic and strategic terms. It is a sober truth that apartheid has no supporters in international society, although South Africa has managed to work out some cooperative relations with other pariah states and commercial relations with some societies.

• *Leverage.* South Africa is strong, prosperous, efficient, and generally stable. Aside from oil it is virtually self-sufficient, and it is planning to replace oil with nuclear energy and coal as quickly and completely as possible. South Africa is likely to remain militarily far stronger than its African neighbors, even if the neighbors should combine forces. A credible military threat would either require superpower backing or would have to be based on a greatly augmented internal liberation movement. South Africa's prosperity could probably be curtailed by economic sanctions, but not its viability as a state. Only a direct large-scale military intervention could produce the external leverage needed to overthrow the regime.

• *Mandate.* The mandate to use pressure against South Africa has been expanding steadily over the past thirty years, and it is now a strong consensus in favor of censure, which is gradually intensifying in support of an enforcement effort. South Africa's pariah status has preoccupied organs of the United Nations for many years, culminating in 1977 with a Security Council decision to impose a boycott on arms sales and deliveries to South Africa. The United States and United Kingdom, with their extensive holdings and ties to the present regime, so far refuse to go farther. But if recent years are any indication, the pressure of Third World opinion will induce even the Americans and British to heighten their antiapartheid posture, although this course of action will also heavily depend on American and British politics. The strength of the mandate, together with the frustrations associated with mounting a coercive response, has led to an emphasis on such symbolic actions as a sports boycott. The concensus against South Africa is also reinforced by a series of reports by such respected human rights NGOs as Amnesty International and the International Commission of Jurists.[31]

• *Legitimacy.* The intensity and unanimity of the mandate has led the formal organs of the United Nations to move toward suspension of sovereign rights of the present government in South Africa and to deny it the benefit of the nonintervention norm. In effect, the constraint of the domestic jurisdiction article of the United Nations charter has been substantially cast aside by characterizing apartheid as a threat to international peace and security, thus opening the way to the application of sanctions and enforcement measures.

The underlying condemnation of South Africa's racist official policies seems fully justified. The abuses arising from them have been documented and clearly contravene basic prohibitions in international law and morality. An overwhelming consensus of governments and public attitudes supports this view. In addition, many years of negotiation and persuasion have failed to induce South African leaders to abandon or even modify apartheid.

• *Resistance.* Sporadic resistance from the black population has occurred for decades. With the advent of Afrikaaner rule the severity of repression has increased, but in recent years grassroots urban resistance has been rapidly evolving more and more into a movement. Predictably, this domestic challenge has led to a tightening of repressive mechanisms of control and intimidation by the government, which, in turn, escalates the international movement against apartheid. The student uprisings of 1976 and 1977 in Soweto and other black townships led to many excesses in the use of police power, as well as to the arrest, detention, and prison murder of a principal leader, Steve Biko, and a general crackdown on even moderate forms of opposition. The resistance movement seems likely to increase in the course of the next decade, although not without suffering setbacks.

Undoubtedly resistance prospects will be significantly affected by the postures of the front-line government policies and leaders, including especially those that emerge in the next few years in Namibia and Zimbabwe, as well as by the policies toward South Africa that prevail in London, Washington, Moscow, and Peking. In essence, the resistance movement will be influenced by the extent of material and psychic support given to liberation activities and by the degree of success that liberation groups have in building a unified movement that receives support within South Africa.

• *Performance.* South Africa's government has experienced a prosperous period of national development and has generally succeeded in running an efficient, stable state. There is no sign of diminished competence in these respects, but economic performance is down and not expected to recover altogether. In any event, the performance record of the government, however impressive, will not dissipate the political forces arrayed against the apartheid system.

The picture that emerges in the South African case is that despite the strong mandate there is no proximate prospect of a strong nonmilitary antiapartheid campaign without some further developments. These include another dramatic escalatory turn in the resistance/repression cycle of the past three years, the further buildup of an internal liberation movement, and a deepened commitment by critical frontline and Western governments to effective action.

If these developments occur and are not offset by other changes—a prolonged recession, preoccupation with strategic issues, rightward drift in American and British politics, or South African nuclear weaponry—then one can imagine the gradual strengthening of the international sanctions program. This program has been conceptualized in considerable detail, yet stops far short of proposing military measures.[32] Stimulating resistance activities may be sufficient to demoralize segments of the white population. Such a shift in the overall political climate might produce deepening splits in the ruling elite and create an accommodationist faction.

The South African case, especially, suggests the limits of what can be done even in the rare situation where all the principal global actors agree on the need to transform an intolerable situation. A determined elite with a firm grip on the governing process can usually exert effective control over the organization of social, political, and cultural life within national boundaries. It is sometimes possible to organize collective security arrangements to deter aggression across boundaries or endorse a geopolitical intervention in internal affairs, but it is far more difficult to mount interventionary operations that have the capabilities and the will required for a humanitarian mission designed to reshape the governing process of a foreign society. International boundaries remain high walls that will be rarely scaled for predominantly human rights objectives.

One general effect, attributable to the strength of the mandate against South Africa, is a tendency for Third World countries to link the overall credibility of Western complaints about human rights to what is done on the South African front. That is, the hue and cry about Amin's barbarism was viewed as "racist" in some quarters to the extent it was not coupled with an equivalently credible hue and cry from the same quarters about Pretoria's barbarism. This Third World attitude impedes the development of the mandate in most non-South African contexts and raises the stakes for the West in moving seriously against South Africa.

A Note on Basic Human Needs

Unlike other dimensions of human rights, the official cluster of obligations that characterize basic human needs imposes affirmative duties on governments. Very few societies, including many of the most prosperous, are organized in such a manner as to discharge these duties satisfactorily. Disagreements persist as to what adjustments would be required in a particular society, because vital economic issues relating to capital accumulation and income distribution are at stake. These matters have been traditionally considered to fall completely within the insulated realm of domestic jurisdiction. However, four sets of developments increasingly have "internationalized" this subject:

- Persistent and worsening poverty despite unprecedented rates of national, regional, and global economic growth.
- Greater emphasis on the responsibility of governments and international economic institutions to provide for basic human needs.
- An intergovernmental consensus supported by academic validation of claims that the international economy is biased against the Third World, which has produced demands for a new international economic order.
- Increased preference on the part of international lending institutions for development projects directed at satisfying basic human needs.

All governments affirm their commitment to the abolition of poverty as a matter of national policy, just as all governments deny the perpetration of any severe domestic violations of human rights. With basic human needs, however, there are no adequate procedures available to brand a particular government as a violator, although a persuasive consensus can often be obtained by media coverage, NGO reporting, and the activities of governments and international institutions.

Nevertheless, effective responses are possible. The first is an increased emphasis on development assistance programs that are oriented to the satisfaction of human needs in recipient countries. This kind of targeted assistance can be objectionable, however, if it assumes a paternalistic, interventionary, or ideological character that attempts to usurp domestic judgments on development priorities.

The second is international economic restructuring that emphasizes equity. However, a fairer division of global wealth and income among countries does not assure fairer allocations within countries.

The two responses raise complex questions of economic and political feasibility. Some development specialists have suggested that a rechanneling of overseas development assistance and modest increases in aid over a fifteen- to twenty-five-year period could do the job if some domestic reforms occurred. Alternatively, others propose that domestic transfers from the upper ten percent to the bottom forty percent of two percent of annual income would generate sufficient purchasing power among the poor to end poverty.[33] Such estimates suggest that the task of eliminating poverty is easily manageable in resource terms even without using some of the more than three hundred billion or so dollars of the annual expenditures that go for military purposes.

Other approaches have emphasized the feasibility and desirability of needs-oriented development strategies that give a developing society the capability of self-sufficiency in meeting its basic needs over time as well as at a given time.[34] Whether ruling elites in either North or South can be induced to move in these directions seems doubtful for a variety of reasons that cannot be dealt with here.[35] Also, to assess the basic needs challenge in terms of resources is misleading: a variety of bureaucratic and societal rigidities would make it unlikely that a decision to transfer and reallocate resources to eliminate poverty would work efficiently. The United States and other advanced industrial societies have witnessed "trickle-up" phenomena whenever assaults on poverty have been attempted without also transforming underlying societal structures. The point is that unlike the coercive responses associated with other severe deprivations of human rights, persuasive tactics can play a major role in the basic needs context.

A Note on Environmental Harm and Ecocide

Activities in this category remain in limbo. The grounds for concerted action seem clearest where the causation is clear. If country X impairs health, destroys life, or harms the environment in countries Y and Z, or more widely—in a region, the oceans, or the globe as a whole—then it is obviously at fault. If evidence mounts that cancer arises from increased radiation and a particular government engages in radiation-producing activities, then this is "ecological aggression." If the victims are geographically dispersed far beyond the territory of the country producing the pollutant, then the more traditional premises for recourse to force are present. The appeal to humanitarian impulses can be buttressed in this case by more elemental considerations of self-preservation.

However, no current situation is of sufficient magnitude to allege ecocidal behavior comparable to the severe violations of human rights that have occurred in Uganda or South Africa. The most comparable "case" may be the Chinese nuclear tests, which pose radiation hazards for inhabitants and animals in the Northern Hemisphere. If further medical evidence of harm is established and more Chinese testing takes place, then an international campaign is likely to be mounted, and support in some circles would be likely to emerge for the use of coercive measures to prevent additional nuclear weapons tests of this sort.

Environmentalists and NGOs can build a greater understanding of environmental rights as a key sector of human rights and generate pressures to translate this understanding into a revised Universal Declaration of Human Rights and a new Covenant on Environmental and Ecological Rights. Such efforts could also focus on specific dangers, such as reactors on space satellites, and seek prohibitions based on the global interest in environmentally sound and sustainable patterns of behavior. At the current stage, fact-finding efforts could make a major contribution. As many individuals now suspect, we may be grossly underestimating the environmental risks and harm associated with various technological innovations.

A Note on War Crimes

This category is also seemingly exotic in the context of human rights. As with ecocide, there is useful work to be done by individuals and NGOs. This includes the articulation of norms, through treaties and international legal customs, that endow the law of war with dimensions grounded in the rights of peoples, governments, institutions, and corporations. Especially important in this regard are procedural initiatives and commissions of inquiry that are secure from governmental interference.[36] By and large, governments are too directly implicated to provide effective leadership in this domain.

Conclusions

On the basis of this discussion some general conclusions can be drawn:

1. The general inability to deal with severe violations of human rights is one of the principal weaknesses of the prevailing system of world order.

2. This weakness is structurally linked to the distribution of power and autonomy among sovereign states and cannot be overcome without the emergence of a new system of world order.[37]

3. However, this structural constraint exhibits considerable variance. It depends on the character of the violator, on how the target regime's survival meshes with geopolitical patterns, and on the orientation of the governments proposing a coercive response to a given human rights challenge.

4. The prevailing world order has a high tolerance for severe violations of human rights, especially if the harmful effects are confined within territorial limits.

5. The prevailing world order, even when significant political actors are aroused by infringements, has a weak potential for effective action against the target polity.

6. Effective international mobilization against a violator usually occurs for reasons largely independent of the denial of human rights.

7. Effective internal mobilization, if it occurs, depends largely on the indigenous will and capabilities of opposition forces, perhaps encouraged and marginally reinforced by international support.

8. The organs of the United Nations, in the event of a substantial consensus, can contribute to the mobilizing process. But they are limited by geopolitical rivalry and partisanship, and as a consequence, the United Nations response to severe violations has been mainly symbolic and highly selective.

9. Partly to offset United Nations weaknesses, human rights and environmental NGOs as well as a variety of private groups and even individuals can play useful roles, especially by establishing the time when violations have occurred, mobilizing public opinion, and exerting informal influence.

Future Prospects and Speculations

Each severe violation is distinctive, setting its particular constraints on external pressures and suggesting special points of leverage. This quality of distinctiveness, evident in my comparison of the Ugandan and South African cases, makes it seem of dubious value to speculate about the future in more general and systemic terms. However, some trends seem likely to affect the structural dynamics of the state system in ways relevant to human rights.

The "Hard State" Hypothesis

The "hard state" hypothesis refers to an aggregation of government powers that insulate the state from outside pressures and enable it to maintain internal order in situations of rising internal pressure. Southern demographic growth, together with frustration about the possibilities of achieving domestic or international goals of equity in the distribution of wealth and income, will induce more generalized patterns of severe repression and the neglect of people living at or below subsistence levels. Anomie, together with disintegration of economic growth, will lead to severe stress and the possible decay of democratic polities (the ungovernability hypothesis) in the liberal societies of the industrial North. An era of extreme statism will ensue with no serious will or capability to overcome human rights violations as more governments will feel implicated or preoccupied and thus may restrict NGOs and individuals concerned about human rights.

In such a future there will be an even greater tolerance of human rights violations than existed in the late 1970s and less of a capacity to respond. The stability of this system will depend on whether it is able to prevent war, economic depression, and ecological breakdown. Such a hard state system has been emerging over the past decade and is likely to establish its preeminence still further in the early 1980s.

The "Moderated System" Hypothesis

This system depends on a reduction of tensions along both the East-West and North-South axes of conflict, with moderation and liberalization prevailing in the domestic arenas of the most significant states. This process could be reinforced by an increasing permeability of the state to measures that assure the achievement of minimum standards of individual economic, social, and political well-being—a drift, in effect, toward an international welfare state. Such moderation is difficult to envision without several concurrent developments: movement toward a new international economic order; an abatement of the strategic arms race; a loosening of security alliances; successful large-scale international cooperation on issues such as oceans, money, and emergency food reserves; the reduction of unemployment and inflation to "acceptable" levels; the elimination of terrorism in the advanced industrial countries; the spread of needs-oriented development approaches in the Third World; increasing acknowledgment and practice of democratic rights in leading Communist countries; and the rapid growth of feelings of human solidarity as a dimension of increasing interdependence. The mere enumeration of preconditions suggests that this optimistic projection for the 1980s is unlikely to take shape.

However, in the happy event that the improbable should occur, a more favorable climate for responding to severe violations of human rights would be present; indeed, the more cooperative premises of such a world order evolution would make severe violations less likely to occur. Those that arise would probably not be insulated by superpower rivalries, which we presuppose to be muted in this hypothesis. Thus, it may be easier to shape a consensus and mobilize the international community for appropriate norm-oriented action. In this climate it seems reasonable to assign greater legitimacy, leverage, and capabilities to the United Nations system. Perhaps a United Nations police force could be established that might, under very carefully restricted circumstances, carry out human rights missions. Such a force could, for example, rescue hostages, safeguard tribal minorities, or release unjustly confined prisoners. In addition, human rights NGOs would probably flourish in a wider range of countries. They might be accorded more significant tasks in relation to fact-finding, mediation, and even implementation procedures, and provided with fiscal security and independence.

If the number of governments relying on repressive rule were to decline, then those that engaged in depraved behavior would be easier to isolate. In other words, although an international system with such moderate features could not guarantee the protection of human rights in every instance, it would probably respond more rapidly and effectively to the sorts of challenges posed currently by the Amin regime in Uganda and apartheid in South Africa. Whether it could also deal in an effective manner with severe violations in countries such as Iran and Indonesia is more problematic.

Furthermore, the spread of equity within and among states would provide positive examples of how to cope with modern socioeconomic pressures in a humane way. In a moderated atmosphere, where humanistic concerns are more successfully protected, repressive regimes would feel more isolated than they do in the current global setting and would be more inclined to avoid depending so blatantly on cruel, repressive tactics.

Also, the shifts in international influences would be important—superpowers and other principal states would generally accept the dynamics of national self-determination and not seek to impose antidemocratic political solutions that promote their geopolitical interests. And aid and capital flows would be contingent on the minimum requirement that the recipient government refrain from any severe violation of human rights.

Regimes with governing styles as deviant as those of Uganda or South Africa are probably not susceptible to major reform despite major changes in the global setting. Even in this highly optimistic projection, the state would remain the dominant organizing entity in international life throughout the 1980s, and thus it would be difficult to change significantly the policy of a medium or large-sized territorial sovereign government without overthrowing it. Powerful states that violate human rights might be more of a pariah minority than is currently the case. But unless they engaged in "aggression" or highly provocative foreign policies, it is unlikely that their domestic policies, however objectionable, would be effectively challenged from without, especially if they were significant participants in the world economy. The fate of certain aboriginal people, such as the Aché Indians in Paraguay, could only be protected against genocidal dangers if human rights NGOs were mobilized in their support and if the strengthening sense of human community embraced in a serious way the fate of such victims.

Conclusions

There are many possible intermediate variations on the course of the 1980s that could be put forward. It seems to me, however, that there is a polarizing of future possibilities, and that the two projections above represent the most plausible central lines of evolution for the world order system in the next decade. Current trends suggest strongly that the hard state hypothesis is much more likely to characterize the future than the moderate system hypothesis. The balance of available evidence points to the intensification of statism, which means that fewer governments will run their countries in a humane fashion, and a callous form of noninterventionism will increasingly inhibit international responses to human rights violations.

Beyond Moderation: The Grounds of Human Governance

As I have argued, even in the most optimistic view of the 1980s, territorial supremacy will insulate severe violations of human rights from international control. The state system imposes structural constraints that set firm limits on global policy. Overcoming these limits presupposes the emergence of a new world order system with enough central guidance capabilities and normative commitment to assure minimum standards of behavior throughout the world. What might this new world order be?

I think that it is most unlikely to suppose that a process of transformation will occur prior to the next century. Change in a world order system is not gradual, but rather occurs in convulsive jolts over a prolonged period, often a matter of several centuries. The "next" world order system is already taking shape within the existing one, although this growth process is obscured by the persistence of the present one. Political ecosystems, like natural ones, tend to maintain their familiar features until the dynamic of transformation has carried so far as to verge on collapse. Hence, system erosion is difficult to identify until long after it occurs.

In world order terms, it seems useful to consider World War I as the time when a new system began to take shape. Because of the destructiveness of that conflict many people were convinced that some reorganization of international society was necessary to avoid another war. Indeed, the creation of the League of Nations, although woefully inadequate to achieve such a goal, was a response to public pressures for some intergovernmental framework devoted to safeguarding world peace. This framework has evolved during the intervening decades. Its contours are indefinite as yet, and likely to remain controversial until a century or so after its dominance becomes evident. This subsidiary evolution has been complemented by the further extension of statism, especially as a consequence of the collapse of colonialism and the effort to build states strong enough to rule effectively and resist outside interferences. Further advances in the technology of war and the global dispersion of sophisticated military equipment has made war even more destructive. Also, the inadequacy of "freedom" as a managerial premise for the oceans has stimulated an expansion of statist control in the form of a massive seaward extension of territorial sovereignty.

The growing constituency for the next world order system is due in part to a deep fear that statism is leading the human race toward a dismal, dangerous future that it is catastrophe prone and lacking in the traditions of capabilities needed to safeguard the peoples of the earth and their descendants. The inverse of such dark forebodings is a visionary contemplation of a future that actualizes spiritual ideals of human unity in the arenas of culture, economics, and politics. In effect, this dualistic interpretation of the human situation has been well embodied in René Dumont's phrase "utopia or else."[38]

In opposition to the "state" as a juristic, teritorial center of military and bureaucratic power is the notion of "community" as an experiential, nonterritorial nexus of affinity and value. Whereas the state is set off by boundaries from other states and acts in the field of international relations, the community is bounded by nonterritorial fields of affinity and affection and has no necessary bureaucratic presence. The notion of "global community" is the animating ideal of an alternative world order system, leading to a dialectical emphasis on the unity of the whole and on the dignity of the individual and distinct substatal human groups. This tension between particular and general is, in essence, the proper foundation for the appreciation and protection of human rights. It implies that there would be no territorial enclave that could flout global community norms.

If this positive image of a new world order were ever realized, the occurrence of severe violations of human rights would undoubtedly become an anomaly. Patterns of ethnic, regional, and class domination that are now so characteristic of the way states are structured would be necessarily dissipated in most societies as this new system crystallized. However, new patterns of conflict would undoubtedly arise so long as the scarcity of valued goods—territory, wealth, status, influence—was not handled by a community of perfect equals. To be sure, territorially strong units would persist for decades, and these might govern in ways that violate fundamental norms of human rights. It is difficult to guess how such residual elements of the old world order system would be handled as the balance of energy swung to the new system and the whole context of political relations in the world changed.

This discussion of global transformation seeks only to posit the view that overcoming the constraints of statism requires a drastically altered world order system that rests on a universalistic view of human identity, and generates appropriate forms for the distribution of power and authority. In fact, the cumulative historical drift is slowly undermining the present world order, based on territorial states, despite the paradoxical short-term show of strength of statist mechanisms.[39] Whether this process of statist decline will lead to a more humane world order system is quite problematic. The centralization of power, nonterritoriality, and the decline of the state do not necessarily entail any normative promise. The outcome could well be tyrannical, chaotic, exploitative, technocratic, demeaning, and unstable.

What can be said with some confidence, however, is that with regard to world order, the 1980s will be a period of learning and experimentation. The multifaceted struggle to uphold basic human rights will be an important way to convey the image of alternative systems of world order and to test their relative potency.

More specifically, stressing the problems of severe violations of human rights may help mobilize constituencies for varieties of global reform that extend to a wider range of issues, including those relating to economic, social, and ecological well-being. Bringing attention to the current situation will underscore how territoriality is serving as a shield for unjust and cruel polities and demonstrate that humane governance can only occur if conditions of security, fairness, and safety can be established at all levels of social organization and in all parts of the planet. Without progress at this fundamental level of human existence there is no way to prevent repressive methods of governance and little potential to correct severe violations. Ultimately, global guarantees of human rights are virtually synonymous with the quest for the next world order system.

The Algiers Declaration of the Rights of Peoples and the Struggle for Human Rights*

Economic and Political Structures of Domination

Contradictory tendencies are very pronounced in this period of world history. On the one side, unprecedented liberation has occurred; since the end of World War II the colonial system has collapsed and in its place have emerged a large number of independent states throughout Asia and Africa. Additionally, socialism has spread its influence almost everywhere, posing an increasingly formidable challenge to reactionary forms of political, social, and economic control. And these developments have contributed to a genuine movement against imperialism, as well as to an affirmation of the rights of people to national self-determination. The United Nations, especially in the General Assembly, has been a principal forum in which the demands for a more just international order have been crystallized in an authoritative manner.

On the dark side, however, have been a series of negative developments. Imperialism of the old direct, formal variety associated with colonial rule has been largely shattered, but often without an accompanying social revolution that displaces the feudal character of the indigenous society. The apparatus of government is controlled by these traditional elites, which have a natural affinity with the main imperial centers of power on a global level. As a consequence national independence has been frequently followed by the reestablishment of reactionary systems of domination often indistinguishable in their effects from colonialist rule. These domestic systems of domination are often reinforced by indirect techniques of external control. These indirect techniques seek to assure the well-being of multinational corporations; these techniques include the capacity and willingness to intervene in the internal affairs of foreign societies to assure the survival of the traditional social structure, as well as a favorable environment for investment and business operations.

The United States is the organizing, ideological center of this new form

*For text of Algiers Declaration, see appendix.

of imperialism, being dominant both with respect to the affiliation of the multinational corporations and with regard to paramilitary support systems required to assure their well-being. This commitment to a liberal international economy has been intertwined with an ideological struggle against the spread of communist influence and with a geopolitical struggle to contain Soviet influence and expansion (the combined effort being known as "the Cold War"). A principal effect of this American-directed system of domination has been to interfere with the dynamics of national self-determination; specifically, counterrevolutionary goals have been consistently pursued, thereby sustaining elite structures of economic and political power in Western Europe and thwarting more progressive tendencies in the Third World that were a natural sequel to the anticolonial independence movement. Additionally, elites with only narrow bases of popular support have been put and kept in power by means of force and intimidation.

Despite recent developments this basic structure persists. The outcome of the Vietnam War has temporarily inhibited direct American interventionary roles on behalf of forms of "stability" suitable for the growth of international capitalism. The Sino-Soviet split and other evidences of pluralism and rivalry within the socialist sector have undermined the image of a monolithic bloc directed from Moscow and/or Peking. As a result, the old rationale for America's global security role has been badly eroded and a new set of ideological justifications is needed that is persuasive to the American public, which is taxed to pay the costs of an imperial role. One adjustment in managerial tactics has been to entrust responsibility to regional superpowers (the Shah's Iran, Nigeria, Brazil, Indonesia) for securing a suitable political and economic atmosphere within their geographic area of influence.

The economic rise of Western Europe and Japan has led to intracapitalist rivalries, including competition for Third World resources and markets that complicates the task of maintaining a world economy that is conducive to the flow of capital and the domestic prosperity of its principal members. In this regard it is significant that the United States is now led by a president whose world view has been shaped to a considerable extent by an association with the Trilateral Commission, a transnational association of the ultraelite dedicated to liberal internationalism, especially the mutually beneficial coordination of monetary, trade, investment, and energy policies among the market economies of Europe, Japan, and North America. In essence, the uppermost political question facing the United States (and the West generally) is how to assure the future of international capitalism in the face of such developments as the outcome of the Vietnam War, the exposé of the CIA's cover interventionary role, the OPEC challenge, and the intensifying competition among the advanced industrial countries for sectors of international trade while avoiding the export of jobs to foreign settings, or worse, to foreign trading partners (e.g., the shift of the color television market from the United States and elsewhere to Japan).

It is essential to understand the human rights "offensive" mounted by the United States amid this background of economic and imperial concerns. First of all, the audience for such moralism is primarily domestic; above all else, the message on human rights is designed to reenlist the enthusiasm of the American people for an activist foreign policy and thereby overcome the disillusionment caused by Vietnam/Watergate. It is worth noting that the Carter cabinet and indeed the president himself do not have notable liberal credentials on international policy; rather, their prime identity is one of close association with the more internationally minded sectors of American business and with an active record of Cold War militancy that included support, and, in several key cases, major responsibility for the Vietnam policies (e.g., Cyrus Vance, James Schlesinger, Harold Brown). Second, the focus of concern about human rights has been overwhelmingly directed so far at the Soviet bloc, thereby helping to sustain domestic support for a high defense budget and appealing generally to the anticommunist segment of American public opinion. Third, the articulation of human rights sentiments seems like little more than a rhetorical posture that does not appear to have adverse behavioral consequences in promoting stability in the nonsocialist sector of the world system.

Despite these realities, the new emphasis on human rights by the United States is a significant development, and may lead to unanticipated effects. It adds legitimacy to initiatives by others who call attention to deprivations and seek to insist upon the real implementation of human rights goals. Beyond this, it inhibits recourse by the United States to some of the most blatant imperialist techniques and affiliations, especially outright support of fascist and quasi-fascist regimes. And finally, it may give some specific aid and comfort to victims of abuse, especially individuals, as well as strengthen the role of international public opinion in opposing drastic forms of repression such as torture. Nevertheless, it is important to appreciate that this renewed emphasis on human rights is not at all responsive to the *structural* or *systemic* circumstances that are the principal explanation for repressive patterns of governance in the world today. In fact, by and large, such official espousal of human rights is associated largely with an affirmation of political rights of dissent. These rights are important, but unless their denial is related to economic factors, misunderstanding arises. How can the United States, for instance, genuinely support political freedoms for the peoples of Latin America when the denial of those freedoms is primarily a consequence of efforts by ruling elites (with American backing) to create the kind of "stability" that will attract foreign capital (i.e., multinational corporations, banks, and international financial institutions)? The structural position of American interests overwhelms (and masks) on the level of *praxis* the sentimental position of lending support to the campaign for human rights. By and large these repressive structures are *functional* for present elites and can be transformed only through struggle.

The linkage of interests produces collaboration between governing elites on the *national level* and imperial elites on the *transnational level*. The rise of militarized patterns of governance in the Third World is directly associated with a crisis of capital accumulation that is afflicting those governments that depend on outside capital and that give priority to private enterprise in development planning. The nature of this crisis is shaped by the tension between rising claims on GNP by the popular sector (in the form of higher wages, greater social services, etc.) and securing savings and profits for the bureaucratic/industrial elite. Put differently, economic development capitalist-style requires the government to squeeze savings from the masses so as to preserve the dynamism of reinvestment and growth. But to squeeze the masses implies either their acquiescence or repression. By and large, political consciousness throughout the Third World has become more alert to injustice and to the indefensible character of distribution systems that confer affluence on the few and misery on the many.

Therefore, to sustain capitalist forms of development increasingly requires coercion, and indeed ever more and more drastic and pervasive forms of coercion as mass outrage mounts. The result has been to eliminate moderate forms of governance and to move increasingly in the direction of imposed rule bearing a military or militarist stamp.[1]

The explanation of these trends is associated with the impulse to achieve "discipline" and "stability." If social services expand, if strikes disrupt production schedules, if terrorism and political conflict create an atmosphere of uncertainty, if wage increases and inflationary spirals eat into returns on capital, then the investment prospects diminish. If investment prospects diminish, then the multinational corporations stay away, go elsewhere, and may even disinvest; international credit from IMF/ World Bank and private sources is more difficult to obtain. This general pattern has been accentuated by the increasing price of oil, which has made fragile economic and political systems more vulnerable to collapse by generating serious balance of payments and indebtedness problems. The trends have also been reinforced by the world recession dating from 1973, which has especially cut into Third World export markets. Fluctuations in commodity prices have also been a factor for several countries.

In the background, also, have been a series of ecological problems that have increased pressure on the governing process. Population growth throughout most of the Third World is at a level of two to three percent per year. Given declines in the death rate, the population is growing at an alarming rate; also the age structure is young. For instance, in Tunisia, a typical case, sixty percent of the population is under twenty-five years of age. In Mexico estimates are that each year before 1980 will have witnessed additions to the potential work force of 1,195,000 and that even if the more optimistic economic projections are realized not more than 300,000 new jobs will be available.[2] The emphasis on urban industrial development leads to a steady migration of the poor to the cities, producing crowding and explosive political possibilities. From the viewpoint of the governing elite, the rationale for "discipline" becomes overwhelming. And "discipline" is a code expression for denying the people of a country the elementary economic, social, and cultural freedoms that underlie a decent human existence.

The Chilean experience is also instructive, if discouraging. It suggests the futility of seeking an electoral or constitutional mandate to transform a given society in a direction oriented around the needs of the popular sector and the poor. With the reactionary apparatus of the state left intact, especially the police and the military, it is virtually impossible to implement a radical program of social change; such bureaucratic resistance is reinforced, as in the Chilean case, by interventionary maneuvers of great variety, ranging from CIA payments to active efforts to defame the Allende policies and governance and so block extensions of credit even by international lending institutions. The downfall of Allende and the Pinochet sequel strongly suggest the limits of legalist and liberal paths of reform in a context where the structures of authority and power remain tied to the imperatives of domestic and international class privilege.

Given this combination of domestic and international factors, it becomes clear that governments cannot be entrusted with the role of serving as the guardian of fundamental human rights. In this regard, the whole tradition of international law is to some extent regressive in the current era. Even the United Nations is an organization of states in which the interests of peoples are misleadingly assumed to be legitimately represented by governments. To the extent that the Third World is pledged to solidarity in its efforts to promote a new international economic order, it represents a coalition of capitalist and socialist governing structures. As such it seeks a *geographical redistribution* of wealth, power, and prestige. This movement does challenge imperialist control, but it does not purport to question the legitimacy of multinational corporations or of capitalist development strategies (except to the extent of a vague insistence on sovereign rights to regulate economic activity within territorial limits).[3] As such, it is only a partial response to the structural base of domination, and must be supplemented from more populist and socialist perspectives. My interpretation suggests that the widespread character of repression attendant upon the current stage of capitalist development makes it naive to expect any international institution composed of states to safeguard in a genuine way the fundamental rights of people. To be sure, even governments are responsive to certain pressures of public opinion and can unite to mount some pressure against special cases, especially against the remnants of colonialism as embodied in the racist regimes of southern

Africa. But the antiapartheid campaign, important as it is, involves mainly an item on the earlier agenda of antiimperialist struggle. The new agenda of antiimperialism can be legitimated to some extent within the United Nations and in various Third World forums; support can be mobilized, legitimacy of demands can be established, but implementation will depend heavily on popular struggles at the national level based on the realization that the protection of human rights requires the dissolution of domestic and international structures of domination and exploitation. A first step is for people to insist upon their own legitimacy as a source of rights, even as against the state.

Although the structural situation associated with the present phase of imperialism is the principal explanation of repression, it is not the only one. There are repressive tendencies evident also in a number of socialist countries in which Stalinist tendencies are evident to varying degrees. As Paul Sweezy and Harry Magdoff have recently noted, " . . . the treatment of democratic rights and liberties as something the working class has had to struggle for and cares about rather than as a mere cover for capitalist interests works to correct a long-standing and all-too widespread misinterpretation of the historical significance of the socialist movement."[4] Such a realization is critical for the successful spread of socialist ideas, especially in North America. And it is for this reason that ruling elites of market economies are so insistent in their allegations that Stalinist patterns are *inherent* in the exercise of power by socialists.

Unlike the structural trap of capitalism (which asserts that there is no other way than repression to sustain capitalist development), socialism offers a potentially humane basis of governance by relating the wealth and income of a country to the needs of its people. The only structural dangers may arise from a tendency in socialist politics to eliminate all populist "checks" on the abuse of power by the state and from unrestrained population growth that could prevent government from meeting even a socialist's needs. Eurocommunism, decentralizing developments in Cuba and China, and critical thinking within the Marxist tradition itself are encouraging signs that socialism can evolve in humane directions with respect to the political and cultural life of the people, and thereby add to the solid achievements already made with regard to economic and social life.

The Algiers Declaration of the Rights of Peoples

International human rights law has been state-centric. Governments have agreed on the standards, their degree of bindingness, and on whatever slight moves in the direction of enforcement have been taken. Such a feature of human rights law reflects the wider pattern of international law-making which tends to view state consent as a precondition to the formation of valid rules of law. In its traditional form each government had a veto over the formation of rules or standards contrary to its policy. In recent years, to some degree *consensus* has started to complement consent as a source of international norm-creation. The law-making stature of General Assembly resolutions, including the Universal Declaration of Human Rights, the resolution affirming the Nuremberg Principles, the Resolution on Permanent Sovereignty over Natural Resources, and the Declaration on the Granting of Independence to Colonial Countries and Peoples, have become milestones in what is properly perceived as the progressive development of international law. The role of consensus as a community-based source of law remains controversial and indefinite. From a strict positivist perspective, General Assembly action is only recommendatory; at the same time, "custom" has traditionally functioned as a source of law in international relations. The existence of a customary norm of international law is, to a certain extent, a matter of majority practice or consensus; the norm can become valid without the consent of every state. The question of norm-creation concerns the *authoritativeness* of norms, not their *effectiveness*. Nevertheless, it seems reasonable to conclude that endowing the General Assembly (and other organs of the world community) with law-making competence is a progressive step. It is especially effective in relation to a pariah state engaged in practices viewed as abhorrent by the vast majority of governments. The antiapartheid campaign has taken advantage of *consensus* to establish the authoritativeness of United Nations pronouncements vis-à-vis South Africa.

But consensus has limits. It can function only when *most* states are in agreement. If international society is split or if a large number of governments are guilty of objectionable policies, then it is impossible to mobilize a meaningful consensus. The principal threat to human rights at the present time derives from structural factors associated with the imperatives of capital accumulation by market-oriented economic systems. As a consequence, nonsocialist international bodies are incapable of forming a consensus that clearly diagnoses the links between multinational corporations, international credit procedures, and the systemic denial of fundamental human rights in the economic, social, political, and cultural spheres. It is taken for granted that institutions of global society constituted by governments are not in a position to do anything effective about a situation sustained by a large number of governments. Without even the pretense of a diagnosis, it is difficult to prescribe therapy. Indeed, the principal basis of repression is obscured by liberal declarations of commitment to human rights that fail to acknowledge structural factors. Put more explicitly, imperial centers of power are unable to pursue human rights without dismantling their economic and political structures of domination. But without those structures current levels of prosperity in the Trilateral countries could not be sustained. These structures are not fortuitous, but are connected with access to resources, markets, and the favorable flow of capital.

The Algiers Declaration of the Rights of Peoples, adopted on July 4, 1976, is responsive to this situation.[5] Its preamble, in highly condensed form, makes it evident that imperialist tactics and structure are the root cause of human misery, including a basic explanation of the general failure to realize those minimal rights associated with the basic needs of the peoples of the world. Issued as a nongovernmental document, with no accountability, it can set forth the realities of the situation without any practical constraints of the sorts operative in United Nations circles. But more than this, the Algiers Declaration is itself an assertion of popular sovereignty, asserting that it is the peoples of the world that are the fundamental source of authority with respect to the governing process. Somehow statist tendencies have distorted this situation, making it appear as if governments are the ultimate, if not the only source of authority with respect to human rights. The Algiers Declaration, drawing inspiration from the Magna Carta tradition, is a framework of rights asserted by and for the peoples of the world over and against the claims and activities of governments, multinational corporations, and international institutions.

Perhaps it is useful at least to refer to the Bertrand Russell War Crimes Tribunal, which claimed the competence on behalf of humanity to examine allegations that United States behavior in Vietnam amounted to a criminal enterprise in a number of distinct respects. The Russell proceedings, although widely attacked in the liberal press, made a persuasive antiimperialist analysis of the criminal character of the Vietnam War, a case that was dutifully ignored in both the United Nations and in the widely hailed free press of the West.[6] More significantly; perhaps, the Russell Tribunal staked out a claim that a panel of distinguished citizens, independent of their nationality, had the competence to act on behalf of humanity on issues of war and peace in Indochina. The precedent, in effect, allows citizens to constitute commissions of inquiry and tribunals of assessment without awaiting any prior governmental or intergovernmental authorization. Daniel Ellsberg's decision to release the Pentagon Papers cuts in the same direction. Ellsberg, acting in part on the basis of his understanding of the Nuremberg experience with war criminals, believed both that the people had a right to know and that a citizen (even if a public employee or official) had a higher duty to the people and to values associated with peace and justice than to his governmental superior.[7]

The Algiers Declaration codifies the popular claims of competence asserted on a more *ad hoc* basis by the Russell Tribunal and the Ellsberg initiative. It extends the scope of such competence to the various spheres of human rights, including those connected with the existence of a people;

economic, political, cultural, and environmental rights are claimed, as well as rights for minority peoples within a state.[8] The explicit reference to environmental rights in the declaration is a progressive acknowledgment that a successful relationship with nature is vital for the fulfillment of human rights and cannot be taken for granted. Even Marxist thinking has been slow to shed its materialist baggage and appreciate the extent to which industrial production and modern technology, if not restrained and guided by humane values, can imperil health and well-being in as fundamental ways as can poverty and inequity.

The importance of the Algiers Declaration also exists on an *ideological* level. In effect, the denial of human rights is associated with capitalism in its international aspect, and their realization associated with the triumph of non-Stalinist forms of democratic socialism. Unlike capitalist governing elites, which must repress to survive in a context of capital shortages, mass misery, and population growth, socialist governing elites are not structurally required to repress (at least once the remnants of the old ruling classes have been either integrated into the new order or rendered harmless in relation to it). Therefore, the antiimperialist struggle, including support for liberation movements, is directly linked to the rights of peoples. Also the declaration makes the point in article 21 that the state *per se* is not opposed as a political form so long as it upholds the rights specified in the course of its activities.

The *legitimacy* of the Algiers Declaration will depend on the degree to which it becomes accepted as a basis of asserting claims in various international arenas. If it enters into the process of opinion formation among those who seek fundamental change in the world, then it may provide content for a broad transnational social movement for peace and justice. Degrees of legitimacy in international relations are not often settled in any authoritative manner. Particular actors can invoke the Algiers Declaration to support their claims. To the extent these claims are satisfied the Algiers Declaration will gain in stature. In the meantime the declaration operates on an inspirational level that gives shape to an ideological position that is progressive and enlightened as formulated. More importantly, perhaps, the Algiers Declaration serves notice on governments, multinational corporations, and international institutions (e.g., the World Bank) that their activities are subject to scrutiny from a vantage point that is higher than that of national governments.

Conclusion

The Algiers Declaration responds to a confusing situation of spreading repression. It calls in dramatic language for a cooperative effort by all anti-imperialist forces. Whether it will be an important instrument in this main struggle is uncertain, depending in part on whether governments can shut down all political activity going on within national boundaries. At the present time rather few governments represent their people(s) as a whole; they tend, rather, to be instruments of class or elite rule that mobilize the coercive apparatus of the state to control the mass by whatever means are necessary.

—————————— VIII ——————————

Keeping Nuremberg Alive

The decision to prosecute German and Japanese leaders as war criminals after World War II, although flawed as a legal proceeding, represents an important step forward. It created a precedent for the idea that leaders of governments and their subordinate officials are responsible for their acts and can be brought to account before an international tribunal. It affirmed the reality of crimes against humanity and crimes against peace, as well as the more familiar crimes arising from violations of the laws of war.

The Nuremberg Judgment was also a promise to generalize the occasion of prosecution so as to make it an ingredient of international order. Justice Robert Jackson, the Chief American Prosecutor at Nuremberg, made his famous pledge in the courtroom: "If certain acts and violation of treaties are crimes, they are crimes whether the United States does them or whether Germany does them. We are not prepared to lay down a rule of criminal conduct against others which we would not be willing to have invoked against us." We know, of course, that what Justice Jackson denied has occurred. After World War II the Allied Powers carried out the sentences passed at Nuremberg (and elsewhere) without subsequently exhibiting the willingness to abide by the commitment embodied in Jackson's statement. To be sure, the legal principles on which the Nuremberg Judgment rested were endorsed by unanimous vote at the first session of the United Nations General Assembly, and some years later these principles were set forth in authoritative form by the International Law Commission, a body of international law experts functioning within the United Nations system[1]. The Nuremberg Principles provide authoritative legal criteria to assess official behavior, and, consequently, are embodied in modern international law.

It is painfully obvious, however, that no willingness has been shown to carry forward the Nuremberg ideas as a practical check on sovereign discretion. Jean-Paul Sartre has suggested:

> It would have been enough if the organ created to judge the Nazis had remained in existence after having carried out that specific task, or if the organization of the United Nations had drawn all the consequences from what had just been done and had, by a vote in its General Assembly, consolidated the body's existence as a permanent tribunal empowered to take cognizance of and to judge all charges of war crimes, even if the accused should happen to be the government of those countries which through the agencies of their judges

delivered the Nuremberg verdicts. *In this way, the implicit universality of the original intention would have been made clear and explicit.* (Emphasis added.)

Sartre, in his role as president of the Bertrand Russell War Crimes Proceedings, concludes that the organized international community has failed to fulfill this crucial promise to the peoples of the world at a historical time when state power is being used for criminal purposes, especially its interference in the liberation struggles of Third World peoples. As Sartre suggests, perhaps overstating the institutional issue and understating the ideological issue, "There is a cruel lack of that institution—which appeared, asserted its permanence and universality, defined irreversibly certain rights and obligations, only to disappear, leaving a void which must be filled and which nobody is filling."[2] The Russell Tribunal, a distinguished jury of conscience, was assembled on an *ad hoc* basis to fill part of the institutional void created by the special circumstances of American military aggression against the peoples of Vietnam. In truth, even if the Nuremberg idea had been embodied in a permanent institutional framework as Sartre urged, I doubt very much whether it would have been capable, for political reasons, of dealing directly with the central issues of oppression and abuse that result from the imperial structure of international society. It hardly needs to be explained that international institutions established and financed by sovereign governments reflect the balance of political forces operative in international society at a given time. The imperial sector, although greatly diminished in significance since 1945, is still able to prevent most adverse initiatives by international institutions, especially if the initiatives move beyond the rhetorical level of censure. Also, the spread of neocolonial influence has led to the emergence of elites in many Third World states who are not at all disposed to subject governmental policy to any system of international moral or legal constraint. For this reason, the assessment of state conduct will depend on innovative paralegal political forms such as took temporary shape in the original Russell Tribunal.

As expected, mainstream media attacked the legitimacy of the Russell initiative, ignored its presentation of evidence (fully vindicated by subsequent inquiries from many sources), and scorned its conclusions. The principal criticism of Russell's initiative was contained in a letter by Charles De Gaulle, then president of France, denying Sartre's request to allow the tribunal to meet on French territory: "I have no need to tell you that justice of any sort, in principle as in execution, emanates from the State. Without impugning the motives which have inspired Lord Russell and his friends, I must recognize the fact that they have no power whatsoever, nor are they the holders of any international mandate, and that therefore they are unable to carry out any legal action."[3] De Gaulle's conception of justice tied to state power was in direct opposition to the vision embraced by the Russell Tribunal. As Sartre said at the outset of the proceedings, "The Russell Tribunal considers . . . that its legitimacy derives equally from its total powerlessness and from its universality."[4] Sartre is using "powerlessness" in an ironic sense as he believes that ultimate power resides in the people, and that the findings of the Tribunal can help guide mass opinion to right action. Again, addressing his fellow members of the Tribunal, Sartre states, "We, the jury, at the end of the session, will have to pronounce on these charges: are they well-founded or not? But the judges are everywhere: they are the peoples of the world, and in particular the American people. It is for them we are working."[5] The exposures of the criminality of the Vietnam enterprise encouraged the mobilization of the peoples of the world, including the American people, and this did contribute, in a small way, to the victory of the Vietnamese people against the American military juggernaut.

Nevertheless, a deeper conviction was desired by those who shaped the Russell initiative. As Bertrand Russell declared in a message to the Tribunal, "I hope this Tribunal will remain in existence, so that it may meet when necessary in the future in order to expose and condemn the future war crimes which will be committed inevitably until the peoples of the world follow the example of Vietnam."[6] Sartre also expressed the same sentiment:

> . . . the Russell Tribunal will have no other concern as in its conclusions, than to bring about a general recognition of the need for an international institution for which it has neither the means nor the ambition to be a substitute. . . . Yes, if the masses ratify our judgment, then it will become truth, and we, at the very moment which we efface ourselves before those masses who make themselves the guardians and the might support for that truth, we will know that we have been legitimized and that the people, by showing us its agreement, is revealing a deeper need: The need for a real "War Crimes Tribunal" to be brought into being as a permanent body—that is to say, the need that it should be possible to denounce and punish such crimes wherever and whenever they may be committed.[7]

The Russell Tribunal, as with Nuremberg, struck a commitment to the future, though one, in my judgment, expressed in overly institution-building terms; it may also be wondered whether "commission of inquiry" or "peoples' hearing" is not more appropriate terminology to identify the quality of the proceedings than the more governmentally coercive image projected by use of the term "tribunal." Quite possibly, such naming is not essential, provided the sense of the undertaking can be adequately conveyed to larger and larger segments of the public. This commitment to keep the Russell process in being, however, failed. Such a failure has had serious consequences. International society at least requires a regular procedure of inquiry and exposure so long as the reality of international crimes persist. More than a decade has passed since the Russell Tribunal was established in 1967, and the spread of imperial and fascist crimes is rampant throughout the Third World. The need to expose the truth about these crimes is greater than ever, especially as their commission is so widespread and disguised by a virtual official conspiracy of silence. In Latin America, in Asia, and in Africa, vicious crimes are committed daily against the peoples of these countries. In the North the stockpiling, deployment, development, and threat of nuclear weapons of mass destruction is a crime against humanity of grave character. In addition, severe abuses of indigenous minorities are being neglected by organized international society. These circumstances demand that something must be done outside the formal structures of conventional diplomacy.

The Algiers Declaration supplements the work of the United Nations in the human rights field, and constitutes a parallel document to the Universal Declaration of Human Rights (1948). Unlike the formulators of the United Nations instruments, the authors of the Algiers Declaration are relatively uninhibited by geopolitical rivalries or by the need to produce agreements that are generally acceptable to principal governmental members. The United Nations' need to please governments virtually nullifies progressive tendencies in the human rights area because a large cluster of governments are the principal violators.

Unlike the mainstream tradition of human rights law and activity, the Algiers Declaration also emphasizes the structural core of oppression. In its preamble it notes that "this is . . . a time" during which "new forms of imperialism evolve to oppress and exploit the peoples of the world . . . using vicious methods, with the complicity of governments. . . . Through direct or indirect intervention, through multinational enterprises, through manipulation of corrupt local politicians, with the assistance of military regimes based on police repression, torture, and physical extermination of opponents, through a set of practices that has become known as neocolonialism, imperialism extends its stranglehold over many peoples." The preamble also endorses the rights of peoples "under subjection, to fight for their liberation and to benefit from other peoples' assistance in their struggle." Specific rights, beginning with the rights of a people to existence and self-determination, are then set forth in the operative provisions of the Algiers Declaration. As with any instrument issued after debate, the consensus reflects some compromises in phrasing and emphasis. I would have preferred more emphasis placed on the rights of individuals (as distinct from peoples), and a more direct endorsement of the political rights of dissent, assembly, and opposition than can be found in the Algiers Declaration. Despite these reservations, I regard the Algiers Declaration as a major progressive juridical step which manifests a serious determination to put the rights of people on a solid legal base and reasserts the legitimacy of nongovernmental initiatives in the area of human rights and criminal responsibility. Furthermore, by comparison with United Nations human rights instruments, the Algiers Declaration is a superior statement of political analysis, connecting the roots of imperialist oppression with its manifestations in an array of abuses. It helps fill the normative and ideological gaps that exist alongside the more obvious institutional void.

It is appropriate to ask the skeptical juridical question: on what basis can a group of individuals gathered together at a meeting give any legal status to a document that purports to set forth the rights of people? No conventional source of law supports such a law-making procedure. Even standards of behavior established by the General Assembly of the United Nations are not generally regarded as binding. The status of such resolutions is controversial, and there is a trend toward treating the General Assembly as the agency of the international community, and hence, possessing a law-making capacity. How, then, shall we regard the Algiers Declaration? Does it purport to be law? On behalf of what community does it speak? Who appointed the authors of this declaration to speak on behalf of "the peoples" of the world?

These are difficult perennial issues for both the international jurist and the international moralist. Naturally, to the extent that law and morality in world affairs are a reflection of the state system, the Algiers Declaration will be dismissed with scorn. Governments did not participate in the norm-shaping process, either directly or indirectly. The fundamental claim of the Algiers Declaration, in contrast, is that the peoples of the world possess the ultimate law-making authority, and that the validity of governmental law-making capacity rests on a prior delegation of competence by the people. How such a delegation takes place and is expressed is admittedly difficult to specify. Implicit in this view is also the contention that there is an inalienable competence that has not been and cannot be delegated. In an earlier period, theories of natural rights were relied upon. Such explanations are still helpful to the extent that they rest upon the conviction that the most fundamental level of moral and legal reality is associated with the will and character of the people.

This affirmation of competence still leaves the question of representation unanswered: who appointed the conveners of these law-declaring initiatives? Are such initiatives entitled to respect? by what criteria? In the world of today, given the pretensions of the absolute state, there is no procedure by which the peoples can gather to express and assert their own demands as to their rights or appoint others to do so on their behalf. At the same time, patterns of exploitation and oppression obviously exist, although much propaganda prevents their clear discernment. The Algiers Declaration is, in the first instance, an argument and appeal, just as was, indeed, the 1776 Declaration of Independence. (Who appointed Thomas Jefferson and colleagues? By what authority did they represent even the opinion of the colonies?) The claim of representation rests ultimately on the popular acceptance of the Algiers Declaration's understanding of exploitation and oppression as a by-product of an imperial world order that needs to be dismantled to allow the peoples of the world to experience lives of dignity and satisfaction. In this sense, the Algiers Declaration is more of a political document than a legal or moral one, and, as such, possesses an educational, mobilizing intention. The founding group, therefore, has no special competence aside from the persuasiveness of its critique and its positive vision. Its legitimacy is inseparable from its potentiality. It deserves a provisional benefit of the doubt partly because its authors and endorsers have no vested economic or bureaucratic interest and have a long, honorable identity associated with progressive politics.

Of course, such a rationale is shaky in some respects, but no more so than other claims of authority at the margins of accepted legitimacy. Whenever a group of individuals asserts the rights on behalf of a wider community, their formal position appears weak. Surely the same doubts that we have been considering with respect to the Algiers Declaration pertain to such earlier inspirational documents as the Magna Carta and Declaration of Independence, as well as to the Universal Declaration of Human Rights. Surely the capacity of governments to act on behalf of the world as a whole, as in creating the League of Nations and United Nations, is subject to challenge on representational grounds.

As this stage in international history, those who endorse the Algiers Declaration and the steps taken to give it impact are expressing their lack of confidence in existing international procedures and their positive conviction that the rights of peoples must be upheld by new kinds of direct action. The validation of this position will depend upon its eventual effects. In the meantime, it advances an appeal to those who understand its arguments to join in the struggle to make its vision of peoples' rights into a reality. Achieving a widening circle of participation in the struggle would be one aspect of validation, and in this regard, it should be noted that the Basso group is not content with declaring intentions and good sentiments. The Algiers Declaration is the premise for a process of political action designed to exert as much influence as possible.

The issue of effectiveness is the central concern. Even the right to meet and discuss can be impaired by governments refusing to allow such activities on their territory. The Russell Tribunal had difficulty finding a government that would tolerate its presence. Furthermore, those who endorse the Algiers Declaration lack any tax base or military establishment, and because of this there is an absence of power in a tangible sense. Nevertheless, power can be gradually acquired with ingenuity and perseverance, and at this early stage, organization and enthusiasm on the part of a few are critical. This has been understood from the outset by the Basso group.

Accordingly, at Algiers in July 1976, the International League for the Rights and Liberation of Peoples was brought into existence to give a continuing institutional backing to the substantive concerns of the Algiers Declaration. The most ambitious project of the League is, of course, to launch an International Peoples' Tribunal that will be available to investigate, assess, and report on allegations of violations of the rights of peoples. This tribunal, operating on a continuing professional and objective basis, may have an historic opportunity to expose the basic structure of imperial abuse in a variety of specific contexts. Its mobilizing potential is enormous, although one must anticipate a hostile response from mainstream media and most governments. An International Peoples' Tribunal carries out one dimension of the promise to the future made at Nuremberg. It keeps the Nuremberg idea alive, and it compensates to some extent for the failure of governments and international institutions to uphold the rights of peoples.

Of course, what Bertrand Russell started and Lelio Basso continued and extended is not the kind of legacy of Nuremberg that was contemplated in 1945. Hopes were higher, at that time, for a permanent international criminal framework agreed to by principal governments. As already discussed, subsequent international patterns of conflict and domination, as well as the reluctance of governments to submit their activities to external scrutiny, have confined the original Nuremberg impulse to its original World War II setting. In the setting of the 1980s, with formal decolonialization virtually complete, only a populist continuation of the Nuremberg idea now seems plausible. The success of an International Peoples' Tribunal will depend upon the support it generates as a means of carrying on the antiimperial struggle in a variety of contexts.

The work of the International Peoples' Tribunal will reflect its energy and capacities. The selection of issues will create its image. As matters now stand, there are many appropriate undertakings for the Tribunal, among them the study of the development and deployment of weapons of mass destruction; the role of the International Monetary Fund and other international financial institutions as repressive agents of international capital in a variety of Third World countries; domestic and international roots of repression in various countries; and unsatisfied obligations of rich countries to give various forms of economic help to the peoples of poor and abused countries.

Each of these illustrative items of potential agenda for the Tribunal could be related to the defense of rights embodied in the Algiers Declaration. The Tribunal would obviously be seeking to influence public opinion, as well as investigating the issues before it in an honest and careful way.

─────────────IX─────────────

Human Rights after the Iranian Revolution

In early 1979 a revolutionary movement toppled the Shah of Iran. It was a startling development for many reasons. Here, we consider only some aspects of its human rights significance. The rationale for the revolution was centered upon the rights of the Iranian people to rise up against the bloody tyranny of Pahlavi rule. Gross violations of human rights by the Shah's regime were attested to by a variety of impartial investigating groups. Indeed, it was widely accepted in international circles that the Shah's human rights record was one of the worst in a world notable for human rights abuse.

After the revolutionary seizure of power under the leadership of Ayatollah Khomeini, a new governing process was responsive to the will of the revolutionary forces and operated without benefit of any framework of constraint. The first of the three parts that comprise this chapter considers the special question of human rights observance and violation in the atmosphere of revolutionary immediacy. In particular, charges against the revolutionary leadership are examined in the context of post-Pahlavi Iran.

As of October 1979 a new situation arose as a consequence of the Shah's admission to the United States to receive medical treatment. On November 4, 1979, militant students seized the American embassy and held hostage there some fifty Americans who were officially connected in various ways with the exercise of diplomatic function. The student leaders, supported by mass demonstrations and Khomeini, demanded the physical return of the Shah to face criminal charges and the return to the Iranian people of wealth allegedly plundered by the Shah and his family. This chapter considers aspects of this situation. The first question is whether it is appropriate to charge a deposed ruler with crimes of state and whether there exist moral and political, if not legal, means by which to achieve jurisdiction to prosecute. At stake here is the effort to enforce human rights against the class of violators in their individual capacity. Such claims are an extension of the Nuremberg idea of imposing criminal responsibility upon defeated leaders in war to the quite different setting of prosecuting deposed tyrants in times of peace.[1] Second is the question as to whether, in the setting of the encounter between the United States and Iran arising from the hostage crisis, the existing structure of international law is not one-sided. That is, international law upholds the immunity claims of the American diplomatic personnel, but it fails to uphold either extradition claims directed at the Shah or charges that the American embassy in Teheran has been used to encroach upon the political and personal human rights of the Iranian people.

The assessment of human rights in revolutionary settings is an unstudied topic of considerable importance. It is in this spirit that this chapter is included in this volume.

Preliminary Notes on Human Rights in a Revolutionary Situation

The Iranian Revolution took power largely by nonviolent means: a general strike, mass demonstrations, cassettes bearing the messages of exiled leader Ayatollah Khomeini, Xerox machines coordinating and reporting on the movement largely through the mosque network of mullahs. It was also a popular revolution enjoying overwhelming support from the Persian masses, as well as more reserved backing from all parts of the country and among all social classes. It was, of course, a revolution inspired by Shi'ia Islamic thought and tradition, indigenous to the Third World, owing virtually nothing to the great Western revolutionary experience emanating from the American, French, and Russian revolutions. It was also a religious revolution, the fervor of the masses and the authority of the leader organized around a sacred mission to overthrow the oppressive Pahlavi dynasty of the Shah and establish in its place an Islamic republic.

The success of this revolution offers great hope to oppressed peoples elsewhere. It demonstrates once and for all that the relation of forces between ruled and ruler in a Third World society has not decisively shifted from the people to the state. Iran is such an important case because the populist possibility seemed so remote until it exploded into success. The Shah's apparatus of state power was immense given the scale of Iranian society, reinforced by a ruthless and large secret police and various categories of armed forces available for use against unarmed opposition to the rulers of the country. Also, the Shah had built up a network of supporting links with outside governments that included, among others, favorable relations with the United States, the Soviet Union, and China, as well as with regional neighbors including Saudi Arabia, Egypt, and Israel. As activists in the Khomeini movement like to put it, "We won although the whole world was against us."

What is important is the confirmation that relative power in a revolutionary situation is more a matter of political will than military and paramilitary capability. The Iranian success resulted from the mobilization of the Iranian people on the basis of leadership and beliefs that had intense mass appeal and deep domestic roots. In that sense, the activation of the Shi'ia perspective by Ayatollah Khomeini and its ideological expression in the influential work of Ali Shariati were crucial catalysts. In the end, however, it was the willingness of the Iranian masses to persist in challenging state power, carrying on with their demonstrations despite the Shah's willingness to inflict widespread casualties with heavy machine guns, helicopter gunships, and tanks. The best estimates are that between twenty thousand and sixty-five thousand Khomeini supporters were killed in the streets during 1978.

At the last stage of the revolutionary struggle—that is, between the time that the Shah left on January 16, 1978, and resistance by the armed forces collapsed a few weeks later—the regime was virtually isolated from the Iranian people as no significant social remnant was willing to lend its support to, much less fight for the survival of, the Pahlavi order. In February small arms were distributed to the people in great numbers. During the last stage of struggle against the Shah, crowds chanted "Leaders, leaders, give us guns." At issue was achieving total control over the state, including its military bureaucracy. The revolutionary leadership was not prepared to reach a negotiated settlement with the military leadership that left the command structure of the Shah period intact. The Allende experience in Chile indicated to Iranian leaders how dangerous it can be if a governing process seeks to implement a radical social and economic program and must rely on a hostile bureaucracy. At the same time, this insistence on a complete victory over the old order led the Iranian revolutionary movement to shift its tactics at the end in the direction of armed struggle. This terminal violent phase was brief, centering on the weekend of February 11, 1978, but it did alter the character of the revolutionary orientation toward the role of violence in the struggle. The dissident elements in the armed forces and the guerrilla groups (People's Fedayeen and Mujahedeen) carried Iran just over the brink of civil war before securing the *de facto* surrender and dissolution of the armed forces loyal to the Shah.

This type of ending also meant, however, that at the moment of victory the stage was set for an orgy of retribution. One of the first tasks for the Khomeini movement was to establish minimum order in an atmosphere of accumulated rage and in a situation in which the means to pursue vindicative justice were available to a population long abused by a repressive, bloodthirsty tyranny. In understanding the early weeks of revolutionary governance, this crucial background element must be kept in mind.

In addition, although the morale of the armed forces was shattered, its leadership remained at large and unreconciled to the revolutionary outcome. Ibrahim Yazdi, originally designated deputy prime minister for revolutionary affairs, contended that a principal reason for the summary executions was the persisting fear that a more orderly process might expose the country to a desperate coup attempt by the remnant of pro-Shah forces. Later developments suggest darker explanations, including some suspicion that the insistence on closed, summary trials followed rapidly by executions was partly designed as a cover-up, designed to avoid compromising elements of the new Iranian leadership which may have cooperated with the Shah's regime or with the United States government at earlier times. A distinctive feature of the Iranian Revolution was the absence of a victorious revolutionary army to protect the new state—in fact, the most experienced promovement armed units formed out of the mass movement were of an essentially left socialist character and found themselves soon at odds with the orientation of the leadership in the postrevolutionary situation. In the early weeks the Khomeini leadership, aside from its hastily organized popular militia, contrived in part to contain the Iranian left, had no way to protect itself against a counterrevolutionary thrust, whether mounted from without or from within the country, or possibly a mixture of the two.

There are other factors. As with any revolution, an artificial unity against a common enemy suppresses cleavage at the moment of victory. The Shah was such a hated enemy that the level of unity temporarily achieved was especially deceptive. With the Pahlavi collapse, however, these cleavages came to the fore. The left was immediately eager to establish its presence and to claim for itself a share of credit for the victory. The armed struggle groups, militant for many years, had given many martyrs to the revolution. They were insistent on being recognized and given a part to play in the emerging postrevolutionary governing process. And the main ethnic minorities—Kurds, Azerbaijanis, Baluchis, Bakhtiaris, Arabs, and Turkomans—who together make up just under half of Iran's population, seized the opportunity, possibly abetted by outsiders, to assert their persistent demands for autonomy and an acknowledgment from the new leadership of their rights of national self-determination. This challenge confronted the new leadership with an immediate threat to the territorial integrity of the state. Besides, ethnic separatism in Iran, while genuine, has also been a fertile ground for foreign intervention. It is reasonable to suspect that both the Soviet Union and the United States will exploit these separatist tendencies to weaken the new government in Iran, especially if eager to show its incapacity to maintain order in the country.

In addition, many special concerns subordinated to the common objective of the revolution surfaced with the explosive ferocity that comes after a long period of confinement. The manifestations of concern over women's rights can be, in part, so understood. Women, who participated so bravely in the struggle against the Shah, were determined that their status in an emergent Islamic republic not perpetuate a cultural tradition of repression.

Never far from the concerns of the new leaders, also, of course, was the fear of outside intervention. Iranian memories of the American-sponsored coup in 1953, which toppled the Mossadegh government, remain vivid. In fact, a preoccupation with avoiding its repetition exists, perhaps accounting for the unexpectedly secular, Westernized quality of Bazargan's cabinet, a reformist orientation out of keeping with the revolutionary climate. Indeed, appointing such a moderate provisional government agitated the more militant and fundamentalist elements in the Khomeini movement. Revolutionaries wondered, in light of this provisional government, about its revolutionary and Islamic content. It is in this light that we must understand the operation of Khomeini's religious entourage as the main source of political direction, to some extent formalized in the Revolutionary Council.

It is against this background that we consider prospects for human rights in Iran. It is, of course, a hazardous moment for conjecture. The situation is changing rapidly. There is, as yet, no coherent governing process. Not everything is known about what is happening, nor do we have access to the full rationale. An unresolved power struggle rages within the revolutionary leadership, with the secular forces on one side (associated with Bani Sadr), and the religious forces on the other (associated with Beheshti). Events will supercede any current diagnosis, and yet the interplay of human rights with a fluid revolutionary situation is itself a focus of attention.

Nevertheless, it is important to put what is now known in some perspective, if only to correct fashionable distortions. Because such powerful outside interests were aligned with the policies of the old order in Iran, an enormous incentive exists to discredit the new order. The most prevalent way to achieve this result is to point up human rights abuses that support a most malicious falsehood, namely, that what has happened in Iran is that one tyranny has been replaced by another.

Such claims are outrageous, and suggest the need for a different assessment. First of all, it is necessary to compare the post-Shah situation with the situation under the Shah. Second, human rights in Iran have to be understood within a regional and cultural context where levels of abuse are widespread and severe. Such comparisons in time and space are not meant to excuse violations of human rights in Iran, but merely to expose the motivation of those who suddenly focus disproportionate attention to Iran. Many of these new "voices of conscience" were exquisitely silent during the long years of repression by the Shah and remain so about the routine of systematic abuse in neighboring states with more Westernized geopolitical orientations.

Here, briefly, the attempt is to take account of context, while exploring the prospects for human rights in the early stages of postrevolutionary Iran.

Repression under the Shah

The evidence of torture, summary execution, denial of minimal rights of the person, and the absence of democratic process were all staple elements of the Shah's rule. Even the most cautious outside observers of the human rights situation in Iran confirmed this impression.[1] Amnesty International issued a report late in 1978 indicating the continuation of systematic torture.

The Khomeini movement emphasized its opposition to the repressive features of the Shah's rule. Many members of the revolutionary leadership were personally abused by the SAVAK, spending years as victims of various forms of harrassment and in jail.

No rights of discussion or criticism were permitted, not even the intellectual preconditions of democratic process. Students periodically disappeared from classes. Signs of opposition, such as demonstrations or meetings, were brutally broken up. Iranians abroad were subject to surveillance and cruel punishment upon their return if political activity was reported.

In every sense, then, the Shah's rule must be perceived as one of severe repression backed up by a willingness to use military power to contain the opposition of a hostile population. Heavy casualties were repeatedly inflicted by the use of modern weaponry against unarmed demonstrators.

Revolutionary Justice

In the aftermath of the revolution a series of summary executions occurred after brief trials before secret revolutionary tribunals. This process was authorized by the Revolutionary Council, originally without the knowledge or backing of Prime Minister Mehdi Bazargan, then head of the provisional government. Bazargan denounced the process and threatened to resign, a threat he subsequently carried out after Ayatollah Khomeini endorsed the student seizure of the American embassy on November 4, 1979.

As matters now stand, the approximately one thousand executions were mainly directed against principal agents of repression in the Shah era, leaders of the armed forces or SAVAK associated personally with massive crimes against the Iranian people. Several Iranians were also executed according to the dictates of Koranic law for alleged criminal acts, including homosexual rape and violent crimes. This mode of assessing guilt and imposing punishment obviously violated the rights of the accused to open trials with due process protection. At the same time, given the revolutionary turmoil, the fear of private vengeance, and the long record of mass abuse associated with Pahlavi rule, extenuating circumstances existed.

The number of executions was relatively limited, and as of early 1980, executions associated with criminal activity on behalf of the Shah's regime have virtually ceased. Khomeini did not repudiate Bazargan despite the harshness of Bazargan's response ("... irreligious, inhuman, and a disgrace") to this method of pursuing "revolutionary justice."

On March 16, 1979, Khomeini called for an end to closed trials and summary executions, a call only partially heeded.[2]

Formation of an Islamic Republic.

The Khomeini movement has been criticized because it assessed popular support for an Islamic republic by a simple yes-no question on a referendum. Critics allege that the choice should have been more subtle, asking whether the people preferred a monarchy, a constitutional monarchy, a nonreligious republic, or an Islamic republic. The constitutional referendum provided an insufficiently democratic sanction, it is argued, on which to base a mandate for an Islamic republic.

In response, however, it should be noted that the Khomeini movement made it clear throughout the revolution that an Islamic republic was its objective. This political outcome was promised to followers of Khomeini, and, in a sense, the extent of popular support for that promise is the only relevant question with regard to the reorganization of the Iranian state. The argument that a range of other options should be presented to the Iranian people is both an academic insistence, given the level of support for an Islamic republic, and probably an overstatement of the political sophistication of the Iranian people, so long victimized by a monochromatic tyranny.

The Role of the Left and Nonreligious Dissent

On numerous occasions before coming to power and shortly thereafter Khomeini has affirmed the rights of Marxists and others to express their views and participate in the political life of an Islamic republic. Such an affirmation has been qualified to the extent that if the left were to establish links with foreign governments, its freedom to operate would be curtailed. The historical memory of the disruptive role played by the Tudeh Party in the early 1950s remains fresh, especially its apparent subordination to the will of Moscow and its contribution to the 1953 collapse of Mossadegh's government. As Khomeini put it, every country is entitled to protect itself "against those who would commit treason."

Underneath Khomeini's attitude lies another, given expression by the first elected president of the Islamic Republic, Abolhassan Bani Sadr; namely, the view that when Marxists in Iran genuinely come to understand the goals of an Islamic republic, they will renounce Marxism and realize that Shi'ia Islam provides a better framework for the pursuit of social justice. And, indeed, the ideas of Ali Shariati have had great appeal for many progressive Iranians, convincing even some Marxists that Islam correctly understood provides a revolutionary ideology that is indigenous to Iran and enjoys a mass following. One of the disappointments with the revolution as of early 1980 is the degree to which Shariati's ideas have been ignored and more conservative conceptions of Islamic social and political policies endorsed. This shift to the right has alienated the secular left, and has even led some religious socialists into a position of guarded opposition to the Khomeini leadership.

As matters now stand a substantial left will remain a critical presence within any Islamic republic; it will test the democratic character of the governing process both by its oppositional style and by the extent to which its rights of expression and activity are allowed. It may also seek to seize power in the event the religious movement fails or is beset by deepening civil strife.

Several ambiguities exist. First of all, there is the Fedayeen, that element on the extreme left that is now heavily armed and has engaged in armed struggle against the Shah. Will it renounce armed struggle at this new stage? Will it be suppressed? If so, by what means? Can this extreme left be integrated in any sense within the framework of an Islamic republic? Second, will the populist mainstream of the revolution tolerate an active left? There have already been indications within university settings of interference by militant religious groups with meetings, with the distribution of literature, and with the carrying of Marxist placards at demonstrations and marches. It remains uncertain, despite some instances where official moves to repress the left occurred, whether the government will discourage such interference and protect the democratic rights of the left. So far, Khomeini has zigzagged between tolerance and repression. Third, there are some disturbing allegations that the religious leadership intends to repress the left as soon as it consolidates its own power, and that reassurances of tolerance are merely tactical. The death of Ayatollah Teleghani, the most liberal of religious leaders, was a serious blow to the hopes for a postrevolutionary government of unity and reconciliation.

The interaction between the left and the emergent governing process in Iran will definitely reveal one dimension of the human rights situation. As suggested, however, this revelation will be two-sided, depending on the political approach of the left (or segments of the left) toward opposition (renunciation of foreign links, of armed struggle), as well as on the attitudes of new political leaders, their religious guides, and the populist tides of the Islamic movement. In the short run, Ayatollah Khomeini's individual guidance is likely to be decisive in setting the tone.

Ethnic Minorities

Iran is a multinational state. The Shah repressed these minorities through military and paramilitary means. With the collapse of the armed forces and the weakening of the central state, these national groups have become insistent to varying degrees on improvements in their economic, political, and cultural situation in Iran. It seems indisputable that these national minorities have been victims of discrimination in the past, receiving a disproportionately low share of investment, social services, and so forth. Also, several of these minorities (e.g., Kurds, Baluchis) are predominantly adherents of Sunni Islam, and, therefore, additionally separate from the Shi'ia adherence of the great majority of Iranians, including all of the leaders of the revolution. Some minority nationalities also contend that in exchange for their support of the Khomeini movement they had received assurances that a larger measure of autonomy and self-rule would be granted in an Islamic republic.

As with the left, it is difficult to assess the situation at this stage. Signs of agitation have been evident throughout the minority territories, and serious fighting has broken out in Kurdish areas. One issue is whether these minorities, or some of them, are secessionist in character, intend to rely on violence to achieve their goals, and maintain contact with outside forces (transnational links with their own people—especially, with Kurds in Iraq and Turkey, Ajerbaijanis and Turkomen in the Soviet Union, Baluchis in Pakistan). The separatist orientation provides, also, fertile areas for covert operations by hostile foreign intelligence organizations seeking to destabilize an Islamic republic in Iran.

These national minorities together dominate the peripheral region of Iran, including the oil-producing region of Khuzistom. These minority populations live in distinct geographic areas, generally close to the borders of Iran, remote from the political and spatial center of the country. Clearly one test of human rights in an Islamic republic will be the capacity of the central government to deal fairly and nonviolently with these national minorities and their claims for some measure of self-determination. At the same time, the role of foreign governments, the reliance by minorities or factional groups in their midst on armed struggle, and the extent to which self-determination becomes a euphemism for secession will shape the setting within which these issues arise.

Religious Minorities

In Iran there are a number of religious minorities, including Sunnis, Armenian Christians, Jews, Zoroastrians, Nestorians, and Bahais. For various reasons the problematic relations are likely to concern Sunnis, Jews, and Bahais. With the exception of the Bahais, the Khomeini leadership has promised freedom of worship and an atmosphere of religious toleration.

The Sunni minority is troubled by the tension it perceives as likely to result from an Islamic republic drawn along strictly Shi'ia lines, especially given the strong hostility expressed by the Shi'ia leaders to Sunni Islam. Furthermore, the concentration of Sunnis among national minority groups hostile to the state may reinforce the perception of Sunnis as subversive elements.

With respect to the eighty thousand or so Jews, the root of the problem involves the hostile relationship between an Islamic republic and Israel. One of the first diplomatic acts of the Khomeini movement was to invite

PLO leader Yasir Arafat to Iran and pledge solidarity, symbolized by turning over the former Israeli embassy to the PLO. The situation is aggravated by the extent to which Israel is perceived as having been a bulwark of support of the Shah, including the role that the Israeli intelligence service, Mossad, is alleged to have played in setting up and working with the SAVAK.

Here again a key issue will be whether Iranian Jews are perceived as Zionists with operational emotional and material links to Israel. The government's capacity and will to discourage antisemitic attitudes within the population are also crucial. Khomeini has given the Jewish community repeated reassurances, including his assertion that it would be a tragedy for Iran if Jews leave. So far, between five thousand and eighteen thousand Jews have left Iran since the fall of the Shah, apparently fearing for their safety and well-being in an Islamic republic. Despite fears, the record of the Khomeini period toward the Jewish community as a whole has been quite positive as of this time. It is difficult to predict what will happen in the future.

The circumstances of the three hundred thousand or so Bahais are of especial concern. Here, alone, Khomeini refuses to provide reassurance. Indeed, he has said that Bahais have no place in an Islamic republic, that they form a political rather than a religious sect, and that their leading members were closely tied up with Pahlavi rule. Reports of abuse of Bahais and their religious property in various parts of Iran by members of Revolutionary Committees have been received and have elicited the first formal acts of protest by human rights groups.

In the background is the Shi'ia view of the Bahai religion—founded by Baha'u'llah, regarded by adherents as a subsequent and superior prophet to Mohammed—as heretical. Nevertheless, maintaining respect for the Bahai religion and people will be one severe test of human rights in an Islamic republic.

Women

The status of women in Iran is another symbolic battleground. It is also a confusing one. Yardsticks for progress cannot be supplied on the basis of Western experience. Since the revolution is Islamic at its core, there are obvious tensions between religious fundamentalism and achieving equality of treatment for women in Iran. The issue, like others in the human rights area, is susceptible to manipulation by those within and without the country seeking to destabilize the new governing process.

Khomeini and other religious leaders have been generally reassuring about the rights of women. After an initial insistence on traditional dress, Khomeini made it plain that the *chador* was optional. Demonstrations by women in Iran were not officially suppressed, and, in fact, those taking part were protected by a peculiar mixture of Fedayeen and some units of the Popular Militia working under the control of the Revolutionary

Committees. At the same time, many incidents of harrassment and intimidation of activist women have been reported in the course of the first year of the revolution.

The main short-run issue is whether women will be able to advance their claims for equality, participation, and dignity within a democratic framework. It will involve a difficult struggle, and by no means are women in Iran united as to their priorities or goals. Also, no Islamic society has yet succeeded in producing a satisfactory readjustment of traditional status and roles of women.

Purges and Purity

In the media and government ministries, allegations are being made that new revolutionary authorities have instituted "purges." Here again, the facts are difficult to sort out. The claim on behalf of the revolution is that those who worked loyally for the old order need to be replaced. The claim of the critics is that anyone who is not subordinate to the religious leadership is neither trusted nor wanted. How much ideological confromity is imposed upon radio, television, and newspaper will certainly determine the atmosphere of freedom in the new Iran. The first twelve months have produced an inconsistent record, one in which the mood has shifted back and forth.

Again, the recent heritage has been one of censorship and control. Iranians were deeply moved in the early days of revolutionary victory when long lines formed to observe the long lines at Tehran newsstands because finally newspapers and magazines contained real news with diverse interpretations. Later on, of course, liberal disenchantment occurred when newspapers and magazines critical of government policy or of divergent outlook were closed down, attacked, or censored.

The issue of "purity" is closely related to the general applicability of Islamic law. How strict and literal will be the lines drawn between Koranic text and behavioral compulsion in the new Iranian state? Already there are indications that liquor will be forbidden in public places and that entertainment featuring violence and sex will not be allowed in any form. Especially in provincial law these new imperatives are likely to be supplemented by harsh punishment for violators. Law enforcement on these matters has been uneven and decentralized, with some very harsh regimes evidently operating in parts of the new Iran.

Assessment

This sketch of human rights prospects for Iran is incomplete and tentative. The unfolding of the Islamic republic will reveal the degree to which human rights will flourish. At present, outsiders should watch, learn, and wait, as well as judge and appraise. The process of post-revolutionary adjustment has been difficult for every polity. There are enemies of the revolution that continue to be active. In Iran's case, outside states have an incentive to provoke the collapse of the Islamic government and the restoration of Western-oriented leadership, this time directly under military rather than dynastic auspices.

At least let us not confuse the tyranny of the past with the problems of the present and future. Ayatollah Khomeini seems dedicated to evolving a form of governance for the people of Iran that includes a central commitment to social justice for the poor, a closing of gaps between social classes, and an elimination of the kinds of wasteful consumption and production patterns that grew up during the Shah's years. He continues to enjoy an intense popular mandate to achieve this goal. Success will enable Iran to demonstrate that a revolutionary victory need not be spoiled by the tensions raised in the postrevolutionary period of consolidation.

Claims Against the Shah: The Rights of Deposed Rulers and the Rights of the People

The international crisis built up around the seizure of American hostages in the United States embassy on November 4 suggests the importance of having some acceptable international mechanism to acknowledge and establish the responsibility of the ex-Shah for crimes against the Iranian people. In the background is a broader problem of dealing with deposed tyrants who are living more or less comfortably in exile. In addition to the Shah, there are such unsavory characters as General Anastasio Somoza, Debayle, Idi Amin, Pol Pot, and Emperor Bokassa I at large in the world at the present time. The dramatic events in Iran, threatening lives of Americans, as well as creating a climate favorable to military intervention and even war, suggest the desperate need in international society for peaceful procedures to resolve conflicts of this type.

One of the great ideas born after World War II was the notion that even heads of state and top government leaders should be held criminally responsible for their gross violations of international law. As a result, war crimes trials were organized at Nuremberg and Tokyo, the surviving German and Japanese leaders prosecuted and, if convicted, punished, in some cases, by death. The trials have been criticized as "victors' justice" and for their failure to consider criminal allegations against the Allied side, especially reliance on strategic bombing techniques against cities and the use of atomic bombs. Nevertheless, the Nuremberg/Tokyo trials were a mechanism that answered the calls at the time for vindication and justice. More important, especially in the German case, the Nazi record of atrocity was publicly recognized.

The United States was centrally associated with this Nuremberg experiment. Our government at that time insisted, over Soviet and British objections, that an orderly, judicial method be relied upon to deal with the irresistible popular demands for some kind of retribution. After the trials the United States led the way in having the United Nations as a whole endorse the Nuremberg Principles as guiding rules of international law. And throughout this experience, prominent public figures, including the distinguished American prosecutor of the German defendants, former Supreme Court Justice Robert Jackson, insisted that the law laid down at Nuremberg included a promise to the future that similar behavior by other rulers and their cohorts would meet with a similar fate. We realize that many governments have violated the Nuremberg guidelines since 1946 and that their leaders could have been indicted if the Nuremberg promise had been kept. As the memory of World War II faded, so did the Nuremberg idea. In retrospect, it seems either unique to the special circumstances of that historical moment, or premature, or possibly both.

The events since the embassy seizure in Tehran on November 4 have made many of us aware that we need a mechanism in international society to assess the criminal responsibility of deposed tyrants. I believe that such a mechanism could be brought into being in the present situation if the minimum political will existed. In other words, there are no legal or moral obstacles that block such action, provided only that the United States and Iran stand aside and allow such a process to come into being. What is possible, and I think desirable, is the establishment of a mechanism within the framework of the United Nations for assessing the Shah's criminal responsibility.

The procedure I have in mind can be outlined to indicate its substance. As a first step a neutral delegation (say, Algeria or Venezuela) in the General Assembly or Security Council could introduce a resolution authorizing the secretary general of the United Nations to appoint a commission of inquiry composed of distinguished international jurists drawn from neither Iran nor the United States. This commission would have two broad functions. First of all, it would receive evidence of the Shah's alleged criminality and make a preliminary assessment as to whether there existed a reasonable basis for supposing the Shah guilty of gross violations of international law and crimes against the Iranian people. If the answer of the commission were affirmative, as is certainly likely, then it would proceed to its second task, that of proposing the establishment of a special tribunal and an operative legal framework for the trial of the Shah. The commission would complete its work by issuing a report containing findings and recommendations, calling upon the United Nations to act accordingly. At this point, assuming there was an affirmative recommendation by the commission, the United Nations would constitute a special tribunal. It could, perhaps, use the facilities, and conceivably even the personnel, of the International Court of Justice, the so-called World Court, that sits, mainly idle, in the quiet Dutch city of The Hague. The World Court, as such, is not a proper forum for a proceeding against the Shah. It is a tribunal limited to deciding legal disputes between sovereign states. Individuals can neither complain nor be the targets of complaint, and the scope of the World Court's activities is confined to noncriminal subject matter. Nevertheless, the independent creation of an emergency structure of adjudication located at The Hague is technically possible and politically attractive.

There are, at least, three technical problems of broad practical consequence with this two-step proposal: securing the participation of the Shah, determining the applicable body of law, and enforcing the final decision. It is highly unlikely that the Shah would agree to participate in his own defense. Indeed, whoever heard of an accused criminal voluntarily agreeing to appear before a court and accept the consequences? The two step procedure outlined above could be flexible on this matter. It could invite the Shah to appear, and failing this, it could urge the government in whose country the Shah was resident to cooperate with the United Nations procedure by turning over his person through some type of extradition process. In all probability, however, the government where the Shah is resident at the time of request will interpose its sovereign right to grant asylum to political leaders of foreign countries. Hence, it is highly likely that the United Nations procedure would have to go ahead *in absentia*. In this circumstance, appointing a counsel for the defense might be appropriate. Such an appointment would add to the credibility and authority of the process.

The problem of applicable law is mainly a technical matter of prescribing for the commission and tribunal the legal criteria for use in their work. At Nuremberg, three categories of crimes were relied upon, specified in advance: crimes against peace, war crimes, and crimes against humanity. Here, the situation is different. The main burden of the charges against the Shah involve crimes against humanity in a context where no war existed. In the Nuremberg Principles, crimes against humanity are defined as follows:

> Murder, extermination, enslavement and other inhuman acts done against any civilian population, or persecution on political, racial or religious grounds, when such acts are done or such persecutions are carried on in execution of or in connexion with any crime against peace or any war crime.[3]

The simplest approach would be for the commission to reformulate crimes against humanity by focusing on the relationship between ruler and population in a setting of international peace and drawing on the authority of the burgeoning international law of human rights, including the Universal Declaration of Human Rights. It would also be necessary, I think, to specify a special category of criminal conduct to cover plundering for private gain the public wealth of a country, possibly calling it "crimes against public well-being and wealth." This last category is important in the case of the Shah, where a main line of allegation is the illegal removal of billions of dollars of Iranian public wealth and the existence of economic corruption as a pervasive feature of government. The challenge here is for the commission to find a legally satisfactory way to formulate authoritative standards without engaging in retroactive law-making.

The final practical issue is that of enforcement. How will the punishment be imposed? What's the point of such a procedure if there are no reliable means to exact the punishment? In essence, I believe, the value of this procedure is to give the Iranian people an opportunity to tell their story in a definitive way. It would, in effect, legitimate their rage over the treatment of the former Shah as an individual deserving of sympathy. The tribunal could also, if so inclined, call upon domestic legal institutions, including courts, to give effect, especially in the property area, to findings establishing that the Shah's assets were criminally acquired.

More substantial than these technical problems are some political problems. There is, first of all, the American sensitivity to exposure by a trial of the Shah of the United States role and that of its embassy in putting and keeping the Shah in power between 1953 and 1979. Such sensitivity must be balanced off against the lives of the hostages, the threats of military intervention, and the growing isolation of the United States in the Moslem world. On a deeper level, it is time our citizenry were more fully informed of our actual foreign policy, and given the opportunity to endorse or reject it. In the present, acutely dangerous situation, the risk of official embarrassment seems small indeed compared to the other risks involved.

Another concern is whether this procedure will satisfy the leaders in Iran, the students at the embassy and Ayatollah Khomeini. We can never be sure until such an initiative is tested. There were indications early in the crisis of favorable response, including statements by two leading members of Ayatollah Khomeini's inner circle—Abolhassan Bani Sadr, then acting foreign minister and later President; also, Sadegh Ghotbzadegh, initially head of Iranian radio and television and later Foreign Minister after Bani Sadr's forced resignation. They have both suggested that the other problems will go away, including the holding of the hostages and the embassy, if some impartial procedure under United Nations auspices can be agreed upon and taken seriously by all parties, but it became increasingly doubtful whether such relatively secular voices of moderation carried any weight with Khomeini or the militants holding the hostages.

Finally, there is the expressed fear that if the Shah is prosecuted, then other former dictators will be pursued as well. More serious than this, it is said, dictators will be disinclined to accept exile if their prospect includes criminal prosecution. Instead, they will fight to the end no matter how bloody the results. Such concerns raise questions about how widespread the procedure proposed here is likely to become. Note that the idea of Nuremberg has been confined to the special political circumstances that existed at the end of World War II although many subsequent international circumstances could logically have produced Nuremberg prosecutions. In the end, the question is one of competing considerations about the drift of world order. I am convinced that the lesser risks at this time involve creating some procedure for the exposure and possible punishment of deposed tyrants for their crimes of state.

In the end, the issue of political will is crucial. Whether the leaders of Iran and the United States, now locked in a death embrace, have the imagination and courage to disengage is the ultimate question. Iran would have to relinquish its literal claim for the physical body of the Shah and the application of Islamic law in exchange for the satisfaction of its most fundamental and principled demand that the responsibility of the Shah for crimes against the Iranian people be established for all to see. The United States would achieve its fundamental and principled demand that all hostages be released, while relinquishing its tactical refusal to allow inquiry into the criminality of the Shah's rule.

Despite difficulties, an international mechanism for investigating crimes of state by deposed rulers seems to be an idea whose time has come. And no better context than the present anguish over the fate of the hostages, of world peace, and of the Shah is likely to present itself.

The Iran Hostage Crisis: The Rights of Diplomats and the Rights of Weak States

The United States government has insisted, since the Iran hostage crisis commenced on November 4, 1979, that international law supports its basic demand that Americans held captive be released. This insistence has been confirmed by a unanimous finding of the International Court of Justice, the highest organ for interpreting international law that exists in the world. For the United States, then, the only inadequacy of international law has involved the inability to enforce its mandate upon a defiant ruler.

Ayatollah Khomeini's refusal to honor the rules of international law relating to diplomatic immunity are among the most serious charges brought against his leadership. Even Hitler, it is alleged, never violated the diplomatic immunity of his enemies. In fact, one has to search the books of diplomatic history to find isolated precedents for the events that have transpired in Tehran since November 4, 1979. And, it is argued, each of these earlier challenges to diplomatic decorum came from a source that could be credibly dismissed as "barbarian." Indeed, condemning Khomeini as a law-breaker and as a backer of terrorism gives rise quite naturally, on a popular redneck level, to the more virulent bumper sticker demands to "nuke Iran" or "hang Khomeini."

Yet one must wonder about this supposed clarity of international law. After all, is it not a serious matter that an embassy is used to subvert the constitutional order of a country, as was done by the United States in staging the coup that brought the Shah back to power in 1953? Is it not also serious that embassy personnel evidently helped establish and train the SAVAK, the secret police that committed so many crimes against the people of Iran?[4] The response to these Iranian grievances is also clear: "Everybody knows that embassies are spy nests." True, vague prohibitions against intervening in the internal affairs of sovereign states exist, but no one takes them seriously. And besides, diplomacy is inevitably interventionary. This is the game of politics played on a global scale, for better or worse.

The law on the subject also supports the American refusal to extradite the Shah. First of all, it is claimed that the Shah was a recipient of the American prerogative to give asylum, especially on this occasion, where a supposed medical necessity existed.[5] Besides, on a more technical level, the absence of an extradition treaty between the United States and Iran would have made it virtually impossible to return the Shah to Iranian custody, even if Jimmy Carter had wanted to do so.[6] Finally, even if an extradition treaty had existed, it is doubtful that an American court would have found the Shah extraditable. The evidence against him is connected with his repressive rule, but extradition is not available against someone accused of "political crimes."

That is, international law as it exists supports the United States claim about the hostages, but it gives Iran almost no comfort. The very clarity of international law, given underlying inequities, raises questions about its one-sidedness. Why should the rules protecting diplomatic immunity be so much clearer than the rules protecting a weak country against intervention? Or why should "asylum" be available to a cruel tyrant associated with the massive commission of state crimes, including torture, arbitrary execution, and economic plunder? What kind of international law is it that protects foreign police and torture specialists by conferring upon them the status of "diplomat"?

In part, the drift of international law reflects the history of international relations since the birth of the modern state system in the middle of the seventeenth century. It is a law of, for, and by governments, and especially powerful governments. In that sense, all governments have a shared interest in upholding the absolute rights of their diplomatic representatives. Relations depend on communication, even in periods of stress, and hence the case for diplomatic immunity seems strong. The United Nations is, as an organization of governments, the world's strongest lobby for diplomatic immunity. On other aspects of the situation, interests are not so clearly shared. Intervention in an interdependent world is not altogether avoidable, and it represents one of the instruments by which the strong control the weak. Nonintervention generally helps the weak, as the prohibition is only meaningful as directed against the relatively stronger party to a conflict. The weaker side, regardless of its intentions, normally lacks an intervention option, although it could in a given instance theoretically ignore its handicaps of power. In fact, however, the history of interventionary diplomacy is overwhelmingly the story of how the strong have used their power in various ways against the weak, and the struggle for norms and regimes based on nonintervention is the contrary story of how weaker states have tried to inhibit intrusions on their territorial integrity and political independence.[7] To renounce intervention seems for a superpower tantamount to renouncing the global extension of power politics. It can be done quite easily in words, but not consistently in deeds.

In this regard, it is true that the protection of diplomatic immunity suggests an invariable constraint whereas the prohibition on intervention is fuzzy, vague, and necessarily conditional and contextual. The rationale for "humanitarian intervention," although itself controversial, suggests that even normative considerations can be ambiguous, as when, for instance, genocide or widespread abuse occurs in the target society. To make nonintervention into an absolute would be to endorse unlimited internal sovereignty, an endorsement quite inconsistent with the protection of human rights. At the same time, there are some core instances of intervention that seem clear, provided some limited assumptions are made. One of these, applicable to the Iranian case, is that in the absence of persistent and severe violations of human rights, the deliberate subversion of the constitutional process of a foreign state is an "illegal" intervention in its internal affairs, especially if a change of regime results.

Regarding the treatment of deposed wandering tyrants, existing governments grow nervous, as well they might. Many rulers are potential defendants in trials alleging state crime. The idea of granting sanctuary to deposed leaders has some appeal as a matter of global policy, thereby creating the option of exile as an alternative to protracted civil strife and bloodshed. Even Idi Amin, Emperor Bokassa I, Pol Pot, and Anastasio Somoza Debayle have found foreign places of refuge; if returned home, they would all almost surely be executed.

What we find, then, is both a proimperial and a progovernmental bias built into modern international law. This double bias is a natural consequence of states' dominating the global scene and of some states' dominating others. Whether such a framework is adequate or not is one of the deeper, unexamined issues posed by the Iranian crisis. Khomeini clearly rejects this bias:

> What kind of law is this? It permits the U.S. Government to exploit and colonize peoples all over the world for decades. But it does not allow the extradition of an individual who has staged great massacres. Can you call it law?[8]

Perhaps, however, Khomeini is mixing up here the law that should be with the law that could be. Given the way that international diplomacy operates, how is it reasonable to expect international law to be different than it is? Let us not sit too quickly in judgment of Ayatollah Khomeini for his evident refusal to shape Iranian policy by reference to the law on the books. American leaders have had their own doubts about whether international law should interfere with the formation of foreign policy in crisis contexts. One recalls, of course, in this connection, Dean Acheson's famous remarks on the Cuban Missile Crisis made at the 1963 Annual Meeting of the American Society of International Law: "The power, position, and prestige of the United States had been challenged by another state; and law simply does not deal with such questions of ultimate power—power that comes close to the sources of sovereignty. I cannot believe that there are principles of law that say we must accept destruction of our way of life."[9] In fact, in the several narrations of the United States decision-making process over the course of the Cuban Missile Crisis, as written by nonlawyers, the legal factor is either not mentioned, or only so slightly as to be of no consequence.[10]

To similar effect, one recalls Leonard Meeker's "legal" defense of the United States Dominican intervention in 1965 by counseling against "fundamentalist views on the nature of international legal obligations" that would make it appear that a nondefensive use of force in a foreign country was a clear violation of the United Nations Charter prohibitions of article 2(4).[11] Mr. Meeker, then legal adviser to the Secretary of State, addressed this defense of American policy to the Foreign Law Association in June of 1965. My point here, as with my earlier reference to the Cuban Missile Crisis, is that American policymakers and their legal experts were quite prepared to bend or ignore international law under the pressure of international circumstances. Why, then, be shocked when others do the same? Of course, the United States didn't violate *this* rule in the past, but why expect Iran to condition its exercise of sovereign rights by a literal imitation of our example? It is the more general example of subordinating legal inhibitions to claims of sovereign necessity that pertains here.

And yet there is another set of possibilities. Why should governments alone establish the rules that govern behavior on the planet? Why should not citizens organize to insist on a framework of law that corresponds to a framework of minimum morality? Part of this pressure can come through the reform of international law, making it less one-sided. The non-Western governments of the Third World have exerted some pressure along these lines with respect to international economic relations, ocean rights and duties, and the status of irregular forces (guerrillas and liberation armies) in time of war.

Perhaps out of the Iranian encounter will come increased possibilities for a more ambitious program of global reform. Perhaps we can look forward to a redrafting of the Vienna Convention on Diplomatic and Consular Immunity so as more nearly to balance the rights of the host country to political independence with the rights of the foreign country to diplomatic security. Already, a commission of inquiry has been established under United Nations auspices to investigate the Iranian grievances. Its role and impact are at this time problematic. From the outset it was evident that the United Nations commission, as established, could not expect to do more than investigate and report, and, as it turned out, even those expectations were never realized. What seems desirable is a permanent, rather than an *ad hoc* mechanism, with a continuing competence to investigate charges of crimes of state filed against tyrants whether deposed or not, with the power to recommend, as appropriate, remedies, including even the formation of special tribunals competent to pass judgment. But to affirm the necessity of such a step should not be confused with a positive attitude toward feasibility. As with such other "necessities" as the Nuremberg enterprise and nuclear disarmament, the need is overcome by the intractable dynamics of statism, keeping power and authority fragmented when it comes to the use of force either internationally or intranationally.

It seems doubtful for a variety of reasons that global reform along the lines proposed above will be undertaken as a consequence of the Iranian hostage crisis. On the contrary. Efforts seem underway in the United States to restore the covert operations mission to the CIA repertoire. The only open question is the degree of accountability to Congress and the stringency of the requirement that the president approve in advance proposed covert operations by the CIA. There is no serious prospect of conditioning CIA operations by the constraints of domestic and international law. Even more clearly, the United States is moving to establish military forces and doctrine for intervention in foreign countries. Indeed, the publicity surrounding the formation of the Rapid Deployment Force, designed especially for use in the Persian Gulf region, is very reminiscent of the 1960s enthusiasm for the Green Berets as the cutting edge of counterinsurgency doctrine, conceived of, especially in those early Kennedy years, as a way to defeat radical insurgencies in the Third World. This approach led to the Vietnam intervention, undertaken by Washington with only the most marginal attention to the constraining role of international law upon its sovereign discretion to use force as national policy-makers saw fit. The one-sidedness of international law is but a reflection of the one-sidedness of international life in general.

Given this reality, have we not reached the stage where citizens, through voluntary associations, should organize to regulate the behavior of governments? At least, it would seem constructive to have a mechanism available for inquiring into the commission of state crime. Some past efforts in these directions exist. In Europe, the British philosopher Bertrand Russell established a "tribunal" to investigate charges of war crimes arising out of the American involvement in the Vietnam War.¹² More recently a group of international legal and cultural figures have joined in an effort to proclaim a legal framework for human rights, issuing the Algiers Declaration of the Rights of Peoples on July 4, 1976. Preliminary steps have been taken by an Italian entity, the Lelio Basso Foundation, to establish a tribunal that would investigate charges against governments and leaders flowing out of violations of the Algiers Declaration.

In other settings, individuals and groups have gathered together to put forward normative demands. In 1978 the Delhi Declaration condemned nuclear weapons and proposed a treaty for their renunciation as weapons of war. Earlier in 1975 a group of economists gathered in Mexico and issued the Cocoyac Declaration, which, called for a new global economic order that went well beyond the demands of governments for "a new international economic order."

How do initiatives such as these gain authoritativeness in international affairs? Suppose other groups issued less congenial declarations as to legal substance. How is it possible to choose among conflicting normative assertions? Would not chaos result if self-appointed law-makers were endowed with legitimacy? These are real concerns that require extended discussion. Suffice it to say here that government-generated law, to achieve effectiveness, also depends often on soliciting respect from the actors in international life. With populist initiatives, the path toward respect and observance is probably more difficult. Yet it is not essentially different from the growth of effective law on the basis of conventional sources. The law-making claim of nongovernmental actors rests on the ultimate competence of individuals and groups to enact authoritative norms for behavior. Such norms do not enjoy an automatic validity and would not be valid at all in those arenas where validity is defined by reference to formal sources (for instance, the International Court of Justice). But in other arenas, including ones where international institutions and governments act, such populist norms can be invoked by participants, and if influential to some degree, then their role in shaping behavior is real and effective, and to that degree establishes part of the legal environment. Particularly with respect to crimes of state, there is an increasingly acknowledged institutional gap in the international legal order that is closed, if slightly, by private, nongovernmental normative initiatives possessing a certain law-creating impact.

Because law is clear on the books does not prove that it deserves respect or that it is adequate. The events in Iran show us that some clear rules of international law have been broken, but they also suggest that the content and impact of this law is arbitrary and one-sided. Given the historical shifts in the world, including the upsurge of power in the Third World, it is not clear why the old law should be kept as is. But it is also not by any means certain that governments will create a more balanced law dealing with embassy use and abuse, as well as with whether someone accused of serious state crime should be entitled to asylum rather than, say, to a fair trial under impartial auspices. This may be the moment for individuals, churches, and voluntary associations of various kinds to assert a human concern—that the future of international law is not a matter for governments *only*.

In time this concern, born of frustration and anxiety, could become a powerful basis on which to impose on sovereign states an effective framework of morally conditioned restraint. At least, it is worth pursuing this way out of surrendering unconditionally our birthright as moral beings to the monopolizing tendencies of the sovereign state.

Appendix

Universal Declaration on the Rights of Peoples

Algiers, 4 July 1976

PREAMBLE

We live at a time of great hopes and deep despair;

—a time of conflicts and contradictions;

—a time when liberation struggles have succeeded in arousing the peoples of the world against the domestic and international structures of imperialism and in overturning colonial systems;

—a time of struggle and victory in which new ideals of justice among and within nations have been adopted;

—a time when the General Assembly of the United Nations has given increasing expression, from the Universal Declaration of Human Rights to the Charter on the Economic Rights and Duties of States, to the quest for a new international, political and economic order.

But this is also a time of frustration and defeat, as new forms of imperialism evolve to oppress and exploit the peoples of the world.

Imperialism, using vicious methods, with the complicity of governments that it has itself often installed, continues to dominate a part of the world. Through direct or indirect intervention, through multinational enterprises, through manipulation of corrupt local politicians, with the assistance of military regimes based on police repression, torture and physical extermination of opponents, through a set of practices that has become known as neo-colonialism, imperialism extends its stranglehold over many peoples.

Aware of expressing the aspirations of our era, we met in Algiers to proclaim that all the peoples of the world have an equal right to liberty, the right to free themselves from any foreign interference and to choose their own government, the right if they are under subjection, to fight for their liberation and the right to benefit from other peoples' assistance in their struggle.

Convinced that the effective respect for human rights necessarily implies respect for the rights of peoples, we have adopted the UNIVERSAL DECLARATION OF THE RIGHTS OF PEOPLES.

226   *Human Rights and State Sovereignty*

May all those who, throughout the world, are fighting the great battle, at times through armed struggle, for the freedom of all peoples, find in this Declaration the assurance of the legitimacy of their struggle.

SECTION 1.—RIGHT TO EXISTENCE

ARTICLE 1.—Every people has the right to existence.

ARTICLE 2.—Every people has the right to the respect of its national and cultural identity.

ARTICLE 3.—Every people has the right to retain peaceful possession of its territory and to return to it if it is expelled.

ARTICLE 4.—None shall be subjected, because of his national or cultural identity, to massacre, torture, persecution, deportation, expulsion or living conditions such as may compromise the identity or integrity of the people to which he belongs.

SECTION II.—RIGHT TO POLITICAL SELF-DETERMINATION

ARTICLE 5.—Every people has an imprescriptible and unalienable right to self-determination. It shall determine its political status freely and without any foreign interference.

ARTICLE 6.—Every people has the right to break free from any colonial or foreign domination, whether direct or indirect, and from any racist regime.

ARTICLE 7.—Every people has the right to have a democratic government representing all the citizens without distinction as to race, sex, belief or colour, and capable of ensuring effective respect for the human rights and fundamental freedoms for all.

SECTION III.—ECONOMIC RIGHTS OF PEOPLES

ARTICLE 8.—Every people has an exclusive right over its natural wealth and resources. It has the right to recover them if they have been despoiled, as well as any unjustly paid indemnities.

ARTICLE 9.—Scientific and technical progress being part of the common heritage of mankind, every people has the right to participate in it.

ARTICLE 10.—Every people has the right to a fair evaluation of its labour and to equal and just terms in international trade.

ARTICLE 11.—Every people has the right to choose its own economic and social system and pursue its own path to economic development freely and without any foreign interference.

ARTICLE 12.—The economic rights set forth above shall be exercised in a spirit of solidarity amongst the peoples of the world and with due regard for their respective interests.

SECTION IV.—RIGHT TO CULTURE

ARTICLE 13.—Every people has the right to speak its own language and preserve and develop its own culture, thereby contributing to the enrichment of the culture of mankind.

ARTICLE 14.—Every people has the right to its artistic, historical and cultural wealth.

ARTICLE 15.—Every people has the right not to have an alien culture imposed upon it.

SECTION V.—RIGHT TO ENVIRONMENT AND COMMON RESOURCES

ARTICLE 16.—Every people has the right to the conservation, protection and improvement of its environment.

ARTICLE 17.—Every people has the right to make use of the common heritage of mankind, such as the high seas, the sea-bed, and outer space.

ARTICLE 18.—In the exercise of the preceding rights every people shall take account of the necessity for coordinating the requirements of its economic development with solidarity amongst all the peoples of the world.

SECTION VI.—RIGHTS OF MINORITIES

ARTICLE 19.—When a people constitutes a minority within a State it has the right to respect for its identity, traditions, language and cultural heritage.

ARTICLE 20.—The members of a minority shall enjoy without discrimination the same rights as the other citizens of the State and shall participate on an equal footing with them in public life.

ARTICLE 21.—These rights shall be exercised with due respect for the legitimate interests of the community as a whole and cannot authorise impairing the territorial integrity and political unity of the State, provided the State acts in accordance with all the principles set forth in this Declaration.

Section VII.—Guarantees and sanctions

Article 22.—Any disregard for the provisions of this Declaration constitutes a breach of obligations towards the international community as a whole.

Article 23.—Any prejudice resulting from disregard for this Declaration must be totally compensated by whoever caused it.

Article 24.—Any enrichment to the detriment of the people in violation of the provisions of this Declaration shall give rise to the restitution of profits thus obtained. The same shall be applied to all excessive profits on investments of foreign origin.

Article 25.—Any unequal treaties, agreements or contracts concluded in disregard of the fundamental rights of peoples shall have no effect.

Article 26.—External financial charges which become excessive and unbearable for the people shall cease to be due.

Article 27.—The gravest violations of the fundamental rights of peoples, especially of their right to existence, constitute international crimes for which their perpetrators shall carry personal penal liability.

Article 28.—Any people whose fundamental rights are seriously disregarded has the right to enforce them, especially by political or trade union struggle and even, in the last resort, by the use of force.

Article 29.—Liberation movements shall have access to international organizations and their combatants are entitled to the protection of the humanitarian law of war.

Article 30.—The re-establishment of the fundamental rights of peoples, when they are seriously disregarded, is a duty incumbent upon all members of the international community.

Notes

Chapter I

1. In fact, of course, a wide range of valuable specialist work on human rights has gone on for years and should not be tainted by these polar pulls of legalism and ideological moralism. Among many others whose work I have found personally stimulating, the following are notable: David Bayley, Ian Brownlie, Thomas Buergenthal, John Carey, Maurice Cranston, Ernst Haas, Louis Henkin, C. Wilfred Jenks, Harold Lasswell, Myres McDougal, Moses Moskowitz, A. H. Robertson, Louis Sohn, and Vernon Van Dyke. And, more recently, Myres McDougal has brought his various writings on human rights into one magisterial volume, coauthored with Harold Lasswell and Lung chu-Chen, *Human Rights and World Public Order* (New Haven: Yale University Press, 1980). In a central respect Professor McDougal's overall orientation toward these issues is mainly implicit in this volume; nevertheless, his approach deeply influences my own, especially his stress upon values as the foundation of public order and his association of values with the promotion of human dignity. What I find encouraging is the convergence of the kind of systemic normative inquiry of McDougal's jurisprudence with various strands of overtly progressive political analysis that rest their case for change ultimately on human rights grounds. One especially persuasive instance of this latter tendency is Edward Said's excellent book *The Question of Palestine* (New York: Times Books, 1979), where the argument for Palestinian self-determination (and, incidentally, Israeli security) is merged with an argument on behalf of human rights; see, for example, p. 52. See, also, Hannah Arendt's relevant argument to the effect that " . . . no cause is left [in politics] but the most ancient of all, the one, in fact, that from the beginning of our history has determined the very existence of politics, the cause of freedom versus tyranny." *On Revolution* (New York: Viking, 1963), p. 1.

2. See their essays in Ralph Pettman, ed., *Moral Claims in World Affairs* (New York: St. Martin's Press, 1979), pp. 52–91.

3. See, for example, many of the contributions to Donald P. Kommers and Gilbert D. Loescher, eds., *Human Rights and American Foreign Policy* (South Bend: Notre Dame U. Press, 1979); Richard Lillich, ed., *Humanitarian Intervention and the United Nations* (Charlottesville, Virginia: U. of Virginia Press, 1973); Tom J. Farer, "United States Foreign Policy and the Protection of Human Rights: Observations and Proposals," *Virginia Journal of International Law* 14 (1974), 623–652; Louis Henkin, "United States and the Crisis in Human Rights," *Virginia Journal of International Law* (1974), 653–671.

4. Raymond Gastil, ed., *Freedom in the World* (Boston and New York: G. K. Hall/ Freedom House, 1978), p. 4.

5. Particularly illuminating here is Lillich's contribution to Kommers and Loescher, *Human Rights*, pp. 278–298.

6. In this regard see statement of May 2, 1979, of United States Deputy Secretary of State Warren Christopher before the International Organizations Subcommittee of the House Foreign Affairs Committee, "Implementing the Human Rights Policy" (mimeographed), pp. 1–23; see also extensive "county reports" annual volume submitted to Congress, "Report on Human Rights Practices in Countries Receiving U.S. Aid," Feb. 8, 1979.

7. Tom Farer's essay "On a Collision Course: the American Campaign for Human Rights and the Antiradical Bias in the Third World" is helpful; published in Kommers and Loescher, *Human Rights*, pp. 263–277.

8. Recent attention in Third World arenas to the distortions of reality associated with the one-sided control of the so-called international information order have brought new attention to such matters in a global context. Despite freedom of expression in the United States, news and its interpretation tend to be presented in a selective and filtered manner that is difficult to elucidate because their modes are subtle and largely informal.

9. Principle VI(c) of the Nuremberg Principles as formulated by the authoritative International Law Commission defined Crimes against Humanity as follows:

> Murder, extermination, enslavement, deportation and other inhuman acts done against any civilian population, or persecutions on political, racial or religious grounds, when such acts are done or such persecutions are carried on in execution of or in connexion with any crime against peace or any war crime. (My emphasis.)

The underlined words suggest the need for a more general formulation not tied to the subject matter of war.

10. On this wider shift see my *Normative International Politics*, forthcoming.

11. Irving Stone, ed., *Dear Theo: The Autobiography of Vincent Van Gogh* (New York: New American Library, 1937), p. 278.

Chapter II

1. For helpful background see Laurie Weissbrodt, "Human Rights Legislation and U.S. Foreign Policy," 7 *Georgia Journal of International and Comparative Law* 231 (1977). I owe much of my appreciation of the congressional role in this period to an excellent paper on the subject written during 1979–1980 by Jo Backer, a graduate student at the Woodrow Wilson School of Public and International Affairs, Princeton University.

2. See R. A. Falk, "Panama Treaty Trap," *Foreign Policy* 30 (1978), 68–82.

3. Noam Chomsky and Edward S. Herman, "The United States Versus Human Rights in the Third World," *Monthly Review*, 29 (1977), 22–45; 29–31.

4. Donald M. Fraser, "Freedom and Foreign Policy," *Foreign Policy* 26 (1977), 140–156.

5. Fraser, p. 141. See also Christopher, "The Diplomacy of Human Rights," p. 2: "Our idealism and our self-interest coincide. Widening the circle of countries which share our human rights values is at the very core of our security interests. Such nations make strong allies. Their commitment to human rights gives them an inner strength and stability which causes them to stand steadfastly with us on the most difficult issues of our time."

6. Fraser, p. 140.

7. Fraser, p. 148–9.

8. "A Foreign Policy Based on America's Essential Character," *Department of State Bulletin*, LXXVI (June 13, 1977), 621–625; at 622.

9. Ibid., p. 632.

10. Interview, "What's Right with Our Foreign Policy," *U.S. News and World Report* (Feb. 13, 1978), 28–32.

11. Cyrus Vance, "Human Rights and Foreign Policy," *Department of State Bulletin*, LXXVI 505–508, at 508.

12. Interview, p. 32.

13. Vance, p. 505.

14. Jimmy Carter, cited note 8, p. 624.

15. D. P. Moynihan, "The Politics of Human Rights," *Commentary* (Aug. 1977), 19–26, at 24.

16. Ibid., pp. 24–5.

17. Ibid., p. 25.

18. Ibid., p. 25.

19. Interview, p. 28.

20. See ch. IV of this book.

Chapter III

1. For an analysis of the Stanleyville Operation along these lines, see Falk, *Legal Order in a Violent World* (Princeton: Princeton U. Press, 1968), pp. 324–335.

2. See, e.g., Hedley Bull, "The Grotian Conception of International Society," in Herbert Butterfield and Martin Wight, eds., *Diplomatic Investigations* (London: Allen and Unwin, 1966), pp. 51–73; Peter F. Butler, "Legitimacy in a States-System: Vattel's Law of Nations," in Michael Donelan, ed., *The Reason of States* (London: Allen and Unwin, 1978), pp. 45–63; R. J. Vincent, *Nonintervention and International Order* (Princeton: Princeton U. Press, 1974).

3. R. J. Vincent, "Western Conceptions of a Universal Moral Order," in Ralph Pettmann, ed., *Moral Claims in World Affairs* (New York: St. Martin's Press, 1979), pp. 52–78, especially pp. 68–72.

4. See Ian Brownlie, "Humanitarian Intervention," and Richard B. Lillich, "Humanitarian Intervention: A Reply to Dr. Brownlie and a Plea for Constructive Alternatives," in J. N. Moore, ed., *Law and Civil War in the Modern World* (Baltimore: Johns Hopkins U. Press, 1974), pp. 217–251.

5. See Dominguez, "Assessing Human Rights Conditions," in Dominguez and others, *Enhancing Global Human Rights* (New York: McGraw-Hill, 1979), pp. 21–116; see also Chapter V of this volume.

6. A more comprehensive framework for the protection of human rights has been embodied in the American Convention on Human Rights, which includes provision for an Inter-American judicial procedure. The treaty is in force despite the absence of United States ratification. Yet it remains to be seen whether it will influence the behavior of the many authoritarian governments within the region.

7. See also Chapter VI of this volume.

8. For a more detailed view, see Falk, *A Study of Future Worlds* (New York: Free Press), 1975.

Chapter IV

1. For specification of values and alternative images of global reform see main work of World Order Models Project: Rajni Kothari, *Footsteps into the Future* (New York: Free Press, 1974); Ali Mazrui, *A World Federation of Cultures: An African Perspective* (New York: Free Press, 1976); Horacio Godoy and Gustavo Lagos, *The Revolution in Being* (New York: Free Press, 1977); Saul H. Mendlovitz, ed., *On the Creation of a Just World Order: Preferred Worlds for the 1990's* (New York: Free Press, 1975), Richard Falk, *A Study of Future Worlds* (New York: Free Press, 1975).

2. See e.g., Albert Fishlow, "Some Reflections on Post-1964 Brazilian Economic Policy" and Philippe C. Schmitter, "The 'Portugalization' of Brazil" in Alfred Stepan, ed., *Authoritarian Brazil: Origins, Policies, and Future* (New Haven: Yale U. Press, 1973), pp. 69–118; 179–232.

3. See, especially, the penetrating assessment along these lines in Guillermo A. O'Donnell, "Corporatism and the Question of the State," in James M. Malloy, ed., *Authoritarianism and Corporatism in Latin America* (Pittsburgh: U. of Pittsburgh Press, 1977), pp. 47–88.

4. See Alfred Stepan, *The Military in Politics: Changing Patterns in Brazil* (Princeton, New Jersey: Princeton U. Press, 1971); for a more general, carefully nuanced assessment see Abraham F. Lowenthal, "Armies and Politics in Latin America," *World Politics* XXVII (1974), 107–130.

5. Empirical confirmation in Schmitter, " 'Portugalization' of Brazil."

6. See Fernando Pedreira, "Decompression in Brazil?" *Foreign Affairs* 53 (1975), 498–512.

7. See discussion to this effect in Carlos Estevan Martins, "Brazil and the United States from the 1960's to the 1970's," in Julio Cotler and Richard R. Fagen, eds., *Latin America and the United States: The Changing Political Realities* (Stanford, California: Stanford U. Press, 1974), pp. 269–301, especially 298–301.

8. For analysis along these lines see Leslie M. Pryor, "Arms and the Shah," *Foreign Policy* 31 (1978), 56–71.

9. E.g., "United States Policies and Programs in Brazil," Hearings of Subcommittee on Western Hemisphere Affairs of Senate Foreign Relations Committee, 92nd Cong., 1st Sess., May 4, 5 and 11, 1971; Michael Klare and Nancy Stein, "Exporting the Tools of Repression," Reprint No. 104, Center for National Security Studies, Dec. 1976, pp. 1–15; Walden Bellow and Severina Rivera, eds., *The Logistics of Repression* (Washington, D.C.: Friends of the Filipino People, 1977).

10. Norman Gall illustrates this characteristic by reference to the callous disregard of human welfare in relation to train safety and service between outlying workers' communities and Rio de Janeiro. See Gall, "The Rise of Brazil," *Commentary,* 63 (1977), 45–55, at 50.

11. For detailed elaboration of this pre-1964 corporatist background in Brazil see Kenneth Paul Erikson, *The Brazilian Corporatist State and Working-Class Politics*, (Berkeley, California: U. of California Press, 1977), pp. 11–46.

12. For elaboration see essays in Malloy, *Authoritarianism.*

13. E.g., Robert L. Borosage and John Marks, eds., *The CIA File* (New York: Grossman, 1976); "Covert Action: Intelligence Activities," Hearings, Senate Select Committee to study Governmental Operations, 94th Cong., 1st Sess., Dec. 4–5, 1975.

14. E.g., for America's role in sustaining the Somoza regime in Nicaragua even while it was in the midst of defending itself against a broad-based opposition, see Penny Lernoux, "Nicaragua's Civil War," *The Nation,* Sept. 16, 1978, 230–231; see related piece by Jim Morrell, "Behind the Scenes at the IMF," *The Nation,* Sept. 16, 1978, 232–235.

15. E.g., "But if Iran is called upon to intervene in the internal affairs of any Gulf state, it must be recognized in advance by the United States that this is the role for which Iran is being primed and blame cannot be assigned for Iran's carrying out of an implied assignment," in "Access to Oil—The United States Relationships with Saudi Arabia and Iran," Senate Committee of Energy and Natural Resources, Dec. 1977, p. 84.

16. Such a course of developments can be inferred from a recent perceptive analysis of the Brazilian experience—José Serra, "Three Mistaken Theses Regarding the Connection between Industrialization and Authoritarian Regimes," Oct., 1978, mimeo.

17. See Stepan, *Authoritarian Brazil,* especially Juan Linz, "The Future of an Authoritarian Situation or the Institutionalization of an Authoritarian Regime: The Case of Brazil," pp. 233–254.

18. Peter L. Berger, *Pyramids of Sacrifice: Political Ethics and Social Change* (New York: Basic Books, 1974).

19. For background see Frank Parkin, *Class Inequality and Political Order: Social Stratification in Communist and Capitalist Societies* (New York: Prueger, 1971); David Lane, *The End of Inequality? Stratification under State Socialism* (Baltimore: Penguin, 1971); see also contribution of Jorgé Dominguez to Council on Foreign Relations volume from The 1980's Project on human rights, *Enhancing Global Human Rights* (New York: McGraw-Hill, 1979), pp. 21–116, for systematic attempt at comparison.

20. The most fundamental consideration of praetorianism as a form of authoritarian rule is Samuel P. Huntington, *Political Order in Changing Societies* (New Haven: Yale U. Press, 1968), pp. 192–263; for refinement and extension of Huntington approach see Henry Bienen's essay "Military and Society in East Africa: Thinking Again about Praetorianism" in Bienen, *Armies and Parties in Africa* (New York: Africana, 1978), pp. 165–186.

21. Roy A. Medvedev, *On Socialist Democracy* (New York: Knopf, 1975).

22. Michael J. Crozier, Samuel P. Huntington, and Joji Watanuki, *The Crisis of Democracy: Report on the Governability of Democracies to the Trilateral Commission* (New York: N. Y. U. Press, 1975).

23. Interview, *U.S. News and World Report,* March 8, 1976, p. 51.

24. Crozier et al., *The Crisis of Democracy,* p. 6.

25. Ibid., pp. 6–7.

26. Ibid., p. 7.

27. Ibid., p. 9.

28. Ibid., p. I.

29. To similar effect see Jean-François Revel, *The Totalitarian Temptation* (New York: Doubleday, 1977).

30. This is, of course, the guiding premise of the World Order Models Project. My own views are spelled out in *A Study of Future Worlds* and in *This Endangered Planet: Proposals and Prospects for Human Survival* (New York: Random House, 1971).

31. David Gompert and others, *Nuclear Weapons and World Politics* (New York, McGraw-Hill, 1977), pp. 4–5.

32. Letter to the editor, *Time,* July 18, 1977.

33. Tom J. Farer, "The Greening of the Globe: a Preliminary Appraisal of the World Order Models Project (WOMP)," *International Organization,* 31 (1977), pp.

34. For discussion of these world order values see Falk, *Study of Future Worlds,* pp. 11–39.

35. The analysis of this paragraph reflects the influence of Kenneth Paul Erikson.

36. See Pedreira, "Decompression," p. 499.

37. Reactions of the *coup* to the 1964 takeover significantly studied in Janice E. Perlman,

The Myth of Marginality: Urban Poverty and Politics in Rio de Janeiro (Berkeley: U. of California Press, 1976).

38.   See Erikson, pp. 97–130.

39.   See Kenneth S. Mericle, "Corporatist Control of the Working Class: Authoritarian Brazil since 1964," in Malloy, Authoritarianism, pp. 303–338, at 306.

40.   Mericle, p. 306.

41.   Schmitter, " 'Portugalization' of Brazil," p. 200.

42.   Ibid., p. 204 (other reinforcing data also collected and presented in Schmitter chapter).

43.   Ibid., p. 193.

44.   Ibid., p. 193.

45.   Table from Ibid., p. 198.

46.   Gall, "The Rise of Brazil," p. 46.

47.   Ibid., p. 47.

48.   Pedreira, "Decompression in Brazil?" p. 502.

49.   For a detailed analysis of American role see Jan Knippers Black, *United States Penetration of Brazil* (Philadelphia: U. of Pennsylvania Press, 1977).

50.   See "The 1964 Revolution—Made in Brazil," *Washington Post,* March 8, 1977, p. A15.

51.   Ibid.

52.   Gall, "The Rise of Brazil," p. 45.

53.   *New York Times,* March 6, 1977, p. 11.

Chapter V

1.   See A. James Gregor, *The Fascist Persuasion in Radical Politics* (Princeton, New Jersey: Princeton U. Press, 1974); Eqbal Ahmad refers to authoritarian/capitalist regimes as partaking of "developmental fascism"; for a useful review of the question of labeling see Herbert Feith, "Repressive-Developmentalist Regimes in Asia: The Search for Hope," World Order Models Project discussion paper, Poona, India, July 1978.

2.   Simone Weil, "Analysis of Oppression," in George A. Panichas, ed., *The Simone Weil Reader* (New York: David McKay 1977), p. 131.

3.   Quoted from the *Boston Globe,* July 25, 1978, p. 6.

4.   For careful, well-documented comparison see Jorge Dominguez's contribution to the 1980s volume on human rights, Jorge I. Dominguez, Nigel S. Rodley, Bryce Wood, and Richard A. Falk, *Enhancing Global Human Rights* (New York: McGraw-Hill, the 1980's Project, 1979).

5.   See Eric Lane, "Demanding Human Rights: A Change in World Legal Order." *Hofstra Law Review* 6, no. 2 (1978); 269–95; H. Lauterpacht, *International Law and Human Rights* (New York: Garland 1950), on links between Westphalian system and the realization of human rights.

6.   For discussion see Dominguez, *Enhancing Global Human Rights;* Fouad Ajami, "Human Rights and World Order Politics," Working Paper no. 4, World Order Models

Projects, 1978, pp. 1–33; Peter Berger, "Are Human Rights Universal?" *Commentary* 64, no. 3 (Sept. 1977), pp. 60-63.

7. See also careful categorization of forms of repression in Ernest Duff and John McCamant, *Violence and Repression in Latin America* (New York: Free Press, 1976), especially pp. 24–55.

8. Cyrus Vance, "Human Rights and Foreign Policy" *Department of State Bulletin*, vol. 76 (May 23, 1977), 505–08; see also manner in which country reports on human rights are organized—"Country Reports on Human Rights Practices," Report of State Department to Congress, February 3, 1978.

9. Quoted from the *New York Times,* July 25, 1978, p. A3.

10. For convenient text see *Development Dialogue,* no. 2 (1974); 88–96; note that rights affirmed here extend beyond what it is reasonable to achieve within the state system.

11. See for example Simon Leys, *Chinese Shadow* (New York: Penguin, 1978); also Donald Zagoria, "China by Daylight," *Dissent* 22 (Spring 1975;, 135–47; Susan Shirk, "Human Rights: What About China?" *Foreign Policy* 29 (1977–78), 109–27; Jerome A. Cohen "Human Rights in China: U.S. Should Press Issues, But Not As Barrier to Ties." *Washington Post,* April 23, 1978, p. D2.

12. See Carl H. Lande, "Letter to the Editor," *New York Times* July 25, 1978, p. A14.

13. D. P. Moynihan, "The Politics of Human Rights," *Commentary* 63, no. 4 (April 1977), p. 24.

14. Mao Tse-tung, "Talk at Enlarged Workers Conference of January 30, 1962," released and printed in *Peking Review* 27 (July 7, 1978), 13.

15. See for example Irma Adelman, "Development Economics: A Reassessment of Goals," *American Economic Review* 65 (1975), 302–09.

16. See Philip Russell, "On Mexico," *New York Times, July 20, 1978, p. 21.

17. See, in general, Henry J. Burton, "Unemployment Problems and Policies in Less Developed Countries," *American Economic Review* 68; 51–55 (May, 1978); Tamos Szentes, "Structural Roots of the Unemployment Problem," *International Social Science Journal* XVIII; 789–80 (1976).

18. See R. J. Barnet, *Intervention and Revolution,* rev. ed. (New York: New American Library, 1972); F. Schurmann, *The Logic of World Power* (New York: Pantheon, 1972).

19. For creative assessment see Lane, "Demanding Human Rights."

20. See Vance, "Human Rights and Foreign Policy," p. 505.

21. See Lane, "Demanding Human Rights," p. 270.

22. *New York Times,* July 30, 1978, see 4, p. 4.

23. For discussion and evaluation of Algiers Declaration see Antonio Cassese and Edmond Jouve, eds., *Pour un droit des peuples* (Paris: Berger-Levrault, 1978).

24. For convenient text see Universal Declaration of the Rights of Peoples, July 4, 1976 (Paris: Francois Maspero, 1977).

25. Algiers Declaration should be read in conjunction with Delhi Declaration on Disarmament and Development, May 1978, also a populist Third World-priented initiative.

26. Moynihan, "The Politics of Human Rights," p. 24.

27. *Ibid.,* p. 25.

28. Berger, "Are Human Rights Universal?" p. 62; note that Carter's middle category of "vital needs" is not embraced by Berger's notion of "grossest cases."

29. See Ajami, "Human Rights and World Order Politics," p. 8.

30. *Ibid.,* pp. 16, 21 respectively; cf. David H. Bayley's more agnostic view of the military in power in *Public Liberties in the New States* (Chicago: Rand McNally, 1964), p. 3.

31. See Ajami, "Human Rights and World Order Politics," p. 25, 28–29 respectively.

32. See Dominguez in *Enhancing Global Human Rights,* pp. 21–116.

33. An observer, "Revolution in Ethiopia," *Monthly Review* 29, no. 3 (July/August 1977), 40–60.

34. See Kathleen Gough, "The Green Revolution in South India and North Vietnam," *Bulletin of Concerned Asian Scholars* 10 (Jan.-March. 1978), 13–23.

Chapter VI

1.   See *Amnesty International Report 1977* (London, England: Amnesty International, 1977), p. 9.

2.   R. J. Vincent, *Nonintervention and International Order* (Princeton, N.J.: Princeton U. Press, 1974), especially pp. 244–249.

3.   The conclusion of "purity" is based, in part, on the fact that the French used troops that might have been needed elsewhere during the period. See ibid., p. 11.

4.   For a useful discussion of the pros and cons of humanitarian intervention see essays by Ian Brownlie and Richard Lillich in John Norton Moore, ed., *Law and Civil War in the Modern World* (Baltimore: Johns Hopkins U. Press, 1974), pp. 217–251.

5.   The Charter of the United Nations makes reference to the promotion of human rights in several of its provisions, especially Articles 1, 55, and 56. On December 10, 1946, the UN General Assembly adopted the Universal Declaration of Human Rights by a unanimous vote of 48–0 (with the seven Soviet bloc members abstaining along with South Africa). The Universal Declaration was regarded as an initial step in the process of setting forth more elaborate and authoritative legal instruments in treaty form. The second step was taken when the General Assembly adopted by resolution on December 16, 1966, three human rights covenants: the International Covenant on Civil and Political Rights; the International Covenant on Economic, Social, and Cultural Rights; and the Optional Protocol to the International Covenant on Civil and Political Rights. The first two covenants have been widely ratified and are in force for those parties. President Carter has submitted these two covenants to the U.S. Senate for ratification, but no favorable action is expected in the immediate future. However, even for nonparties these covenants are generally regarded as evidence of widely shared governmental views as to the human rights requirements of international law. For convenient texts of the Universal Declaration and the covenants see Ian Brownlie, ed., *Basic Documents in International Law*, 2d ed. (Oxford, England: Oxford U. Press, 1972), pp. 144–186. For a more complete collection of human rights documents see Brownlie, *Basic Documents on Human Rights* (Oxford, England: Oxford U. Press, 1971).

6.   "Pathological" in the text refers to psychologically deviant behavior on the part of a political leader, and should be distinguished from "structural" repression that is perceived by the leadership as functionally related to maintaining stable rule.

7.   See Richard Arens, ed., *Genocide in Paraguay* (Philadelphia: Temple U. Press, 1976), especially pp. 132–164.

8.   See Shelton H. Davis, *Victims of the Miracle: Development and the Indians of Brazil* (Cambridge, England: Cambridge U. Press, 1977).

9.   For depiction by an American ambassador and his wife, who were in Uganda from 1972 to 1973, see Thomas and Margaret Melady, *Idi Amin Dada: Hitler in Africa* (Mission, Kansas: Sheed, Andrews and McMeel, 1977). The Meladys contend, for instance, that during Amin's first year in office "about two-thirds of the Langi and Acholi soldiers in the army were killed." Under the prior regime the Ugandan army had been dominated by members of these two tribes.

10.   For a fully documented account of the events considered, including the argument that genocide occurred, see Subrata Roy Chowdhury, *The Genesis of Bangladesh: A Study of International Legal Norms and Permissive Conscience* (New York: Asia Publishing House, 1972).

11.   Article II(b) of the Genocide Convention defines genocide as extending to serious "mental harm"; also Article II(c) regards as genocide "Deliberately inflicting on the group conditions of life calculated to bring about its physical destruction in whole or in part." In effect, ethnocide is encompassed by genocide to the extent that if the identity of a people can

be preserved only under certain conditions, then removing those conditions becomes tantamount to destroying the group.

12. For full account see "The Report of the Mackenzie Valley Pipeline Inquiry," vols. I and II (Ottawa, Canada: Minister of Supply and Services, 1977).

13. Rhodesia has been recently transformed into a majority-ruled, multiracial, independent state. An altered status is expected soon also for south-west Africa. Their transformed condition will be expressed by the formal adoption of their liberation names, Zimbabwe and Namibia, respectively. Each currently has a different status and each is likely to take a different route away from racism.

14. See Jean-François Revel, *The Totalitarian Temptation* (New York: Doubleday, 1977); see also Michael Crozier, Samuel Huntington, and Joji Watanuki, *The Crisis of Democracy: Report on the Governability of Democracies to the Trilateral Commission* (New York: N.Y.U. Press, 1975).

15. For a systematic inquiry into the scope of human rights see the essay by Jorge Dominguez in *Enhancing Global Human Rights*, pp. 21–116.

16. Official conceptions of human rights under the Carter Administration have expanded, at least on the rhetorical level, to include "such vital needs as food, shelter, health care, and education," as well as such standard liberal fare as the rights of persons to be free from arbitrary governmental action and the right to enjoy the civil and political liberties necessary for genuine participation in the political life of the state. For a typical formulation of this enlarged conception of human rights see Warren Christopher, "Human Rights: Principle and Realism," *Department of State Bulletin*, vol. 77, no. 1992 (August 29, 1977), pp. 269–273, especially pp. 269–270.

17. For impressive results along these lines see Amilcar Herrera and others, *Catastrophe or New Society: A Latin American World Model* (Ottawa: International Development Center, 1976); Graciela Chichilnisky, "Development, Basic Needs, and the International Order," *Journal of International Affairs*, vol. 31, no. 2 (1977), pp. 275–304.

18. See, for example, Simone Weil, *The Need for Roots* (New York: Harper & Row, Colophon edition, 1971; originally pub. 1952), pp. 3–39; see also John McHale and Magda Cordell McHale, *Basic Human Needs: A Framework for Action* (New Brunswick, N.J.: Transaction Books, 1978).

19. David Morris and Florizelle B. Liser, "The PQLI: Measuring Progress in Meeting Human Needs," *ODC Communique* (1977).

20. Discussed by Johan Galtung in many places. See, for example, his essay in Saul H. Mendlovitz, ed., *On the Creation of a Just World Order* (New York: Free Press, 1975), pp. 152–153.

21. For my argument along these lines see Chapter IV.

22. A. James Gregor gives the figure of one to three million persons on the basis of "conservative estimates" in *The Fascist Persuasion in Radical Politics* (Princeton, N.J.: Princeton U. Press, 1974), p. x.

23. See, for example, Samir Amin, "Self-Reliance and the New International Economic Order," *Monthly Review*, vol. 29, no. 3 (July/August 1977), 1–21, especially pp. 2–3.

24. See Nicos Poulantzas, *Fascism and Dictatorship* (London: New Left Books, 1974), pp. 119, 191, 220–221.

25. More typical, however, has been to regard "humanitarian" rules of the international law of war as an aspect of human rights. These rules, however, are of limited scope. Their concern is to avoid unnecessary suffering for civilians and to confirm the obligation of countries to give medical treatment to all sick and wounded, even if enemy soldiers.

26. Michael Walzer writes in his preface: "I want to suggest that the arguments we make about war are most fully understood . . . as efforts to recognize and respect the rights of

individual and associated men and women. The morality I shall expound is in its philosophical form a doctrine of human rights. . . . " See Walzer, *Just and Unjust Wars: A Moral Argument with Historical Illustrations* (New York: Basic Books, 1977), pp. xv–xvi.

27.   See Gareth Porter, *A Peace Denied: The United States, Vietnam, and the Paris Agreement* (Bloomington, Ind.: Indiana U. Press, 1975).

28.   For consideration of the extent of U.S. complicity in Trujillo's assassination see "Alleged Assassination Plots Involving Foreign Leaders," Interim Report. Select Senate Committee on Intelligence Activities, November 20, 1975, pp. 191–215.

29.   See for example, Richard H. Ullman, "Human Rights and Economic Power: The United States Versus Idi Amin," *Foreign Affairs*, vol. 56, no. 3 (April 1978), pp. 529–543; James H. Mittelman, "The Amin Phenomenon," unpublished ms., March 1978; for a positive assessment of the impact of sanctions on Amin's Uganda see Judith Miller, "When Sanctions Worked," *Foreign Policy* 39 (Summer 1980), pp. 118–129.

30.   Contrary to some popular misconceptions, South African gold and diamonds are not "essential" to other countries, and constraints on their export would seriously deprive South Africa of foreign exchange.

31.   For a report on the role of NGOs see "Actions of International NGOs in the Implementation of U.N. Resolutions on the Problem of Apartheid and assistance provided by them to the oppressed people of South Africa," Centre Against Apartheid, UN Dep't of Political and Security Council Affairs, March 1978, No. 78–04681; parallel study on role of national NGOs issued at the same time, No. 78–04682.

32.   See Clyde Ferguson and William R. Cotter, "South Africa—What Is to Be Done," *Foreign Affairs*, vol. 56, no. 2 (January 1978), 253–274.

33.   See Roger D. Hansen, "Major U.S. Options on North-South Relations: A Letter to President Carter," in John W. Sewall and staff, *The United States and World Development: Agenda 1977* (New York: Praeger, 1977), pp. 67–68.

34.   For example, see Herrera and others, *Catastrophe or New Society: A Latin American World Model*, and Chichilnisky, "Development, Basic Needs, and the International Order."

35.   See Albert Fishlow et al., *Rich and Poor Nations in the World Economy* (New York: McGraw-Hill for the Council on Foreign Relations, 1978).

36.   For a populist approach to human rights, see "The Universal Declarations of the Rights of Peoples," approved in Algiers July 4, 1976, International Documentation (IDOC), Bulletin no. 46, September, 1976; also see essays inspired by Algiers Declaration in Antonio Cassese and Edmond Jouve, eds., *Pour un droit des peuples* (Paris: Berger-Levrault, 1978).

37.   For extended argument to this effect, see Falk, *A Study of Future Worlds* (New York: Free Press, 1975).

38.   Rene Dumont, *Utopia or Else* . . . (New York: Universe Books, 1975).

39.   For elaboration, see Falk, "A New Paradigm for International Legal Studies," *Yale Law Journal*, vol. 84, no. 5 (April, 1975), 969–1021.

Chapter VII

1. For presentation and analysis of these trends see Falk, "Militarization and Human Rights in the Third World," *Bulletin of Peace Proposals* (1977), 220 ff.; see also Chapter IV of this book.

2. See Lyons, "Inside the Volcano: the Mexican Revolution is Always Possible," *Harpers* (June, 1977), 41–55, at 42.

3. Consider, for instance, the treatment of these issues in such a representative document as the Charter of Economic Rights and Duties of States, a principal ideological achievement of the Third World insistence on a new international economic order (NIEO).

4. "The Editor's Reply," *Monthly Review* (June 1977), 15–24, at 15.

5. For the text of the Algiers Declaration of the Rights of Peoples see the appendix to the paper of F. Rigaux in Weston, Falk, and D'Amato, *Basic Documents in International Law and World Order* (St. Paul: West Publishing, 1980), pp. 413–15.

6. For interpretation and documentation of the Russell Proceedings see Duffett, ed., *Against the Crime of Silence: Proceedings of the International War Crimes Tribunal*, New York; Bertrand Russell Peace Foundation, 1968.

7. See Ellsberg, *Papers on the War* (New York, Simon and Schuster, 1972), especially pp. 9–41.

8. The text has some imperfections. For instance, article 4, as formulated, seems to imply that "massacre, torture, etc." are not objectionable unless occasioned by "national or cultural identity." Of course, this is a perverse reading of the text that only suggests the need for further drafting to achieve a final text.

Chapter VIII

1. General Assembly Resolution 95(1); for text of Nuremberg Principles as formulated by the ILC see R. A. Falk, G. Kolko, and R. J. Lifton, eds., *Crimes of War* (New York: Random House, 1971), pp. 107–08.

2. Sartre's Inaugural Statement, John Duffett, ed., *Against the Crimes of Silence: Proceedings of International War Crimes Tribunal* (New York, Bertrand Russell Peace Foundation, 1968), pp. 41, 42.

3. Text of De Gaulle's letter in Duffett, pp. 28–29.

4. Duffett, p. 43.

5. Duffett, p. 45.

6. Duffett, p. 39.

7. Duffett, p. 44.

Chapter IX

1. See chapters VII and VIII of this book for further background.

2. On executions, see the *New York Times,* March 17, 1979, p. 1.

3. Text in R. A. Falk, G. Kolko, R. J. Lifton, editors, *Crimes of War* (New York: Random House, 1971), p. 108.

4. Perhaps the most reliable interpreter of Iranian political developments refers to the Shah as having come to power in 1953 "as a result of a CIA-backed and in large part CIA-directed coup. . . . " Richard Cottam, *Nationalism in Iran* 2nd rev. ed. (Pittsburgh: Pittsburgh U. Press, 1979), p. 332; for an insider account see Kermit Roosevelt, *Counter-coup: The Struggle for the Control of Iran* (1979).

5. For a convincing dissent on the claim of medical necessity see Bloom, "The Pahlavi Problem: A Superficial Diagnosis Brought the Shah into the United States," *Science* 270 (1980), 282–286; see also front page journalistic account by Richard A. Knox to same effect, *Boston Globe,* Nov. 24, 1979, pp. 1, 4.

6. According to United States law, extradition cannot be granted by the president apart from treaty, unless authorized by legislation. Even if a special statute authorizing extradition of the Shah had been validly enacted, it would almost certainly have been struck down by the courts as an *ex post facto* law. For brief summary of legal situation pertaining to extradition in absence of treaty see Marjorie Whiteman, *Digest of International Law* 6 (1968), 732–737; cf. also Valentine v. United States ex rel. Neidecker, 299 U.S. 5, esp. 8–9 (1936).

7. An excellent analysis of the dependence of international order upon upholding the norm of nonintervention as much as possible is to be found in R. J. Vincent, *Nonintervention and International Order* (Princeton, New Jersey: Princeton U. Press, 1974).

8. Interview, *Time,* Jan. 7, 1980, p. 27.

9. Remarks, Proc. Amer. Soc. Int'l. L. 1963, 13–15, at 14.

10. For skeptical assessment of the relevance of international law to the Cuban missile crisis see W. P. Gerberding, "International Law and the Cuban Missile Crisis," in L. Scheinman and David Wilkinson, eds., *International Law and Political Crisis* (Boston: Little, Brown & Co., 1968), pp. 175–210. Cf. much more positive view in Abram Chayes, *The Cuban Missile Crisis* (New York: Oxford U. Press, 1974).

11. Leonard Meeker, "The Dominican Situation in the Perspective of International Law," *Dept. State Bull.* 53 (1965), 60–66, at 60.

12. The results of this investigation remain impressive as a moral and legal indictment of United States tactics in the Vietnam War. See John Duffett, ed., *Against the Crime of Silence: Proceedings of the International War Crimes Tribunal* (New York: Simon & Schuster, 1970).

Books Written Under the Auspices of the Center of International Studies, Princeton University, 1952-1980

Gabriel A. Almond, *The Appeals of Communism* (Princeton University Press 1954)

William W. Kaufmann, ed., *Military Policy and National Security* (Princeton University Press 1956)

Klaus Knorr, *The War Potential of Nations* (Princeton University Press 1956)

Lucian W. Pye, *Guerrilla Communism in Malaya* (Princeton University Press 1956)

Charles De Visscher, *Theory and Reality in Public International Law*, trans. by P.E. Corbett (Princeton University Press 1957; rev. ed. 1968)

Bernard C. Cohen, *The Political Process and Foreign Policy: The Making of the Japanese Peace·Settlement* (Princeton University Press 1957)

Myron Weiner, *Party Politics in India: The Development of a Multi-Party System* (Princeton University Press 1957)

Percy E. Corbett, *Law in Diplomacy* (Princeton University Press 1959)

Rolf Sannwald and Jacques Stohler, *Economic Integration: Theoretical Assumptions and Consequences of European Unification*, trans. by Herman Karreman (Princeton University Press 1959)

Klaus Knorr, ed., *NATO and American Security* (Princeton University Press 1959)

Gabriel A. Almond and James S. Coleman, eds., *The Politics of the Developing Areas* (Princeton University Press 1960)

Herman Kahn, *On Thermonuclear War* (Princeton University Press 1960)

Sidney Verba, *Small Groups and Political Behavior: A Study of Leadership* (Princeton University Press 1961)

Robert J. C. Butow, *Tojo and the Coming of the War* (Princeton University Press 1961)

Glenn H. Snyder, *Deterrence and Defense: Toward a Theory of National Security* (Princeton University Press 1961)

Klaus Knorr and Sidney Verba, eds., *The International System: Theoretical Essays* (Princeton University Press 1961)

Peter Paret and John W. Shy, *Guerrillas in the 1960's* (Praeger 1962)

George Modelski, *A Theory of Foreign Policy* (Praeger 1962)

Klaus Knorr and Thornton Read, eds., *Limited Strategic War* (Praeger 1963)

Frederick S. Dunn, *Peace-Making and the Settlement with Japan* (Princeton University Press 1963)

Arthur L. Burns and Nina Heathcote, *Peace-Keeping by United Nations Forces* (Praeger 1963)

Richard A. Falk, *Law, Morality, and War in the Contemporary World* (Praeger 1963)

James N. Rosenau, *National Leadership and Foreign Policy: A Case Study in the Mobilization of Public Support* (Princeton University Press 1963)

Gabriel A. Almond and Sidney Verba, *The Civic Culture: Political Attitudes and Democracy in Five Nations* (Princeton University Press 1963)

Bernard C. Cohen, *The Press and Foreign Policy* (Princeton University Press 1963)

Richard L. Sklar, *Nigerian Political Parties: Power in an Emergent African Nation* (Princeton University Press 1963)

Peter Paret, *French Revolutionary Warfare from Indochina to Algeria: The Analysis of a Political and Military Doctrine* (Praeger 1964)

Harry Eckstein, ed., *Internal War: Problems and Approaches* (Free Press 1964)

Cyril E. Black and Thomas P. Thornton, eds., *Communism and Revolution: The Strategic Uses of Political Violence* (Princeton University Press 1964)

Miriam Camps, *Britain and the European Community 1955–1963* (Princeton University Press 1964)

Thomas P. Thornton, ed., *The Third World in Soviet Perspective: Studies by Soviet Writers on the Developing Areas* (Princeton University Press 1964)

James N. Rosenau, ed., *International Aspects of Civil Strife* (Princeton University Press 1964)

Sidney I. Ploss, *Conflict and Decision-Making in Soviet Russia: A Case Study of Agricultural Policy, 1953–1963* (Princeton University Press 1965)

Richard A. Falk and Richard J. Barnet, eds., *Security in Disarmament* (Princeton University Press 1965)

Karl von Vorys, *Political Development in Pakistan* (Princeton University Press 1965)

Harold and Margaret Sprout, *The Ecological Perspective on Human Affairs, With Special Reference to International Politics* (Princeton University Press 1965)

Klaus Knorr, *On the Uses of Military Power in the Nuclear Age* (Princeton University Press 1966)

Harry Eckstein, *Division and Cohesion in Democracy: A Study of Norway* (Princeton University Press 1966)

Cyril E. Black, *The Dynamics of Modernization: A Study in Comparative History* (Harper and Row 1966)

Peter Kunstadter, ed., *Southeast Asian Tribes, Minorities, and Nations* (Princeton University Press 1967)

E. Victor Wolfenstein, *The Revolutionary Personality: Lenin, Trotsky, Gandhi* (Princeton University Press 1967)

Leon Gordenker, *The UN Secretary-General and the Maintenance of Peace* (Columbia University Press 1967)

Oran R. Young, *The Intermediaries: Third Parties in International Crises* (Princeton University Press 1967)

James N. Rosenau, ed., *Domestic Sources of Foreign Policy* (Free Press 1967)

Richard F. Hamilton, *Affluence and the French Worker in the Fourth Republic* (Princeton University Press 1967)

Linda B. Miller, *World Order and Local Disorder: The United Nations and Internal Conflicts* (Princeton University Press 1967)

Henry Bienen, *Tanzania: Party Transformation and Economic Development* (Princeton University Press 1967)

Wolfram F. Hanrider, *West German Foreign Policy, 1949–1963: International Pressures and Domestic Response* (Stanford University Press 1967)

Richard H. Ullman, *Britain and the Russian Civil War: November 1918– February 1920* (Princeton University Press 1968)

Robert Gilpin, *France in the Age of the Scientific State* (Princeton University Press 1968)

William B. Bader, *The United States and the Spread of Nuclear Weapons* (Pegasus 1968)

Richard A. Falk, *Legal Order in a Violent World* (Princeton University Press 1968)

Cyril E. Black, Richard A. Falk, Klaus Knorr and Oran R. Young, *Neutralization and World Politics* (Princeton University Press 1968)

Oran R. Young, *The Politics of Force: Bargaining During International Crisis* (Princeton University Press 1969)

Klaus Knorr and James N. Rosenau, eds., *Contending Approaches to International Politics* (Princeton University Press 1969)

James N. Rosenau, ed., *Linkage Politics: Essays on the Convergence of National and International Systems* (Free Press 1969)

John T. McAlister, Jr., *Viet Nam: The Origins of Revolution* (Knopf 1969)

Jean Edward Smith, *Germany Beyond the Wall: People, Politics and Prosperity* (Little, Brown 1969)

James Barros, *Betrayal from Within: Joseph Avenol, Secretary-General of the League of Nations, 1933–1940* (Yale University Press 1969)

Charles Hermann, *Crises in Foreign Policy: A Simulation Analysis* (Bobbs-Merrill 1969)

Robert C. Tucker, *The Marxian Revolutionary Idea: Essays on Marxist Thought and Its Impact on Radical Movements* (W. W. Norton 1969)

Harvey Waterman, *Political Change in Contemporary France: The Politics of an Industrial Democracy* (Charles E. Merrill 1969)

Cyril E. Black and Richard A. Falk, eds., *The Future of the International Legal Order*. Vol. I: *Trends and Patterns* (Princeton University Press 1969)

Ted Robert Gurr, *Why Men Rebel* (Princeton University Press 1969)

C. Sylvester Whitaker, *The Politics of Tradition: Continuity and Change in Northern Nigeria 1946–1960* (Princeton University Press 1970)

Richard A. Falk, *The Status of Law in International Society* (Princeton University Press 1970)

Klaus Knorr, *Military Power and Potential* (D.C. Heath 1970)

Cyril E. Black and Richard A. Falk, eds., *The Future of the International Legal Order*. Vol. II: *Wealth and Resources* (Princeton University Press 1970)

Leon Gordenker, ed., *The United Nations in International Politics* (Princeton University Press 1971)

Cyril E. Black and Richard A. Falk, eds., *The Future of the International Legal Order*. Vol. III: *Conflict Management* (Princeton University Press 1971)

Francine R. Frankel, *India's Green Revolution: Political Costs of Economic Growth* (Princeton University Press 1971)

Harold and Margaret Sprout, *Toward a Politics of the Planet Earth* (Van Nostrand Reinhold 1971)

Cyril E. Black and Richard A. Falk, eds., *The Future of the International Legal Order*. Vol. IV: *The Structure of the International Environment* (Princeton University Press 1972)

Gerald Garvey, *Energy, Ecology, Economy* (W. W. Norton 1972)

Richard Ullman, *The Anglo-Soviet Accord* (Princeton University Press 1973)

Klaus Knorr, *Power and Wealth: The Political Economy of International Power* (Basic Books 1973)

Anton Bebler, *Military Role in Africa: Dahomey, Ghana, Sierra Leone, and Mali* (Praeger Publishers 1973)

Robert C. Tucker, *Stalin as Revolutionary 1879–1929: A Study in History and Personality* (W. W. Norton 1973)

Edward L. Morse, *Foreign Policy and Interdependence in Gaullist France* (Princeton University Press 1973)

Henry Bienen, *Kenya: The Politics of Participation and Control* (Princeton University Press 1974)

Gregory J. Massell, *The Surrogate Proletariat: Moslem Women and Revolutionary Strategies in Soviet Central Asia, 1919–1929* (Princeton University Press 1974)

James N. Rosenau, *Citizenship Between Elections: An Inquiry Into The Mobilizable American* (Free Press 1974)

Ervin Laszlo, *A Strategy For the Future: The Systems Approach To World Order* (Braziller 1974)

John R. Vincent, *Nonintervention and International Order* (Princeton University Press 1974)

Jan H. Kalicki, *The Pattern of Sino-American Crises: Political-Military Interactions in the 1950s* (Cambridge University Press 1975)

Klaus Knorr, *The Power of Nations: The Political Economy of International Relations* (Basic Books Inc. 1975)

James P. Sewell, *UNESCO and World Politics: Engaging in International Relations* (Princeton University Press 1975)

Richard A. Falk, *A Global Approach to National Policy* (Harvard University Press 1975)

Harry Eckstein and Ted Robert Gurr, *Patterns of Authority: A Structural Basis for Political Inquiry* (John Wiley & Sons 1975)

Cyril E. Black, Marius B. Jansen, Herbert S. Levine, Marion J. Levy, Jr., Henry Rosovsky, Gilbert Rozman, Henry D. Smith, II, and S. Frederick Starr, *The Modernization of Japan and Russia* (Free Press 1975)

Leon Gordenker, *International Aid and National Decisions: Development Programs in Malawi, Tanzania, and Zambia* (Princeton University Press 1976)

Carl Von Clausewitz, *On War,* edited and translated by Michael Howard' and Peter Paret (Princeton University Press 1976)

Gerald Garvey and Lou Ann Garvey, eds., *International Resource Flows* (Lexington Books, D. C. Heath 1977)

Walter F. Murphy and Joseph Tanenhaus, *Comparative Constitutional Law Cases and Commentaries* (St. Martin's Press 1977)

Gerald Garvey, *Nuclear Power and Social Planning: The City of the Second Sun* (Lexington Books, D. C. Heath 1977)

Richard E. Bissell, *Apartheid and International Organizations* (Westview Press 1977)

David P. Forsythe, *Humanitarian Politics: The International Committee of the Red Cross* (Johns Hopkins University Press 1977)

Paul E. Sigmund, *The Overthrow of Allende and the Politics of Chile, 1964–1976* (University of Pittsburgh Press 1977)

Henry S. Bienen, *Armies and Parties in Africa* (Holmes & Meier 1978)

Harold and Margaret Spout, *The Context of Environmental Politics* (The University Press of Kentucky 1978)

Samuel S. Kim, *China, the United Nations, and World Order* (Princeton University Press 1979)

S. Basheer Ahmed, *Nuclear Fuel and Energy Policy,* (Lexington Books, D. C. Heath 1979)

Robert C. Johansen, *The National Interest and the Human Interest: An Analysis of U.S. Foreign Policy* (Princeton University Press 1980)

Richard A. Falk and Samuel S. Kim, eds., *The War System: An Interdisciplinary Approach* (Westview Press 1980)

James H. Billington, *Fire in the Minds of Men: Origins of the Revolutionary Faith* (Basic Books, Inc. 1980)

Bennett Ramberg, *Destruction of Nuclear Energy Facilities in War: The Problem and the Implications* (Lexington Books 1980)

Gregory T. Kruglak, *The Politics of United States Decision-Making in United Nations Specialized Agencies: The Case of the International Labor Organization* (University Press of America 1980)

James C. Hsiung and Samuel S. Kim, eds., *China in the Global Community* (Praeger Publishers 1980)

W. Phillips Davison and Leon Gordenker, eds., *Resolving Nationality Conflicts: The Role of Public Opinion Research* (Praeger Publishers 1980)

Index

Ache Indians, 159, 180
Acheson, Dean, 221
Afghanistan, 30
Agency for International Development (AID), 14
Ajami, Fouad, approach to human rights, 144–45
Albania, 68, 90–1, 99, 164
Algeria, 87, 215
Algier's Declaration, 53, 140–42, 146, 190–94, 198–201, 223, 225–28
Allende, Salvador, 41, 60, 69, 83, 189, 205
Alliance for Progress, 13
American Revolution, 204
Amin, Idi, 43, 47, 79, 154, 159, 160, 170–72, 180, 214, 220
Amnesty International, 1, 48, 50, 51, 153, 173
Angola, 85, 111
Appalachia, 156
Arabs, minority in Iran, 206
Arab-Israeli conflict, 163
Arab League, 47
Arafat, Yasir, 212
Argentina, 14, 68, 79, 81, 163, 164; U.S. aid cutoff, 139
Armenian Christians, 211
Asun, Juan Pereda, 133
Azerbaijanis, 206, 211

Bahais, 211, 212
Baha'u'llah, 212
Bakhtiaris, 206
Baluchis, 206, 211
Bangladesh, 39, 161
Bani Sadr, Abolhassan, 207, 209, 217
Bazargan, Mehdi, 38, 207, 208
Beheshti, Ayatollah Mohammed, 207
Belgium, 35
Bengali nationalism, repression of, 160
Berger, Peter, approach to human rights, 143–44
Bertrand Russell War Crimes Tribunal, 50–51, 192, 196–97, 222
Biko, Steve, 161, 174
Biyogo, Masie Nguema, 163
Bodin, Jean, 35
Bokassa I, Emperor, 214, 220
Bolivia, 133
Branco, Castelo, 110
Brazil, 6, 61, 66, 67–83, 97, 152, 163, 186; anti-Zionist vote, 80; as example of Brazilianization, 104–11

Brazilianization, 66–83, 84, 96–103; ascendent military establishment, 74–76; capitalist development strategy, 72–73; coalition with technocrats, 77–78; geopolitical links, 78–79; militarist politics, 73; and military governance, 70–72; public enterprise and investment, 78; repressive politics and apparatus, 76–77; rightist ideology, 72; statism, 79–83
Brezhnev era, 164
Bricker, John, 12; amendment, 26
Brown, Harold, 187
Brzezinski, Zbigniew, 22–23, 30, 93
Buckley, William, 19
Bulgaria, 164
Bull, Hedley, 1, 2
Bull/Vincent approach, 3
Burundi, 160

Calcutta, 156
Cambodia, 43, 46, 99, 134, 140, 148, 149, 161, 163
Canada, 161
capitulary regimes, 35
Carter Administration, 1, 2, 10, 14, 15, 19–31, 36, 55, 56, 57, 79, 100, 111, 155–57, 219; and approach to human rights, 139–41; Notre Dame speech, 22, 38, 57, 58, 59
Castro, Fidel, 46, 58, 104, 132
Central Intelligence Agency (CIA), 9, 28, 59, 64, 71, 78, 186, 189, 222
Chile, 41, 42, 47, 49, 60, 70, 79, 81, 83, 99, 148, 189, 205
China, Peoples Republic of, 40, 84, 134, 135, 149, 152, 166, 190, 204; nuclear tests, 177; support for anti-Soviet regimes, 41
China initiative, Nixon, 13
Chomsky, Noam, 20
Clark, Ramsey, 19
Cocoyoc Declaration, 134, 223
Cold War, 12, 17, 30, 40, 41, 100, 103, 186, 187
Commission on Human Rights, 49
Congo, 36, 47
Convention on the Elimination of Racial Discrimination, 162
Council on Foreign Relations, 1980s Project, 95
Crisis of Democracy (Trilateral Commission Report), 92